NORMAN C. MILLER

García Lorca's

POEMA DEL CANTE JONDO

NORMAN C. MILLER

García Lorca's

POEMA DEL CANTE JONDO

TAMESIS BOOKS LIMITED
LONDON

Colección Támesis

SERIE A - MONOGRAFIAS, LXV

Depósito Legal: M. 40074.—1978

Printed in Spain by Talleres Gráficos de SELECCIONES GRÁFICAS (EDICIONES)
Paseo de la Dirección, 52 - Madrid-29

for
TAMESIS BOOKS LIMITED
LONDON

To the memory of Professor Francisco García Lorca to whom I am deeply indebted for his encouragement and personal example.

I should like to express my sincere gratitude to the following people for their help in making this book possible: my wife Paulina whose invaluable assistance was often a crucial factor, Professors Dorothy C. Shadi and Francisco García Lorca who guided my early attempts to formulate this study, my colleagues in the Department of Spanish and Portuguese at Tulane University for their valuable suggestions, Mr. Terence Keenan and Mr. Charles Merrill, Jr. who introduced me to this rewarding field of knowledge.

CONTENTS

INTRODUCTION

The purpose of this study is to present a close analysis of Federico García Lorca's *Poema del Cante Jondo,* an early work that in our opinion has been undeservedly overlooked or treated too superficially by most contemporary critics. This short collection of poems represents the poet's attempt to capture or to recreate the essential spirit of the *cante jondo* rather than to copy superficially its formal structure in the manner of a Manuel Machado who, a decade earlier, had utilized the *cante* as a source of inspiration for his own works. Lorca, as we shall see, consistently avoids a facile imitation of what is essentially a folk art and seeks always to delve beneath the surface, to bring forth the intense dramatic-emotional qualities inherent in the genuine *cante jondo,* and to express these qualities in a highly original poetic form.

Since the *cante* is inseparably linked to the Andalusian people who were its originators and present-day continuers, the poems in this collection go beyond the thematic limitations of music and dance and evoke a wider, more general Andalusian setting. Consequently, in many compositions the poet utilizes the landscape as a theme or attempts to capture the spirit of the region's cities, the flamenco cafes, the religious processions, and above all, the spirit of its people, chief of whom are the Gypsies since their role in the creation of the *cante jondo* was unique.

Because it would be futile to attempt any analysis of the poetry without some familiarity with the *cante jondo* itself, we have devoted the first chapter to a general discussion of the *cante*'s definition, origin and history, and to a description of its most important forms. Chapter II contains a detailed account of the series of events and influences that led to the writing of the *Poema del Cante Jondo* and a comparative study of the known variants of those poems published prior to the first edition of the book in 1931. Chapter III is an analysis of the work's content and structure with an evaluation of the various critical interpretations that have been offered for each of its poems.

Chapters IV-V are devoted to a detailed technical analysis of the poetry. In Chapter IV the reader will find a discussion of Lorca's poetic vocabulary and its classification into categories, followed by a description and illustration of each of the individual poetic techniques used in this work. Chapter V attempts to demonstrate how these poetic processes function together within the poem to convey a unified poetic effect. Our method here has been to explicate in detail a representative poem from each of the major sections of the book.

CHAPTER I

THE *CANTE JONDO*

The terms *cante flamenco* and *cante jondo* have been defined variously by Spanish musicologists. In spite of the many differences of opinion, however, there seems to be a general tendency among recent critics to include under *cante flamenco* all those songs, regardless of origin, which are adapted to a flamenco style of performance. Such a broad definition therefore includes songs of probable Gypsy origin, a number of folk songs from Andalusia and other parts of Spain, and some from foreign countries, such as the Cuban *guajira* or the Colombian *colombiana. Cante jondo,* on the other hand, refers to a very limited number of songs within the general corpus of the *cante flamenco* which share certain common characteristics: (1) Their lyrics have a serious, profound content or expressive depth (hence the name *jondo,* the Andalusian form of *hondo* meaning deep), and they deal with those life situations that provoke the deepest human emotions, usually despair or grief. The *cante jondo* normally expresses personal or familial sorrows and rarely contains allusions to events of a more general or national interest. (2) They are traditionally sung in a *voz afillá,*[1] a rough, coarse, or raucous voice deliberately lacking melodious refinement. (3) The music is slow and serious in tone. (4) Originally, they were probably sung without guitar accompaniment. (5) They generally have a *macho* or personal refrain typical of the singer. (6) Until very recently they were never danced or in any way asociated with the *baile flamenco.* (7) They are all from a much earlier date than the majority of the *cantes flamencos.*

Other critics, however, would disagree with the classification of the *cante jondo* as a subdivision of the *cante flamenco.* For them the two are diametrically opposed because the lyrics and music of the *cante flamenco* are generally less serious, gayer, and frequently festive in their mood; the *cante flamenco* always utilizes a guitar accompaniment; it never has a dramatic *macho*; it is normally danced, and, finally, it is usually considered to have descended from the *cante jondo.* García Lorca subscribed to this point of view concerning the basic opposition between *cante jondo* and *cante flamenco.* His ideas, which were influenced greatly by the opinions of Manuel de Falla, are set fort in his 1922 lecture on the *cante jondo* in which he states:

> Las diferencias esenciales del cante jondo con el flamenco consisten en que el origen del primero hay que buscarlo en los primitivos sistemas musi-

---

[1] This term is derived from the singing style of Diego el Fillo, an early nineteenth century *cantaor.*

cales de la India, es decir, en las primeras manifestaciones del canto, mientras que el segundo, consecuencia del primero, puede decirse que toma su forma definitiva en el siglo XVIII. El primero es un canto teñido por el color misterioso de las primeras edades; el segundo es un canto relativamente moderno, cuyo interés emocional desaparece ante aquél. Color espiritual y color local, he aquí la honda diferencia.[2]

The *cante flamenco,* often held in lesser esteem than the *cante jondo,* is considered by some to be a mere commercialization and vulgarization of the latter.[3]

Frequently, the *cante jondo* is called *cante grande* whereas the *cante flamenco* is named *cante chico* by those who wish to differentiate between these two art forms. This distinction is not universally accepted, however, for some critics believe that these two expressions refer more to a song's difficulty of performance than to a basic distinction in character.[4] Furthermore, the designation of a particular song as *jondo* or *flamenco* can be the result of the way in which it is performed rather than because of its inherent qualities. Anselmo González Climent states: «Todo, pues, absolutamente todo, depende del intérprete-creador: el cantaor. Unas cañas en la voz de Juanito Valderrama o Manolo el Malagueño pueden ser flamencas. Unas bulerías en la voz de Manuel Torres o Manolo Caracol pueden ser jondas. Ultima consecuencia: el jondismo o el flamenquismo no radican en la estructura formal de los cantes, sino en la calidad vital de los cantaores.»[5] In addition to the two basic classifications of *cante grande* and *cante chico,* some critics assert that there is an intermediate group of songs or *cantes intermedios,* largely of Andalusian rather than Gypsy origin, that expresses the tragedy of the *cante grande,* but with «la ligereza y el barroquismo» associated with the more melodic *cante chico.*[6]

Traditionally the *cante jondo* is performed in the following manner: There is first the *temple,* a guitar introduction or prelude during which the singer accompanies the guitar by modulations of his voice, often without the use of words other than the repetition of «ay.» Secondly, we find a *planteo* or *tercio de entrada,* the introduction of the song itself, which is then followed by the *tercio grande,* the main part of the *cante.* Next comes a *tercio de alivio* which lessens the emotional qualities of the preceding phase. Finally, there is often a *cambio* or *remate,* the closing of the song with a thematic variation. This phase may be substituted by a *macho,* the personal

[2] «El cante jondo (primitivo canto andaluz)» in *Obras completas,* 6th ed. (Madrid: Aguilar, 1963), pp. 1824-25.

[3] ANTONIO MACHADO Y ALVAREZ, for example, stresses the fact that whereas the *cante jondo* is genuine folk music, the *cante flamenco* is essentially a commercial-theatrical form of entertainment derived from folk music and dance, but now distinct from them. *Colección de cantes flamencos recogidos y anotados por Demófilo* (Sevilla: Imprenta y Lit. de El Porvenir, 1881), p. viii.

[4] See HIPÓLITO ROSSY, *Teoría del cante jondo* (Barcelona: Credsa, 1966), p. 15.

[5] *Flamencología* (Madrid: Editorial Escelicer, 1964), p. 158.

[6] *Ibid.,* p. 178 and D. E. POHREN, *The Art of Flamenco* (Jerez de la Frontera: Editorial Jerez Industrial, 1962), p. 49.

refrain or individual touch that the singer gives the traditional lyrics.[7] This series of phases can be interrupted at any point by various exclamations which, when used to denote sorrow, are called *quejíos,* laments.

The question of the *cante jondo*'s origin has given rise to various theories. The popular belief that both the *cante jondo* and the *cante flamenco* are primarily creations of the Spanish Gypsies is almost universally rejected by critics and musicologists. The fact that the Gypsies settling in other European countries and even in other parts of Spain did not produce anything analogous to the *cante* strongly indicates that its main elements are of Andalusian and not Gypsy origin. As the critic Hipólito Rossy has pointed out: «Si el cante jondo es judío, o árabe, o gitano, ¿por qué no cantan flamenco los hebreos de Alemania o Norteamérica, o los gitanos de Polonia o Hungría, o los árabes de la Arabia y demás países ismaelitas?»[8] Such an affirmation does not, however, exclude the possibility that the musical traditions of immigrant Gypsies did contribute to the formation of the *cante* as we now know it. It is generally acknowledged that the *cante* is, in fact, a hybrid art form which amalgamates the Gypsy tribes' musical traditions with Andalusian folk music whose origins long predate the arrival of the Gypsies. García Lorca, again paraphrasing Manuel de Falla, comments: «Se trata de un canto puramente andaluz, que ya existía en germen en esta región antes que los gitanos llegaran a ella.»[9] Later he continues: «. . . Y estas gentes, llegando a nuestra Andalucía, unieron los viejísimos elementos nativos con el viejísimo que ellos traían y dieron las definitivas formas a lo que hoy llamamos 'cante jondo.'»[10] The majority of the critics tends to agree with this point of view. Julián Pemartín, for example, restates the same concept in the following way:

> Esta gente gitana, de dotes poéticas autóctonas muy pobres, pero con notable facultad para el arte del ritmo y la recreación imitativa, se encontró en la campiña y en los barrios populares de las ciudades andaluzas con un rico y brillante folklore, de excepcional gracia poética. Y excitada y alentada su genialidad interpretadora, absorbió . . . las substancias musicales de ese espléndido cancionero popular, y alumbró algo distinto, ya que no nuevo, y en cierto modo original: el «cante», como forma artística, ya diferenciada de los cantos folklóricos de Andalucía, aflora en el seno de la familia gitana, pero es producto de dos factores, ambos ineludibles: el andaluz y el gitano.[11]

The same idea is also presented more succinctly by Ricardo Molina and Antonio Mairena: «Los gitanos crean o forjan el cante primitivo; son los agentes creadores. Pero lo forjan con metales en su mayoría andaluces.»[12]

---

[7] See POHREN, pp. 53-54.
[8] *Op. cit.,* p. 39.
[9] *Op. cit.,* p. 39.
[10] *Ibid.,* p. 41.
[11] *El cante flamenco, guía alfabética* (Madrid: Afrodisio Aguado, 1966), pp. 35-36.
[12] *Mundo y formas del cante flamenco* (Madrid: Revista de Occidente, 1963), p. 27.

However, other critics who take a less enthusiastic view of the Gypsies' contribution to the *cante jondo* tend to minimize their influence on the *cante*'s basic structure and to limit their contribution to external refinement only. Domingo Manfredi Cano, for example, claims: «Los gitanos no enseñaron a los andaluces a cantar y a bailar, sino que ellos fueron los que aprendieron en Andalucía; los gitanos no hicieron más que poner el salero, la gracia, el misterio del duende. . . .»[13]

According to Manuel de Falla, this Andalusian folk music which formed the necessary precondition for the *cante* was greatly influenced by two historical factors: the adoption of the Byzantine liturgical chant by the Spanish church and the long occupation of the region by the Arabs.[14] Using the *siguiriya gitana* as an example, Falla describes the Byzantine elements as follows: «En la 'siguiriya' hallamos los siguientes elementos del canto litúrgico bizantino: los modos tonales de los sistemas primitivos (que no hay que confundir con los modos que ahora llamamos griegos, aunque éstos participan a veces de la estructura de aquéllos); el enharmonismo inherente a los modos primigénicos, o sea la división y subdivisión de las notas sensibles en sus funciones atractivas de la tonalidad; y por último, la ausencia de ritmo métrico en la línea melódica y la riqueza de inflexiones modulantes en ésta.» [15] He points out, furthermore, that in the rhythmic dance patterns found in the Arabic music still played today in Morocco, Algiers, and Tunisia under the name of *música andaluza de los moros de Granada,* one can easily recognize the origin of the flamenco *sevillanas, zapateados, seguidilla,* and others. Although Falla does not mention it in this discussion, it is interesting that many critics believe that the word *flamenco* may be derived from two Arabic words, *fellah-mangu,* meaning peasant song or song of the peasants,[16] or, possibly, from the Arabic *fellah-mengo* which means poor or errant peasant.[17] Falla then concludes that it was this combination of elements from early Christian liturgical music and the Moorish music of Granada that formed the early Andalusian substrata which, when combined with those elements brought specifically by the Gypsies who entered Spain in 1447, coalesced to form the primitive *cante jondo.*

Falla describes five essential characteristics of the *cante jondo* which he believes are oriental elements contributed specifically by the Gypsies who came from India. The first is «el enharmonismo como medio modulante.» The various scales in primitive Indian music were quite numerous, and each one was capable of originating a new melodic series by means of the free alteration of four of its seven tones. In other words, Falla explains, only three of the notes are invariable, and each of the tones susceptible to alteration is divided and subdivided, with the result that, in

---

[13] *Geografía del cante jondo* (Madrid: Gráficas C.I.O., 1955), p. 51.
[14] «El cante jondo,» in *Escritos sobre música y músicos* (Madrid: Espasa-Calpe, n.d.), pp. 121-147.
[15] *Ibid.,* p. 124.
[16] ROSSY, p. 16.
[17] RAMÓN SENDER, «Sobre los gitanos cantaores,» *D.H.* (19 julio 1953).

some cases, the notes of attack and resolution of some fragments of the phrase remain changed, which is exactly what occurs in the *cante jondo*. Furthermore, both primitive Indian music and the *cante jondo* make use of a wide range of semitones, those infinite gradations of pitch existing between two notes whether contiguous or far apart. In both kinds of music the musical scale is a direct consequence of the oral scale. The second characteristic is «el empleo de un ámbito melódico que rara vez traspasa los límites de una sexta.» Through the use of *enarmonía* the number of sounds accessible to a singer is greatly increased beyond the nine semitones common to the tempered scale. The third characteristic is «el uso reiterado y hasta obsesionante de una misma nota, frecuentemente acompañada de apoyatura superior e inferior.» This trait (often used in certain types of incantations) destroys any impression of a rhythmic meter and produces the effect of chanted prose, though in reality the compositions are in poetry. As the fourth characteristic Falla points out: «. . . aunque la melodía gitana es rica en giros ornamentales, éstos, lo mismo que en los cantos primitivos orientales, sólo se emplean en determinados momentos como expansiones o arrebatos sugeridos por la fuerza emotiva del texto.» Consequently, they are usually more like vocal inflexions than true ornamental flourishes. Regarding the fifth characteristic he states: «. . . las voces y gritos con que nuestro pueblo anima y excita a los 'cantaores' y 'tocaores' tienen también origen en la costumbre que aún se observa para casos análogos en las razas de origen oriental.»[18]

The possible Indian origin of the Spanish *cante jondo* is discussed in greater length in a monograph by Aziz Baloch who claims that the primitive *cante jondo* is derived from the folk music of the Sind region in what is now Pakistan. He points out the amazing melodic similarities between such forms as the *seguidilla, soleares, cañas,* and *polos* and the melodies of the *Sindhi Sufi Kalam,* the mystic songs of the Sind. Even the Spanish *saetas* have their counterparts in the Pakistani *Osaras,* sung to commemorate the martyrdom of Imam Husain. More specifically, he feels that the melodic patterns of the *Marui* or *Sindhi Bhairivin* have direct counterparts in the *seguidilla, soleares,* and the flamenco *fandangos,* while the *Lorraoo* is the ancestor of the flamenco *campanilleros.* These melodies were carried from India by the professional singers called *lora* or *loree* who, in the fifth century A.D., transmitted their music to Iran and in the course of time brought about a synthesis between Sindhian and Iranian music. This music, in both its original Sindhian and mixed Sindhian-Iranian forms, was subsequently absorbed by the Arabs who then introduced it into Spain. Such indirect transmission, however, was not the only source. Later migrations of Sindhi communities carried their music to Spain in its original form from about the eighth century on. The various ethnic groups that comprised the Sindhian communities who passed through Iran, Syria, Palestine, and Egypt before reaching southern Spain constituted a proto-Gypsy stock from which some of the later European Gypsies may have descended. These early

---

[18] *Op. cit.,* pp. 127-130.

Sindhian emigrants who settled in Andalusia during the Arabic period included a large number of the *lora* or *loree* singers. The melodies and musical forms brought by these groups were then transmitted to the Spanish-Christian communities that subsequently absorbed them into their own folk music.[19]

It is interesting to note that another musicologist, Hipólito Rossy, disagrees with both Falla and Baloch concerning the origin of the *cante*'s oriental features. Rossy states that the undeniable similarities between the *cante jondo* and certain oriental—Indian folk music are not due to either an Arabic or a Gypsy influence on the *cante*, but to an entirely different and, in many ways, opposite set of historical circumstances. He maintains that the characteristic features of Andalusian folk music in general and the *cante jondo* in particular are primarily of Greek-Byzantine origin, implying that it was the Arabs who, upon invading Spain and encountering a superior culture, incorporated Andalusian music into their own:

> . . . los ochenta años que los bizantinos ocuparon militarmente el sur de la península Ibérica tuvieron gran importancia para la cultura hispánica porque le inyectaron nueva savia de la civilización greco-bizantina. . . . De esta forma, el arte musical griego, que se extendió desde el Indus hasta España e Irlanda, y que estaba influido por la música de Asiria, Mesopotamia, Israel, Canaán y Persia, influyó, a su vez, por más de mil años, en el folklore sureño español; de tal modo, que la escala fundamental del sistema griego (la escala en «mi»), conocida como modo dórico, sigue siendo el tronco estructural y básico del cante jondo más puro y antiguo.
>
> La hora de los árabes en la Historia sonó con la aparición de Mahoma. . . .
>
> A España llegaron unos noventa años después de la Hégira. Su cultura era la que asimilaron con la conquista de Siria, Palestina, Egipto, Cirenaica, Armenia y Persia; y, por improvisada, inferior a la existente a la sazón en España.[20]

Although Rossy does not deny the inevitable cultural interchange between the two civilizations during the eight centuries of Arab occupation, he emphasizes that Arabic music was more influenced by that of the native inhabitants than Andalusian music was by the Arabs: «Lejos de haber sido los árabes quienes enseñaron a cantar a murcianos y andaluces, el hecho ha sido al revés. . . .»[21] Later, after the Arabs were driven from southern Spain at the end of the fifteeenth century, they carried this music to India and Pakistan, which explains why the folk music of these two countries bears such striking similarities to the Spanish *cante jondo* and flamenco:

> Cuando la hora de los árabes había pasado en España, su resurgir, por Oriente, daba otra de sus portentosas sorpresas: la de extender su imperio

[19] *Spanish Cante Jondo and its Origin in Sindhi Music* (Hyderabad, Pakistan: The Mehran Arts Council, 1968), p. 49.

[20] *Op. cit.*, pp. 32-33.

[21] *Ibid.*, p. 47.

hasta la India. . . . Con la invasión del sur asiático llevaron el acopio de la ciencia musical griega y de los cantos sirios y persas, que plasmaron en la música hindú, dándole la apariencia —externa, puramente externa— de cante flamenco que aún conservan hoy los cantos de la India y el Pakistán, para desorientación y desesperación de nuestros aficionados al cante jondo, que no explicándose estos parecidos por olvidar las circunstancias que los produjeron, llegan a pensar si el cante jondo lo importaron los andaluces de la India o lo trajeron los gitanos indostánicos prendidos en sus harapos. Error en el que parece haber incidido el maestro Falla, el más glorioso de los músicos españoles.

A cambio de sus aportaciones, los andaluces dieron a los mogrebinos todo un estilo de música —ésta, sí, de igual estructura a la flamenca—, que se conoce con el nombre de «garnatí,» es decir, de Granada, último bastión de su gran aventura en España.[22]

Thus, before leaving their homeland, the Gypsies were at least partially acquainted with those tonal systems which they would later encounter again in southern Spain: «En apoyo de la tesis de Manuel de Falla, que considera trascendental la presencia del gitano en el arte flamenco, puede admitirse que antes de abandonar su patria indostánica tuvieron la oportunidad de conocer sistemas tonales que habrían de encontrar más tarde extendidos por el sur de España.»[23] Hence their easy absorption of the *cante* which they recognized as something familiar. In Rossy's view the Gypsy contribution to the *cante jondo* was minimal, for the *cante* is essentially an Andalusian folk music which the Gypsies learned after their arrival in southern Spain. Their importance in the early history of the *cante* was that of preserving it rather than of shaping its development.[24] Such a view ignores, however, the possibility of early Indian (proto-Gypsy) immigrations to Andalusia during the Arabic period of Spain's history, and it suggests that the musical influence was not from the Indians, to the Arabs, to the Spaniards, as Baloch thinks, but rather the other way—from the Spaniards to the Arabs and then to the Indians, the latter stage beginning, presumably, no earlier than the sixteenth century. We know of no other musicologist who subscribes to this theory.

Other critics, like Molina and Mairena, are more inclined to admit a more pervasive Arabic influence on Andalusian music, and they view the Gypsies' role in a somewhat different manner. They emphasize the importance not only of the eight centuries of Arab occupation, but of the large number of peasants of Moorish descent who remained in Andalusia after the expulsion of the Moors in 1492. It was precisely the contact between these people and the Gypsies that enabled the latter, who were already arriving in Andalusia by the last third of the century, to familiarize them-

---

[22] *Ibid.*, pp. 33-34.
[23] *Ibid.*, p. 36.
[24] This observation becomes suspect in view of the strongly anti-Gypsy bias shown throughout the book. Rossy goes to great pains to demonstrate that the *cante* is almost entirely a Spanish-Andalusian phenomenon owing very little to outside sources. He therefore minimizes not only the Gypsy, but the Arabic and Jewish influences as well, and he emphasizes the important role played by the folk music of other regions of Spain.

2

selves with Andalusian folk music. Molina and Mairena give a convincing account of the way in which this music was absorbed by the Gypsies:

> Lo que conviene subrayar es el fenómeno de convivencia durante los siglos XVI y XVII. La población morisca campesina debió de ser numerosa en las campiñas de Sevilla y de Jerez. Allí se formaron sedentarios grupos gitanos que en el transcurso de los siglos se andaluzaron por completo. . . .
>
> Pues bien, el primitivo cante flamenco se ha debido formar lentamente (siglos XVI al XVIII) en las provincias de Sevilla y Cádiz. En trescientos años, la aclimatación de los gitanos sedentarios fue total. Es probable, por no decir seguro, que las tierras bajas de Andalucía conservasen un numeroso porcentaje de moriscos, pese al decreto de expulsión, y, en todo caso, la entrañable tradición musical arábigo-andaluza pervivió con fuerza y pureza en el campo. Los gitanos procedían de la India, y en los cantes «propios», muy alterados por sus seculares errancias, latían melodías, ritmos, giros ornamentales, procedimientos característicos del folklore oriental. En Andalucía encontraron un folklore hermano, que les recordaba y refrescaba el suyo. Entonces, con su innata capacidad de asimilación, absorben los cantos y danzas diseminados en el pueblo. Refunden elementos dispersos y crean algo por completo nuevo: el flamenco primitivo.[25]

Most musicologists also point to a third possible source of the *cante jondo* in the synagogue chants of the Andalusian Jews. According to this theory, the names *cante flamenco* and *cante jondo* originally referred to Jewish religious music. One such theorist, Medina Azara, states: «. . . los judaizantes y marranos españoles designaron como 'cante flamenco' aquellas melodías, entonces religiosas, que sus hermanos emigrados a Holanda y Flandes podían cantar en su culto sinagogal tranquilos y sin miedo a la Inquisición.»[26] These songs were performed on Jewish festival days. He maintains that *jondo* is very likely a corruption of the Hebrew words *Jom tob,* signifying «buen día» or «día de fiesta.»[27] If this theory is correct, *jondo,* then, has no connection with the Spanish word *hondo.* Medina Azara asserts that today many of the Jewish synagogue chants are nearly indistinguishable from some of the older forms of the *cante jondo*: «El parecido entre 'cante jondo' y multitud de cánticos hebreos es tan estupefaciente, que a los estudiantes o gente del pueblo que lo ejecutaron los creían 'jassanim', es decir, cantores de sinagoga. Lo que casi asusta a los judíos que escuchan el 'cante jondo' es que, no sólo coincide en tonalidad y color con ciertos cantares sinagogales, sino que también el estilo de la dicción, el donaire, es el mismo.»[28] He believes that the older *saetas,* the *siguiriya gitana,* the *fandanguillo* and, to a certain extent, the *soleá* still show marked traits of their Jewish origin. Although the Jewish element in the latter three songs is debatable, many critics agree

---

[25] *Op. cit.,* p. 33.
[26] «Cante jondo y cantares sinagogales,» *Revista de Occidente,* XXX, 88 (oct.-dec., 1930), p. 53.
[27] *Ibid.,* p. 54.
[28] *Ibid.,* p. 56.

that the older *saetas* are very likely of Jewish origin, as we shall see later in our discussion of the *saeta*.

Although there is a considerable difference of opinion as to which songs of the *cante flamenco* deserve to be classified as *cante jondo*, there seems to be a general agreement among the critics that at least the following ten should be so designated: the *caña, carceleras, debla, martinete, polo, saeta, serrana, siguiriya gitana, soleá,* and the *toná.* Other forms of the *cante flamenco,* such as the *malagueñas* and *peteneras,* normally regarded as *cantes intermedios,* may be classified as *cante jondo* or *grande* when they are sung in an appropriate *jondo* style.

The *caña* was formerly considered the oldest form of the *cante jondo* and the origin of its name has been the subject of considerable speculation. Estebánez Calderón believed that it was derived from the Arabic word *gannia* which means «song,»[29] but more recent critics, like García Matos, feel that the name is borrowed from the verses of an older Andalusian folk tune. According to this theory, the word *caña,* appearing in the refrain, came to designate all the folk songs whose lyrics centered around that word, and one of those tunes, upon being adopted by the Gypsies, gave rise to the flamenco *caña.*[30] Another theory maintains that the name is derived from the fact that before the guitar came to be used as the chief instrumental accompaniment for the *cante,* the stanzas of this song were accompanied by *golpes de caña.*[31]

Like most forms of the *cante jondo,* it is a song of melancholy or despair that originally was never danced and was most likely sung *a palo seco,* without guitar accompaniment. The *caña* consists of an introductory, prolonged «ay» followed by a stanza of four octosyllabic verses with the even lines rhyming in assonance. After the fourth verse there is a *quejío* or lament, usually in the form of «¡ay!», and then a *macho* or refrain of indefinite length. Usually the meter of the *macho* differs from that of the preceding strophe. Example:

> a . . . . y.[32]
> Aunque toque a rebato
> las campanas del olvío,
> en mí no s'apaga el fuego
> que tu queré ha encendío.
> Aaaa, aaaa, aaaa, aaaa,
> ¡Viva Ronda!
> Reina de los sielos,
> flor d'Andalusía.
> ¡Quien no t'ha visto que se ponga
> aquí! [33]

---

[29] Related by Julián Pemartín, p. 52.
[30] *Ibid.,* p. 52.
[31] Rossy, p. 180.
[32] *Ibid.,* p. 181.
[33] José Carlos de Luna, *De cante grande y cante chico* (Madrid: Escelicer, 1942), p. 24.

Rossy has pointed out that the *copla* of the *caña* is not as old as its music and that most of its surviving lyrics are of a later date than those of the *siguiriya gitana* and the *soleá*. Furthermore, the *machos* are probably of a much later date than the *coplas,* as are the *ayes* or *quejío* that precede the *macho*. In fact, the use of the *quejío* probably did not become widespread until the song was accompanied by a guitar.[34] Although there may have originally been many melodic forms of the *caña,* only one has survived, and it seems to be closely related to the *soleá*.

The *carcelera* is a song expressing the loneliness and suffering of the imprisoned. Its melodic forms are the same as the *martinete,* and both are frequently considered to be variations of the *toná*. The *carcelera's* strophes usually consist of four octosyllabic verses with the even lines rhyming in assonance:

> Maldita sea la cárcel,
> sepultura de hombres vivos,
> donde se amansan los guapos
> y se pierden los amigos.

or

> Conocí a un hombre de bien,
> tan cabal como un «reló,»
> y por causas del querer
> en un presidio murió.[35]

Occasionally, the repetition of either the first or the fourth line adds a fifth verse to the stanza. The *carcelera* is, above all, a song of stoic acceptance of whatever fate has befallen the singer who rarely sings of revenge or escape. The song is intended to be sung without guitar accompaniment.

The *debla,* one of the oldest forms of the *cante jondo,* is known only by its modern versions, for its original form disappeared about the middle of the nineteenth century.[36] According to Molina and Mairena, all the modern versions are based on the one introduced by Tomás Pavón,[37] but there is considerable doubt whether this singer was acquainted with the original *debla,* supposedly created by an early nineteenth century *cantaor* called El Lebrijano,[38] or whether he transmitted a personalized version of that older form. Although José Carlos de Luna claims that the *debla* is descended from the *martinete,*[39] Molina and Mairena believe that it may be described more correctly as a *toná,* originally of religious character.[40]

Its name is derived from two words of *caló,* the Andalusian Gypsy dialect: *deblica barea,* which appear as the song's refrain, but whose

---

[34] *Op. cit.,* pp. 178-179.
[35] MANFREDI CANO, p. 141.
[36] PEMARTÍN, p. 83.
[37] *Op. cit.,* pp. 166-167.
[38] MANFREDI CANO, p. 145.
[39] *Op. cit.,* p. 62.
[40] *Op. cit.,* p. 166.

meaning is uncertain. According to Machado y Álvarez, the words may mean simply *mírala* and are used at the end of the song to infer «there you have it.» He also states that others believe they mean *mentira,* «lie,» and are used because the *debla* often begins like a *martinete,* but ends in an entirely different manner. Thus, *deblica barea* implies *te engañé*: «I deceived you.» Machado y Álvarez then mentions a third theory—that *deblica* means *diosa,* «goddess,» and that *barea* means «great» or «excellent.»[41] Molina and Mairena support this hypothesis and point out that the words are of Sanskrit origin. The Indo-European root word *dei* means «brilliant sky,» and by extension it came to mean «goddess.» They state a different meaning for *barea,* however, which they believe may be related to the Indo-European word *bher,* meaning «dark.»[42]

The *debla* consists of strophes of four octosyllabic verses with lines two and four rhyming in assonance. Each stanza is always followed by the *macho, deblica barea.*

> Comparito de mi alma,
> dígale usté a mi mujé
> que vaya a pedir limosna,
> le dé pan a mi chavé.
> Deblica barea.
>
> Los ojitos tengo secos
> de mirar hacia el camino
> y no veo de venir
> el espejo en que me miro.
> Deblica barea.[43]

Molina and Mairena affirm, however, that the two final words are no longer used by modern singers.[44] Of all the *cante jondo* forms, the *debla* is probably one of the most expressive of anguish and despair. It has been described by Rossy as: «el canto del hombre que ha conocido todas las claudicaciones, todas las humillaciones, amarguras y ruindades de la vida, que vegeta sin esperanzas de redención.»[45] It is a song with neither fixed rhythm nor musical accompaniment, and it is rarely performed by professional entertainers.

The *martinete* is very likely of Gypsy origin and is thought to have originated as a work song among the ironworkers, blacksmiths, and others whose tools are the hammer, anvil, and forge.[46] Molina and Mairena believe that the *martinete* is, in fact, identical to the *carcelera* in its musical structure and that the two songs differ only in their lyrics. Both are in reality different names for the *toná.*[47] The verses of the *martinete*

[41] *Op. cit.,* pp. 167-168.
[42] *Op. cit.,* p. 166.
[43] PEMARTÍN, p. 84.
[44] *Op. cit.,* p. 166.
[45] *Op. cit.,* p. 151.
[46] MANFREDI CANO, pp. 167-168.
[47] *Op. cit.,* p. 165.

are always of a sober and dramatic nature and are arranged in stanzas of four octosyllabic lines. There are two forms for the *martinete*: *natural* and *redoblado*, neither of which is meant to be performed with guitar accompaniment. The *martinete natural* is sung without repeating any of its verses as in the following:

> Así como está la fragua
> hecha candela de oro,
> se me ponen las entrañas
> cuando te recuerdo y lloro.[48]

The second form, the *martinete redoblado*, does repeat some verses. For example:

> Nadie diga que es locura,
> nadie diga que es locura
> esto que estabaíto ya aparentando
> que la locura,
> que la locura se cura
> y yo vivo agonizando.[49]

The *martinete* is one of the oldest forms of the *cante jondo*, and it was well on its way to being forgotten when attention was focused on its importance by the *Primer Concurso del Cante Jondo* in 1922.

The *polo* is often associated with the *caña* insomuch as many of their *coplas* are nearly identical and their music shares some similarities.[50] The *polo*, however, does not generally have the *caña*'s emotional depth. Some musicologists assert that the *polo* is, in fact, an Andalusian folk song which was adapted to the flamenco style around the beginning of the nineteenth century.[51] Its shorter length and comparatively light-hearted, gayer mood makes it the least prestigious form of the *cante jondo*, and its survival in our time has been due largely to its incorporation into the repertoire of the Ballet Español. In Ricardo Molina's opinion: «. . . el polo es un cante brillante, de inspiración más bien exterior que intimista, que parece compuesto para el teatro.»[52] This author differs from most other critics in that he feels that it is related more directly to the *soleares* than to the *caña*.

Its octosyllabic verses are arranged in four-line strophes introduced by a prolonged *ay*, and they usually have a *macho* at the end. It is always performed *with* guitar accompaniment. An example of the *polo* is the following:

> ¡De qué me sirvió el querer
> ni el pasar por ti quebranto,

[48] PEMARTÍN, p. 118.
[49] *Ibid.*, pp. 118-119.
[50] MANFREDI CANO, p. 180; MOLINA and MAIRENA, p. 243. The latter authors believe that the *polo* is derived directly from *la caña*.
[51] PEMARTÍN, p. 130 and MOLINA and MAIRENA, p. 243.
[52] *Cante flamenco* (Madrid: Taurus, 1965), p. 35.

si no habías de ser mía
de no hacer Dios un milagro! [53]

Another of its *coplas*, this one in a more characteristically light-hearted spirit, is:

En Carmona hay una fuente
con catorce o quince caños
con un letrero que dice:
¡Viva el polo sevillano! [54]

The *polo* is at best a marginal form of the *cante grande*, for although its structural similarities to the *caña* (or *soleares*) and its use of a *macho* would normally classify it as *cante jondo*, nevertheless, its gayer lyrics, grandiloquent tone, and affected style make it more typical of the *cante chico*.

The *saeta*, which probably originated in Seville, is essentially an octosyllabic, four or five-line poem or musical prayer without refrain. It is sung to Christ or the Virgin as their statues are carried on floats or by penitents during the religious processions of Holy Week. The *saetas* are always sung without guitar accompaniment from a balcony or sidewalk by a single individual as the statues enter or leave the church or when they reach a point along the route directly in front of the singer. At the first notes of the *saeta*, the procession stops in order to receive the offering of song. When it has ended the trumpets sound and the procession continues. Musically, the *saeta* makes use of semitones and fluctions between major and minor modes that create the impression of ancient song. [55] The verses usually depict or comment on the sufferings of Christ or the Virgin Mary. Many Biblical incidents—the Last Supper, the seizure of Jesus, Calvary—as well as the apocryphal legends like the Veronica are utilized in its stanzas. [56] Examples of both the four and five verse *saetas* are as follows:

Er cuerpo yeva doblao
por el peso de la crú,
y los sayones asotan
su cara yena de lú. [57]

Madre de santa ternura,
que lloras sin descansar
por el hijo sin ventura;
¡Bien te podemos llamar
la Virgen de la Amargura! [58]

[53] PEMARTÍN, p. 130.
[54] ROSSY, p. 182.
[55] See EDWARD F. STANTON, «Federico García Lorca and Cante Jondo,» Diss. Univ. Calif., Los Angeles 1972, p. 137.
[56] *Ibid.*, p. 138.
[57] LUNA, p. 52.
[58] PEMARTÍN, p. 137.

Medina Azara believes that the *saeta* was originally of Jewish origin and that its melody was based primarily on the fourteenth-fifteenth century prayer of atonement, the *Kol Nidrei,* in which the penitent asked Jehovah to annull all the oaths that he had been forced to make against his will—specifically his abjuration of Mosaic law and his profession of Christianity, which had been forced upon him by the Inquisition. Ironically, however, the verses sung to the melody were devout Catholic lyrics calculated to reassure the Christian populace of the convert's religious sincerity. For this reason the original *saetas* tended to combine the most ardent appearance of devotion (to Christ) with the genuine despair and grief of the singer (the Jewish convert).[59]

Although this theory is generally accepted by many critics, others, including Molina and Mairena, object that there is no historical evidence to support such a hypothesis.[60] In their opinion the *saeta* dates from the early nineteenth century and was created about the same time as the *cante flamenco* itself. They believe that the *saetas* come basically from three sources: (1) The largest group is descended from the folk *tonás*; (2) next, are those derived from the *siguiriya gitana*; (3) finally, there are those related to Christian liturgical music.[61] This theory holds that these songs, called *calvarios,* were spontaneous Easter prayers that had been assimilated into the folk culture of Andalusia and were later adapted to a flamenco style of singing in the early nineteenth century.[62]

Hipólito Rossy presents a similar theory, but he insists that there are essentially two kinds of *saetas*: the older, traditional ones derived from popular religious songs and the more modern *saetas flamencas.*[63] The *antiguas* or *clásicas,* which were still widely sung during the first two decades of this century, are examples of religious folk poetry, but they have been almost entirely supplanted by the modern *saetas* which are usually referred to as *saetas por siguiriyas, ... por martinetes,* or *... por fandangos.* The term «por siguiriyas» means that the words of the *saeta* are sung in the meter appropriate to the *siguiriya.* A *saeta por martinetes* or *fandangos* is, in reality, a *martinete* or a *fandango* with the words of a *saeta.* According to Rossy, the originator of the modern *saeta* was Manuel Centeno whose creations surpassed the older *saetas* in popularity within a very few years.[64]

A final theory concerning the possible origin of the *saetas* (that of Edward F. Stanton) suggests that these songs represent the survival of an ancient fertility rite involving violent, blood sacrifice. Many of their traditional verses seem to suggest the use of the god's blood to fecundate the earth. Furthermore, there often seems to be a cyclical quality to the events described: life - death - rebirth. Citing the findings of Arcadio de Larrea, Stanton points out that the music itself has a tonal system representing a

---

[59] *Op. cit.,* pp. 58, 62.
[60] *Op. cit.,* p. 255.
[61] *Ibid.,* p. 255.
[62] See EDWARD F. STANTON, p. 144.
[63] *Op. cit.,* p. 146.
[64] *Ibid.,* p. 150.

symbolic life - death dualism. With the advent of Cristianity, these pagan rites were then altered to suit the new religion and were absorbed into the celebrations of the Church. Eventually, through a process of secularization, the music and poetry of these religious ceremonies were assimilated into the folk culture of Andalusia, and from there they were absorbed into the *cante jondo,* possibly in the mid-nineteenth century.[65]

The next type of *cante,* the *serrana,* presumably originated in the mountainous regions of Andalusia, possibly around Córdoba,[66] and it may have been based on a rural folk song that was adapted to the flamenco-*cante jondo* style around the mid-nineteenth century.[67] Its music bears certain similarities to the *caña,* since both use the same tonal system in «mi,» and to the *siguiriya gitana.* The *copla* of the *serrana* has the same structure as the *seguidilla castellana* with each stanza consisting of four verses, the first and third having seven syllables, and the second and fourth, five. Each strophe has a three line *macho* whose first and third verses contain five syllables and whose second has ten. In the four-verse stanza, the even verses rhyme in assonance, as do the first and third lines of the refrain.

The *serranas'* themes concern shepherds, mountaineers, robbers, and other fugitives who hide in the mountains. For example:

> Por la Sierra Morena
> va una partía.
> Y al capitán le llaman
> José María.
> No pasará preso
> mientras su jaca torda
> tenga pesuezo.[68]

Frequently, the figure of the *ventera* appears as the confidant and ally of these people. She is usually portrayed as a rough peasant woman, quick with a knife or shotgun.[69] A large group of *serranas* consists of ironic commentaries on human nature. In all cases, the *macho* or refrain completes or summarizes the meaning of the *copla* and frequently presents a moral or a confirmation of the idea in the preceding strophe. For example:

> Yo crié en mi rebaño
> una cordera.
> De tanto acariciarla
> se volvió fiera.
> Que las mujeres
> de tanto acariciarlas
> fieras se vuelven.[70]

---

[65] *Op. cit.,* pp. 145-158. STANTON uses the theories of ARCADIO DE LARREA PALACÍN as a starting point, but then modifies them to propose the hypothesis summarized above.
[66] PEMARTÍN, p. 144.
[67] MOLINA and MAIRENA, p. 238.
[68] *Ibid.,* p. 238.
[69] ROSSY, p. 204.
[70] PEMARTÍN, p. 144.

The *serrana* was not originally sung with guitar accompaniment, and it is traditionally performed only by male singers.[71]

The *siguiriya gitana* has achieved a preeminent place as one of the two most basic forms of the *cante jondo*. There are several theories regarding its origin. Hipólito Rossy believes that its current forms date from the late fifteeenth or early sixteenth centuries, that it was given its final form by the Gypsies (as the name implies), and that it has little to do with the *seguidilla castellana*. He feels that the *siguiriya gitana* is based on Andalusian funeral laments in the doric mode which are at least two thousand years old and are of pagan origin.[72] The remnants of these songs still existed in Andalusia in the fifteeenth century and were adopted and modified by the Gypsies who first called them *plañideras*. This name was later changed to *playera* and, finally, to *siguiriya*. The reason for these changes is unknown, though Rossy theorizes that the Gypsies used the name *seguidilla* out of ignorance, since this type of song was very much in vogue at that time.

> A su arribo a Al-Andalus (hacia 1470), ahítos de caminos en su peregrinar sin tregua, esclavizados del mal sino que les echó de su tierra indostánica, los gitanos encuentran en la plañidera la más cabal expresión de su infortunio, de sus penas sin fin. Y se apoderan de ella, la ornan de policronías melismáticas orientales, le dan ese hálito fatalista que la distingue del resto del cante jondo. . . .
>
> El porqué y el cuándo del nombre de este cante no es problema fácil de resolver. Por su carácter desolado y llorón, la melodía tuvo primero el nombre de plañidera—de plañir, llorar—, que por corrupción pasó a planiera y a playera. Fueron los gitanos quienes dieron su nombre definitivo al cante: el de seguiriya gitana.
>
> Cuando los gitanos llegaron a España, comenzaba la boga de la seguidilla; y oyendo hablar de ella hasta el abuso, tal vez tomaron el nombre y se lo aplicaron al cante de su predilección, sencillamente por ignorancia.[73]

Other critics, like Manfredi Cano, feel that the *siguiriya gitana* was not formed until the late eighteenth century and that it is based directly on the *seguidilla castellana*: «Ellos tomaron de los castellanos del siglo XVIII la seguidilla y la adaptaron a su peculiar manera de ser; se canta en compás de tres por cuatro o de tres por ocho; al final, como un alivio, la seguidilla lleva un macho, no sujeto a regla fija, sino brotado casi siempre por impulso intuitivo del gitano que canta.» [74]

A third view, that of Molina and Mairena, combines certain aspects of the two theories stated above. Although they are quite hesitant to accept the idea that the *siguiriya gitana* originated in the late fifteenth or early sixteenth centuries, and they reject as fanciful Rossy's belief that the *siguiriya* is based on ancient Andalusian funeral chants, nevertheless, they agree with the etymology of the *siguiriya*'s earlier name, *playera*, as a cor-

---

[71] ROSSY, p. 207.
[72] *Ibid.*, p. 167.
[73] *Ibid.*, pp. 161-162.
[74] *Op. cit.*, p. 188.

ruption of *plañidera,* a word chosen to describe the song's pathos. Furthermore, they do not deny the presence of certain ancient musical influences on the *cante.* These include: (1) a resemblance of the verse structure of the *siguiriya* to some of the *jarchas mozárabes* of the eleventh century; (2) the undeniable presence of a few qualities found in primitive Hindu music (a fact they explain by the Indian homeland of the Andalusian Gypsies); (3) the possible resemblance of the *siguiriya* to the Jewish sinagogal chant *Kol Nidrei,* which they feel originated in Spain during the late Middle Ages. They also admit, however, that the question of Jewish influence is debatable and that other critics have denied it altogether. Like Manfredi Cano, Molina and Mairena believe that the *seguidilla castellana* did influence the development of the *siguiriya gitana* and that the presence of some ancient elements does not preclude the possibility of its originating in the late eighteenth century, although an earlier date is more likely: «. . . en un plano objetivo, es imposible conceder que las siguiriyas sean anteriores a 1780 porque no hay prueba documental en que apoyar semejante afirmación. Ahora bien, el hecho de que nuestras noticias no vayan más allá de 1780 no invalida la suposición de que existiesen con anterioridad a dicha fecha. Incluso opinamos que lo más probable y natural es que se cantase antes de 1780.»[75] This date nearly coincides with the edicts of Charles III (1783) which granted freedom of movement to the Gypsies and thereby facilitated their intermingling with the rest of society. Since the *siguiriyas* became known almost immediately thereafter, it is logical to suppose that they were already a fully developed *cante,* but known and sung only among the Gypsies prior to that date.

The genealogy of the *siguiriya gitana* has given rise to many theories. Molina and Mairena believe that it is descended from the older *tonás,*[76] whereas José Carlos de Luna affirm the opposite, that the *tonás* were derived from the *siguiriya,*[77] which in turn is a direct descendant of the *soleá.*[78] Tomás Borrás, on the other hand, believes that the *siguiriya,* as well as most other forms of the *cante,* is derived from the *caña.*[79] Finally, some critics, like Eduardo Martínez Torner[80] and Manuel de Falla,[81] regard the *siguiriya gitana* as the original parent form of the *cante flamenco* from which all others are descended.

The standard copla for the *siguiriya gitana* theoretically contains four verses, the second and fourth of which rhyme in assonance. All have six syllables except the third which has eleven. The third verse is divided into two hemistiches of five and six syllables with a pause or *caída* after the fifth.[82] In reality, the *siguiriya gitana* has many forms and is apt to vary considerably depending on the locality where it is sung and the individual style

---

[75] *Op. cit.,* p. 177.
[76] *Ibid.,* p. 178.
[77] Reported by MOLINA and MAIRENA, p. 179.
[78] MANFREDI CANO, pp. 120-121.
[79] According to MANFREDI CANO, p. 115.
[80] Also reported by MANFREDI CANO, p. 113.
[81] *Op. cit.,* p. 126.
[82] PEMARTÍN, pp. 145-146.

of the performer. Like most forms of the *cante jondo,* it was originally sung without instrumental accompaniment although now it is almost always performed with a guitar. Usually there are two separate rhythms that form a counterpoint. The basic rhythm is carried by the guitar and the secondary rhythm is supplied by the singer or by the *palmas* or clapping of hands by the other performers.[83] The *siguiriya gitana* begins with a guitar introduction that helps establish the mood of the song. This guitar prelude, called a *temple,* is followed by a prolonged *quejío* or *grito* of the singer who dramatizes the emotions to be expressed in the lyrics. The *quejío* is often, but not necessarily, succeeded by a silence which is then followed by two *coplas,* one of which is expanded. These are generally sung on an emotionally ascending scale and may be interrupted at any point by exclamations, cries of *¡ay!,* or by sudden, unexpected silences which often come after the moments of greatest emotional intensity. The third and fourth *coplas* are usually sung on a descending scale with the fourth normally shorter than the third. The song ends with the gradual fading away of the singer's voice and the guitar accompaniment.

The lyrics of the *siguiriya gitana* are especially noted for their tragic content, for the *siguiriya* is, above all, a song of despair, of the *situación límite* described by A. González Climent as follows: «Las siguiriyas se destacan por la hondura trágica de sus giros sonoros y por el contenido agonista de sus coplas, monadas de los dramas más intensos del ser . . . Es la rebelión del albedrío humano, expuesta con la quejumbrosidad extrema del jipío que nace ante la situación límite. No hay nada, desde el punto de vista de la filosofía flamenca, más allá de las siguiriyas. Son el salto al vacío, donde la razón humildemente tiene que atreverse a no ver, a no explicar, solamente a gritar. Tras las siguiriyas sólo cabe Dios o la Nada.» [84] Because of the *siguiriya's* extreme artistic and emotional demands, it is normally considered the culminating point in a singer's career when he has mastered this form of the *cante jondo.* Its *coplas,* often of a very personal nature, cover the gamut of human emotions:

> Ni el sudó de mi cara
> lo pueo secá
> porque yevo a la espalda, con una caena,
> las manos atrás.[85]

> Tengo yo una pena
> que me jase yorá;
> la de vé a mis hijos sin pare,
> con hambre y sin pan.[86]

> Cuando yo me muera
> mira que te encargo:

[83] MOLINA and MAIRENA, p. 172.
[84] *Op. cit.,* p. 175.
[85] LUNA, p. 44.
[86] *Ibid.,* p. 45.

> que con la jebra de tu pelo negro
> me amarres las manos.[87]

> To er mundo e rodiyas:
> Dios está pasando;
> va a yevale a mi mare consuelo,
> qu'está agonisando.[88]

> Liao en mi manta,
> tumbao en el suelo
> pensando en tus ojos y en tus pinos blancos
> encuentro consuelo.[89]

Other *coplas,* however, reflect moments of serenity, like these verses cited by Manfredi Cano:

> No sarga la luna
> que no tié pa' qué;
> con los ojitos e mi compañera
> yo m'alumbraré.[90]

Some even portray humor as in this *copla* quoted by José Carlos de Luna:

> Ve y dile a tu mare
> qu'esté reposá,
> porque tu ropa junta con la mía
> no se va a lavá.[91]

or this one collected by Antonio Machado y Álvarez:

> ¿Que un beso es pecao
> te dise tu mare?
> Que te diga si eya era una santa
> y un santo tu pare.[92]

If the *siguiriya gitana* represents the first of the two fundamental forms of the *cante jondo,* the *soleá* is the second. While lacking the emotional intensity of the *siguiriya,* the *soleá* has a tremendous diversity of forms and is highly adaptable to other types of music. Hence, there are *soleares de Alcalá, de Triana, de Utrera, de Cádiz, de Jerez, de Córdoba* (almost every locality in Andalusia has its own form of *soleá*) as well as an innumerable variety of other folk and flamenco songs that are sung *por soleares,* in the style of the *soleá.*

Many opinions exist concerning its date of origin. Hipólito Rossy

---

[87] PEMARTÍN, p. 146.
[88] LUNA, p. 47.
[89] *Ibid.*, p. 48.
[90] *Op. cit.*, p. 189.
[91] *Op. cit.*, p. 45.
[92] *Cantes flamencos* (Buenos Aires: Espasa-Calpe Argentina, S. A., 1947), p. 161.

feels that its music is extremely old because it is in the *modo dórico*: «La melodía del canto es antiquísima, anterior en muchos siglos a la música de guitarra sobre la que se canta, que a su vez pertenece, como la melodía, al modo dórico.» [93] He also affirms that it was not sung with guitar accompaniment until the middle of the sixteenth century. [94] Julián Pemartín, on the other hand, claims that the *soleá* dates from the beginning of the nineteenth century and that its origin is found in the *jaleo,* a form of chanted dance which had been known for some time in Cádiz and Jerez. [95] Other critics, like Molina and Mairena, believe that the *soleá* is entirely of Gypsy origin and that it originated during the first half, rather than at the very beginning of the nineteenth century. They also think that it was originally a *cante bailado*: «Es muy probable que la soleá haya surgido de algún cante gitano para bailar en el primer tercio del siglo XIX, pues mientras más antiguas son, más ligero y bailable es su compás. . . . Pero, en rigor, no puede hablarse de soleá anterior a la mitad del siglo XIX.» [96] They feel that the song does not bear any recognizable resemblance to any other form of the *cante*. Thus, they reject the theory that it descended from the *jaleo* or from the *caña,* which is considered by some to be the source of all forms of the *cante flamenco.*

Although originally written as a *cante para bailar,* the *soleá* was gradually transformed into a *cante para cantar* independent of the dance. This transformation was the work of individual performers who, through their personal interpretations, also converted the *soleá* to a *cante grande* by the last quarter of the nineteenth century. [97] This trend has continued into the modern period, as most singers have chosen to maintain its characteristically serious, solemn style.

The music of the *soleá* is normally in a tempo of 3/4 or 3/8 and the chords that accompany it cover the entire range encompassed by the Greek scale in «mi.» [98] The melody is usually like a prolonged lament, and, in contrast to most forms of the *cante jondo,* the guitar accompaniment has always played a major role in its performance.

There are basically three types of *copla* for the *soleá*. The most frequent, the *copla clásica,* consists of three octosyllabic verses with the first and third rhyming either in assonance or full rhyme. There is also a *copla* of four octosyllabic lines with assonance or full rhyme in the second and fourth verses, though Rossy considers this form to be a later adaptation. [99] Manfredi Cano, however, believes the *cuarteta* is, in reality, the original form and that the four-verse structure was later reduced to three. [100] The third type of *copla,*

[93] *Op. cit.,* p. 171.
[94] *Ibid.,* p. 177.
[95] *Op. cit.,* p. 149.
[96] *Op. cit.,* pp. 211-212.
[97] *Ibid.,* p. 212.
[98] ROSSY, pp. 172-173.
[99] *Ibid.,* p. 177.
[100] *Op. cit.,* p. 194.

30

the *soleariya,* consists of three verses. The first has between three and six syllables and the second and third are octosyllabic.

The *soleá* is characterized by sobriety, dignity, and a certain proclivity toward philosophical speculation or even sententiousness:

> Aquel que nunca lloró
> y nunca tiene una pena
> vive feliz, pero ignora
> si la vida es mala o buena.[101]

> Voy como si fuera preso:
> detrás camina mi sombra,
> delante mi pensamiento.[102]

Often the *soleares* express aphorisms, such as:

> El queré quita el sentío;
> lo digo por esperiensia,
> porque a mí me ha sucedío.[103]

In spite of its seriousness, however, the *soleá* rarely expresses the intense emotional dramas or the extremes of tragedy found in the *siguiriya gitana.* The *soleá* is more subdued, more serene and refined; its mood is suggestive of stoic resignation rather than despair. González Climent has described the essential difference between these two forms of the *cante jondo* as follows: «La soleá es la siguiriya experimentada, en sosiego, sin prisas, sabia, sentenciosa. La siguiriya es la expresión de lo que está pasando, el embargo dinámico del drama. La soleá desarrolla el comentario de lo transcurrido, como la entrada en carena después del temporal. La soleá es el descenso sosegado de la siguiriya.»[104] He concludes his comparison saying that «los soleares son el tono menor de las siguiriyas.»[105] There is also a tendency, particularly evident in the three-verse *coplas,* to concentrate an entire drama, to state a particular problem and provide its solution, all within the limits of the three verses. For example:

> El tomillo ha florecío.
> Su flo se yevó el aroma
> der queré que te tenío.[106]

The next *copla* describes an incipient amorous relationships, its results, and suggests the woman's reaction to gossip—all in three verses:

> Mira lo que andan hablando:
> sin tené naíta contigo,
> tós nos están criticando.[107]

---

[101] ROSSY, p. 177.
[102] PEMARTÍN, p. 150.
[103] LUNA, p. 35.
[104] *Op. cit.,* p. 177.
[105] *Ibid.,* p. 202.
[106] LUNA, p. 33.
[107] *Ibid.,* p. 37.

Although the *soleá* is usually serious in content, its verses do not always deal with transcendental matters. Molina and Mairena remind us that some of its *coplas* express trivial, everyday situations of no particular importance, as the following example shows:

> Quise cambiarle, y no quiso,
> un pañuelo de lunares
> por otro de fondo liso.[108]

Molina and Mairena emphasize that «las letras son fragmentos volanderos de vida, circunstancias de tal o cual existencia determinada, episodio, sentimiento, gesta individual . . . el tan celebrado 'estilo sentencioso' no monopoliza ni mucho menos a la soleá. Es una de sus facetas y nada más.»[109] Finally, it should be noted that the *soleariya* tends to be in a lighter, happier vein than the *soleá*. The following rather sarcastic commentary is an example:

> Tu queré
> es como el oro del moro
> y el salero del inglé.[110]

The last form of the *cante jondo* is the *toná*. Its name is derived from *tonada* which, according to García Matos, was previously used throughout Andalusia, Castile, León, and Extremadura to designate a generic category that included a large variety of traditional, popular folk songs.[111] The *tonadas* as well as *tonadillas* appeared in the early seventeenth century,[112] though the first specific reference to the flamenco *toná* occurs in Estébanez Calderón's *Escenas Andaluzas* (1847) in which he speaks of the *tonadas de Sevilla*.[113]

The *toná* is extremly flexible in its melodic patterns, and Machado y Alvarez believes that there were at one time twenty-six types of *tonás*, most of which were named after the singer who invented or popularized them.[114] According to Molina and Mairena, however, a popular Gypsy-Andalusian tradition claims that there were previously as many as thirty-one different *tonás*. Most of these have disappeared so that at present they report only eight to ten forms in actual use.[115] The situation is further complicated by the fact that the name *toná* is gradually falling into disuse, and most of

[108] *Op. cit.,* p. 208.
[109] *Ibid.,* p. 209.
[110] MANFREDI CANO, p. 195.
[111] Quoted by MOLINA and MAIRENA, p. 159.
[112] *Ibid.,* p. 159.
[113] Cited by MOLINA and MAIRENA, p. 160.
[114] *Op. cit.,* pp. 161-162.
[115] *Op. cit.,* p. 164. This statement, which is generally supported by the findings of other critics, is curiously contradicted two pages before by the assertion: «Todas las 'tonás' que hoy se conocen acusan un estrecho parentesco entre sí y un aire familiar melódico que permitirá reducirlas a variaciones de dos o tres tipos substanciales de melodía; acaso a un tipo único.» In a later work Molina reduces the number of extant forms for the *toná* to seven or eight. See *Cante flamenco,* p. 39.

its existing forms are now designated as *martinetes,* a misnomer, because the *martinete* is really a sub-category of the *toná.* Molina and Mairena believe that the *toná* is undoubtedly one of the oldest forms of the *cante jondo.* They stress the fact that some of its lyrics refer to persecutions, torture, and murder of Gypsies, and to events that occurred long before the end of the eighteenth century. They claim, in fact, that the *toná* may well be the parent *cante* from which the *siguiriya gitana* as well as most of the other forms of the *cante jondo* descended.[116] This view seems to have found acceptance among other musicologists as well, like Julián Pemartín and Manuel Ríos Ruiz.[117]

Other critics, however, have arrived at conclusions that differ considerably from those of Molina and Mairena. Manfredi Cano, for example, feels that the *toná* is a *cante de fragua,* that it is, in reality, a *seguiriya gitana* without the initial *tercio de entrada,* and that for anyone but an expert, there are no appreciable diferences between the two.[118] Far from being a *cante para escuchar,* the *toná* was originally intended to accompany an Andalusian dance. In time the music became independent of the dance and was taken over as a work song by the Gypsy *fragueros.*[119]

Hipólito Rossy presents a third theory concerning its origin. He believes that formerly there may have been many forms of the *toná,* but only one has survived rather than eight or ten. He further states that the *toná* probably originated during the later years of the high Middle Ages and that it may be of Jewish origin.[120]

Although there are many musical forms of the *toná,* its *letras* are generally composed of stanzas of four octosyllabic verses with irregular rhyme in the even lines; but it is not unusual to find occasional verses of more than eight syllables. Each strophe is followed by a refrain consisting of either three verses or a couplet whose lines are of unequal length. Melodically, the refrain is a prolongation of the preceding stanza, but in a slowly descending scale. The *toná* is never accompanied by the guitar nor by *palmas,* clapping of the hands. Its melody is invariably sad and often expresses despair like the *siguiriya gitana.* The oldest *coplas* of the *toná* usually contain many words in *caló,* the Andalusian Gypsy dialect, and relate incidents of persecutions, suffering, and death. Examples of the *toná* are as follows:

> Los «geres» por las esquinas,
> con velones y farol,
> en voz alta se decían
> «matarlo» que es «calorró.» [121]

---

[116] See pp. 159-169.
[117] *Op. cit.,* p. 161 and *Introducción al cante flamenco* (Madrid: Ediciones Istmo, 1972), p. 70.
[118] *Op. cit.,* p. 200.
[119] *Ibid.,* pp. 200-201.
[120] *Op. cit.,* p. 141.
[121] MOLINA and MAIRENA, p. 163.

3

Cuando te encuentro en la calle
me causa gran sentimiento;
que pasas y no me hablas
y agachas la vista al suelo.[122]

The following is a typical refrain:

Y si no es verdad,
que Dios me mande la muerte,
si me la quiere mandar.[123]

Two additional *cantes* mentioned by García Lorca in his *Poema del Cante Jondo* are the *malagueña* and the *petenera*, both of which are usually regarded as *cantes intermedios*. Neither was originally considered an integral part of the *cante jondo*, but in recent years there has been a tendency to elevate them to this category due to the prestige of their most famous performers. It is generally agreed that the *malagueña* was created during the first half of the past century by the *aflamencamiento* of a popular Andalusian *fandango*, and that it was promoted from the status of *cante chico* by Enrique el Mellizo and Antonio Chacón, two famous singers of the late nineteenth and early twentieth centuries. The *malagueña* is never danced and its lyrics, always of a serious, dramatic nature, frequently mention Malaga, its monuments and districts, or they relate events from the lives of mariners and others who make their living from the sea. Its *coplas* are normally composed of either four or five octosyllabic verses with the even lines rhyming in assonance. Examples:

¡Barrio de la Trinidá,
cuántos paseos me debes!
¡Cuántas veces me han tapao
las sombras de tus paredes! [125]

Por esos mares de Dios
navegando, me perdí;
y con la luz de tus ojos
a puerto de mar volví.[126]

Cuando me pongo a pensar
lo lejos que estoy de ti
no me canso de llorar,
porque sé que te perdí
para no verte jamás.[127]

[122] PEMARTÍN, p. 163.
[123] MOLINA and MAIRENA, p. 168.
[124] PEMARTÍN, p. 112.
[125] LUNA, p. 166.
[126] ROSSI, p. 242.
[127] *Ibid.*, p. 242.

The *petenera* is now considered by most critics to be either a part of the *cante jondo* or to belong to that special category midway between *jondo* and *flamenco*. Rossy admits: «de la petenera se ha hecho más literatura que de todas las demás canciones que componen el folklore andaluz y levantino. Los profesionales del cante y los aficionados exigentes la tienen en poca estima; incluso algunos le niegan su naturaleza de cante jondo y, a lo sumo, la admiten como una particularidad inclasificable del cante chico. Pero esto es un juicio equivocado.»[128] He goes on to explain that because of its supposed modern origin, its creation by a single, known individual, the fact that it is fairly easy to sing tolerably well, and, finally, because it enjoyed a tremendous popularity around the turn of the century, it has been unjustly disdained by contemporary performers and *cognoscenti* of the *cante jondo*. Rossy remarks that in the hands of a skillful performer like Pastora Pavón («La Niña de los Peines»), the *petenera* is fully a *cante grande*. Molina and Mairena also observe: «La 'Niña de los Peines' hizo de la petenera algo de admirable grandeza, rompiendo el molde primitivo del cante chico en que fue modelada.»[129] Other critics, like González Climent, regard it as a *cante fronterizo* between the *situación límite* of the *cante grande* and the *situación cotidiana* of the *cante chico*.[130] José Carlos de Luna limits himself to saying: «No son 'cante grande' ni 'chico.'»[131]

If the exact classification of the *petenera* lends itself to confusion, the question of its origin is no clearer. The musicologist Arcadio de Larrea Palacín states that it is from a foreign source, but he does not mention which.[132] José Carlos de Luna notes its similarities to the *soleá* and remarks: «'El Punto de la Habana' y la canción popular de 'El paño moruno' son los únicos ascendientes de 'las peteneras.'»[133] Molina and Mairena also point out the song's resemblance to the *soleá*, but reject the possibility of its being descended from it.[134] The likelihood of a Cuban origin is based both on its possible relationship to the first song mentioned above and on one of its *coplas* which reads:

En la Habana nasí yo
debajo de una parmera,
ayí me echaron el agua,
¡Niña de mi corasón!,
ayí me echaron el agua
cantando la petenera.[135]

Many critics believe that it is the creation of an early nineteenth century singer from the village of Paterna de la Rivera, near Cádiz. Manfredi Cano

[128] *Op. cit.*, p. 255.
[129] *Op. cit.*, p. 317.
[130] *Op. cit.*, pp. 174-188.
[131] *Op. cit.*, p. 39.
[132] *Op. cit.*, p. 156.
[133] *Op. cit.*, p. 39.
[134] *Op. cit.*, p. 317.
[135] MACHADO Y ÁLVAREZ, p. 173.

is of the opinion that she amalgamated two popular songs of the day, «El Punto de La Habana» and «El Paño Moruno,» and that the resulting *petenera* was an original composition unlike either of its predecessors.[136] Molina and Mairena claim, however, that although the flamenco *petenera* may have originated with her, its music is much older, since the basic melody is to be found in certain *composiciones cultas* of the eighteenth century.[137] Still another version of its origin, that of Machado y Álvarez, combines many of these hypotheses into a single theory. In his collection of *cantes flamencos* he states: «Aunque las 'Peteneras' no han estado de moda en Sevilla hasta el año de 1879, convienen todos los cantadores en que son antiguas y en que deben su origen a una cantadora de flamenco llamada la 'Petenera,' a quien unos hacen natural de Málaga, y otros, de la Habana.» [138] He admits that the name is probably a corruption of «Paterna» and that the *petenera* probably originated in Paterna de la Rivera. However, if these oral traditions are correct, then the song and its originator are much older than the early nineteenth century. Finally, there is the theory of the song's possible Jewish origin based on one of its *coplas:*

> ¿Dónde vas, linda judía,
> tan compuesta y a deshora?
> —Voy en busca de Rebeco,
> que estará en la sinagoga.[139]

This theory, rejected by most critics for lack of sufficient evidence, is regarded seriously by Rossy who states that the musical structure of the *petenera* indicates a much earlier date than the nineteenth century: «Es errónea la creencia de que la petenera data del siglo XIX. Su estructura melódica y armónica corresponde al período de transición de los modos griegos antiguos a los modos mayor y menor modernos, y el ritmo en compás alterno se corresponde con el de algunas villanescas del XVI, aunque hay indicios de que sea de época anterior . . . .» [140] Noting that some *coplas* of the *petenera* are still found among the folk music of Jewish communities in the Balkans and that these communities are descended from Jewish emigrants expelled from Spain in 1492, Rossy concludes that a semitic influence on the *petenera* is, indeed, quite possible.[141] The implications of this theory are that the *petenera* dates from at least the fifteenth century, that it is probably a form of Andalusian folk song, that its musical estructure was modified by the Spanish Jews, and that it was a modern version of this form that was adapted to a flamenco style in the early nineteenth century.

The typical *copla* of the *petenera* consists of four octosyllabic verses

---

[136] *Op. cit.,* p. 178.
[137] *Op. cit.,* p. 317.
[138] *Op. cit.,* pp. 171-172.
[139] PEMARTÍN, p. 128.
[140] *Op. cit.,* p. 259.
[141] *Ibid.,* p. 259.

with the even lines rhyming in assonance. Usually there is an exclamatory extra verse, such as «Niña de mi corazón,» included after the third line. The third verse is then repeated before proceeding to the fourth so that the stanza actually contains six rather than four lines. The most typical of the *coplas* would be sung as follows:

> Quien te puso petenera
> no te supo poner nombre,
> que debió de haberte puesto,
> ¡Niña de mi corazón!,
> que debió de haberte puesto
> la perdición de los hombres.[142]

The *petenera* is always accompanied by the guitar and is intended to be a *cante para bailar*. It is a melancholy, sentimental song whose fundamental themes are similar to those of the *soleá*.[143]

Opinions differ regarding the various forms of music for the *petenera*. Julián Pemartín believes that there are essentially two: the traditional one and that of Pastora Pavón, the song's most famous interpreter.[144] Molina and Mairena state that the melody of the *petenera* has at least three distinct variations: the folklore version, the flamenco, and the personal interpretation of Pastora Pavón.[145] Rossy has a similar theory which he states in greater detail. For him the song has two basic forms, the *antigua* and the *moderna,* and the latter can be subdivided into *corta* and *larga.*[146] The *forma antigua,* in the doric mode, is no longer heard and is known only to scholars. The *petenera corta,* however, is widely known, and the ease with which it can be performed has made it the most popular of the three. It is this version which is usually danced. The *petenera larga* was, according to Rossy, a much older form, and it was almost totally forgotten when Pastora Pavón rediscovered it. Its melody is similar to the *petenera corta,* which is undoubtedly descended from it, but it requires variations that make it undanceable and extremely difficult to sing. Its strophes consist of five-line stanzas rather than the usual four. Probably the most highly popularized *copla* of the *petenera larga* is the following, made famous by Pastora Pavón around 1918:

> Niño que en cuero y descalzo
> va llorando por la calle,
> ven acá y llora conmigo,
> que tampoco tengo madre,
> que la perdí cuando niña.[147]

The history of the *cante flamenco* can be divided into four stages. The first, its pre-history, dates from the second half of the fifteenth century,

---

[142] MACHADO Y ÁLVAREZ, p. 171.
[143] MANFREDI CANO, p. 178.
[144] *Op. cit.,* p. 129.
[145] *Op. cit.,* p. 318.
[146] *Op. cit.,* p. 256.
[147] *Ibid.,* p. 261.

when the Gypsies began settling in southern Spain, to the latter third of the eighteenth century, when history records the name of the first known singer of the *cante flamenco:* Tío Luis «el de la Juliana,» born in Jerez de la Frontera around 1750.[148] During this span of three centuries, the Gypsies combined their own musical traditions with the native Andalusian folk music and created the primitive *cante jondo.* Many critics, including José Carlos de Luna, Manfredi Cano, and Arcadio de Larrea Palacín, believe that the *cante* probably originated in the triangular territory limited by Morón de la Frontera, Jerez de la Frontera, and Ronda.[149] Another view holds that its birthplace was more likely the geographical triangle bounded by Jerez, Seville, and Cádiz.[150] A third opinion, that of Molina and Mairena, is that it began in the area of Ronda, Triana, and Cádiz, with Jerez as its geographical center.[151] Still another view, advanced by Manuel de Falla, suggests that the *cante* originated in Granada.[152] This idea, however, has not been widely supported by other musicologists.

The earliest verses of the *cante jondo* were not intended to be sung before an audience, but were considered a form of self-expression that was frequently autobiographical, as the following stanza from a *siguiriya gitana* shows:

Por Puerta Tierra
no quiero pasar
porque me acuerdo de mi amigo Enrique
y me echo a llorar.[153]

During this period the *cante jondo* was virtually unknown outside Gypsy circles, because, living as a persecuted race, the Gypsies formed an independent sub-culture and had only minimal contact with the rest of Andalusian society.

The second stage of the *cante*'s history may be said to begin with the decade of the 1780's, when, through the edicts of Charles III in 1783, official persecution of the Gypsies came to an end, and they were accorded the same civil rights as other Spanish citizens. This period of the *cante* extends to about 1860. It was during these years that the *cante jondo* was developed fully, and, as a result of a freer intermingling of peoples in Andalusian society, the *cante flamenco* began to evolve. The word *flamenco* came to be used as a synonym for the Gypsies and their music. The romantic and *costumbrista* writers of the period helped to popularize the Gypsy legend and to bring public attention to the typically

---

[148] MOLINA and MAIRENA, p. 34.
[149] LUNA, p. 21; MANFREDI CANO, p. 62; ARCADIO DE LARREA PALACÍN, *La canción andaluza* (Jerez de la Frontera: Publicaciones del Centro de Estudios Históricos Jerezanos, 1961), pp. 154-155.
[150] GONZÁLEZ CLIMENT, p. 183.
[151] *Op. cit.,* p. 48.
[152] *Op. cit.,* p. 125.
[153] MOLINA and MAIRENA, p. 22.

Andalusian forms of Spanish folk art. Generally, these writers made no distinction between Andalusian and specifically Gypsy music and song. Gradually the Gypsies, who had their own distinctive styles, began to acquire the reputation as the most skillful performes of Andalusian folk music. Gypsy artists were sought as paid professional performers, and, in a short time, public interest in flamenco led to the opening of the first *cafés cantantes* which specialized in the performance of *cante y baile flamenco* for the entertainment of its patrons. Although the first such *café* opened in Seville in 1842, they did not become an important institution in the history of the *cante* until 1860: «El más antiguo del que tenemos dudosas noticias es el mencionado (sin nombre) por Fernando de Triana como existente en Sevilla en 1842. Pero el que consiguió un éxito con esta institución flamenca fue Silverio Franconetti, cuyo café se hizo famoso en la sevillana calle de Rosario.» [154]

The advent of the *cafés cantantes,* and in particular that of Silverio Franconetti, marks the third stage in the development of the *cante flamenco.* This period, which has come to be regarded as the *cante*'s golden age, lasted until around 1910. It was at this time that the transition towards professionalism took place among flamenco singers and dancers whose number rapidly increased to include many non-Gypsies. These years saw a rapid absorption of new songs into the flamenco repertoire, not only from Andalusia, but from other regions of Spain and Latin America as well. The *bulerías, tientos, cantiñas,* and many other modern forms of flamenco were perfected, and there was a corresponding growth in the *baile flamenco* as well. The *café cantante,* which became a feature of almost every Andalusian town of moderate size, has been described by Rossy as follows:

> El café cantante, por lo general, tiene un pequeño escenario o tabladillo (plataforma elevada) en el que actúa «el cuadro flamenco». Por «cuadro» se entiende el formado, al menos, por un guitarrista, un cantaor y una o más bailaoras, o una pareja de baile, hombre y mujer.
>
> La actuación del cuadro flamenco en el tablado se caracteriza por la formación del semicorro—cuando el cuadro se compone de seis o más artistas—, que viene a ser una imitación y recuerdo del corral o patio andaluz. Los artistas, arrimados a la pared, sentados en fila a los lados del guitarrista, esperan su turno para salir a bailar o cantar cuando llegue su momento. Entretanto, subrayan con acompasadas palmas la actuación del que en aquel instante canta o baila, o dicen olés o frases animadoras, por lo general, en elogio que encierra una fineza, para alentar al artista que actúa.[155]

It is precisely during this period that the *cante flamenco* began to diverge markedly from the older *cante jondo* which had been cultivated exclusively by the Gypsies. Many of the *cante jondo*'s oldest forms, such as the various *tonás, deblas, caña* and *polo,* were almost forgotten and were surpassed in popularity by the *siguiriya gitana* and the *soleares.* According

[154] *Ibid.,* p. 46.
[155] *Op. cit.,* pp. 68-69.

to Machado y Álvarez, the term *cante jondo* was first used at this time
to distinguish those songs of deeper emotional content from the general
repertoire of the *cantes flamencos*. Originally, the word *jondo* was applied
only to the *siguiriya gitana,* but it quickly came to include the *soleares,
caña, polo, serranas, martinete,* and *carceleras*.[156] The prestigious position
accorded the *siguiriya gitana* and the *soleares* gave rise to a number of
cantaores especialistas whose principal artistic achievement was in singing
either to perfection. This demand for specialized singers quickly spread
to other forms of the *cante* and led inevitably to a decline in the number
of *cantaores generales* who could perform all or most of its major styles.
According to Molina and Mairena, this tendency towards greater and greater
specialization resulted in the eventual separation of flamenco singers into
two groups, Gypsy and non-Gypsy. The former tended to show a marked
preference for the *siguiriyas gitanas, soleares,* and *martinetes* and to be
more restrained, traditional, and less flamboyant in their style of singing.
The non-Gypsy performers were drawn to the *cantes levantinos,* such
as the *malagueñas, granadinas,* and *fandangos,* and they tended to cutliv-
ate a more ornate style with a deliberate display of virtuosity for its own
sake in the accompanying dance.[157] These tendencies, all of which evolved
from the institution of the *café cantante,* produced what José Monleón
has called the *aburguesamiento del cante*: «Lo que era un arte del pueblo para el pueblo lo convertimos, primero, en un arte del pueblo para
la burguesía, y, casi inmediatamente, en un arte aburguesado para la burguesía. Las letras se ajustaron a la poética propia de la cultura 'paya'
y los cantes fueron valorados en función de su riqueza musical y las posibilidades líricas ofrecidas al cantaor.» [158]

This led to the fourth or present stage of the *cante*'s history known as
the *época teatral*.[159] If the previous era was represented by Silverio Franconetti, whose *café cantante* gave impetus to and symbolized the entire
period, the modern era may well be representd by Antonio Chacón who
was a specialist in the *malagueña* and the lighter *cantes levantinos*. In this
period the *cante* has acquired an even larger public by adapting itself to
the affectations of the *zarzuela,* the opera, and the falsetto, an innovation
introduced by Antonio Chacón and widely imitated to this day: «...él
inauguró el reinado del falsete: frente a la bronca voz 'afillada' . . . pre-
dominante en casi todo el siglo XIX, Chacón, de voz atenorada, inició la
moda del falsete, que le permitía gorjear y desplegar toda una gama pres-
tigiosa de recursos, que le ayudó a ganar fama sin precedente.» [160]

The early years of the modern era saw the transition of the *cante* from
the *café cantante* to the theatrical stage and with it the ascendancv of the
dance over the singing. In this period of the *Ballet Español!,* the single
guitarist of the *café cantante* was replaced by an orchestra whose function

---

[156] Reported by MOLINA and MAIRENA, p. 48.
[157] *Ibid.,* p. 54.
[158] «Cante y sociedad española,» *Cuadernos Hispanoamericanos,* No. 22 (1968),
p. 524.
[159] MOLINA and MAIRENA, p. 59.
[160] *Ibid.,* p. 60.

was to provide musical accompaniment for the dancers. Previously, the *baile* was considered to be only a complement to the *cante* and was limited solely to the *cante chico*. It was generally conceded that the *cante grande* could not be danced and that to do so would detract from its essential, ritualized solemnity:

> Era uso en la época clásica del flamenquismo ordenar un programa en el que el cante constituía la materia primordial y la danza un relleno escénico, un paréntesis festivo, salpimentador. Incluso los cantaores que acompañaban a las bailaoras no eran más que los jaleadores de turno o los principiantes de la carrera flamenca. Los ases, los maestros, constituían espectáculo por sí solos, y su prestigio no podía acceder al baile. Sólo por contadísimas razones, el cantaor consagrado hacía una excepción. De común, tanto el cantaor como el público exigían de las sesiones flamencas un culto absorbente y riguroso del cante por el cante. No se concebía otra técnica ni otra consideración respecto al baile.[161]

Although it is generally admitted that this situation doubtlessly retarded the development of the *danza flamenca,* it is quite probable that these restrictions had the beneficial effect of insuring that the dance would be firmly rooted in the *cante*'s traditions of sobriety, formality, and discipline before embarking on a more independent course. This relationship between the *cante* and the *danza* persisted until the time of the First World War.[162] Soon thereafter their respective roles were reversed, as the public's attention focused increasingly on the dance as the primary spectacle and viewed the singing as secondary. This new emphasis on the possibilities inherent within the dance led to an increase in the dance repertoire and, later, to the creation of the *baile grande*. Accordingly, the *siguiriya gitana, serrana, martinete,* and other forms of the *cante jondo* were soon danced, a development that would have been unheard of during the previous era. The creation of these new dances also resulted in the development of more complicated styles, further and further removed from their folk origins. The *baile grande* was an invention of professional dancers and had little connection with the folk dances still cultivated by the people.[163] However, this extension of the dance to include the formerly forbidden area of the *cante grande* had the beneficial effect of resurrecting older forms of the *cante jondo,* like the *caña* and the *polo,* that by not being performed, had been almost forgotten. This fact has created a somewhat paradoxical situation in that the preservation of the *cante jondo* now seems to be more the result of an interest in the dance than in the song.

The advent of the *ópera flamenca* in recent years was perhaps an attempt to reverse this tendency and to reassert the primacy of the *cante,* but the attempt was unsuccessful as the opera failed to gain widespread popularity. According to many critics interested in the *cante* as a genuine folk art, such modern developments as the *ballet flamenco* or the *ópera*

---

[161] GONZÁLEZ CLIMENT, p. 219.
[162] *Ibid.,* p. 220.
[163] ROSSY, pp. 70, 73.

flamenca have had a pejorative effect resulting in a greater commercialization and, what is worse, in an increase in the distortions, artificiality, and affectations that inevitably result from trying to adapt a folk art to a cultural tradition that is alien to it. It was precisely this sense of dismay at the degeneration of the *cante,* already apparent by the 1920's, that prompted Manuel de Falla and García Lorca to undertake its rehabilitation. The *Primer Concurso del Cante Jondo,* held in Granada in June 1922, was to be the first step in accomplishing this task.

Chapter II

HISTORY OF THE *POEMA DEL CANTE JONDO*

There is a considerable difference of opinion concerning when the *Poema del Cante Jondo,* first published in 1931, was actually written. Rafael Alberti, Edwin Honig, Guillermo Díaz-Plaja, Marie Laffranque, and Alfredo de la Guardia state that the work was completed ten years earlier, in 1921.[1] Other critics, including Howard Young and Albert Henry, believe it was written between 1921 and 1922.[2] Still others, like Vázquez-Ocaña and Eduardo Molina Fajardo, claim that it was completed between 1921 and 1923.[3] In a subsequent work, Marie Laffranque suggests that some of the poems may have been written as late as 1924: «Le 'Poema del cante jondo,' publié en 1931, est daté de 1921. On n'a aucune raison de croire que l'auteur ait menti. On sait d'ailleurs qu'il a lu dès 1922 certaines de ses pièces et que d'autres ont paru en 1924. Rappelons seulement qu'il a très bien pu, selon son habitude, remanier et surtout corriger légèrement certains poèmes.»[4] Unfortunately, she does not mention which poems appeared in 1924, nor does she attempt to ascertain if they were written at that time or earlier. To our knowledge only one other critic, María Teresa Babín, believes the poems were composed from 1921 to 1924.[5]

Whatever the actual date of composition may be, all critics are unanimous in believing that the original inspiration for the *Poema del Cante Jondo* is to be found in the series of events that led to the *Primer Concurso del Cante Jondo* held in Granada on the 13th and 14th of June 1922.[6]

---

[1] Rafael Alberti, «García Lorca,» *Los Hombres de la Historia* (Centro Editor de América Latina, Buenos Aires), No. 15 (1968), pp. 141-147; Edwin Honig, *García Lorca* (Norfolk, Conn.: New Directions, 1963), p. 53; Guillermo Díaz-Plaja, *Federico García Lorca* (Madrid: Espasa-Calpe, 1961), p. 108; Marie Laffranque, «Pour l'Étude de Federico García Lorca, Bases Chronologiques,» *Bulletin Hispanique,* LXV, 3-4 (1963), p. 338; Alfredo de la Guardia, *García Lorca, persona y creación* (Buenos Aires: Editorial Schapere, 1952), p. 147.

[2] Howard T. Young, «The Magic of Reality,» in *The Victorious Expression* (Madison: Univ. of Wisconsin Press, 1966), p. 154; Albert Henry, «Les Grands Poèmes Andalous de Federico García Lorca,» *Romania Gandensia,* VI (1958), p. 99.

[3] F. Vázquez Ocaña, *García Lorca* (México: Biografía Gandesa, 1962), p. 140; Eduardo Molina Fajardo, *Manuel de Falla y el cante jondo* (Granada: Imprenta Urania, 1962), p. 68.

[4] *Les Idées Esthétiques de Federico García Lorca* (Paris: Centre de Recherches Hispaniques, 1967), p. 87.

[5] *García Lorca, vida y obra* (New York: Las Americas Pblg. Co., 1955), p. 20.

[6] José Mora Guarnido, *Federico García Lorca y su mundo* (Buenos Aires: Losada, 1958), p. 160; Federico García Lorca, «El cante jondo (primitivo canto andaluz)» in *Obras completas* (Madrid: Aguilar, 1963), p. 1823; Albert Henry, *op. cit.,* pp. 98-99; Laffranque, *Les Idées...,* p. 97; Fernando Sierra Gago, «Cante flamenco, orígenes, evolución y estado actual,» in *Falla y Granada* (Vitoria, España: H. Fournier, 1963), n.p.; Cesco Vian, *Federico García Lorca, Poeta e Drammaturgo* (Milano: La Goliardica, Edizioni Universitarie, n. d.), p. 25; E. Molina Fajardo, *op. cit.,* p. 49.

As we noted in the preceding chapter, this *Concurso* was primarily the work of Manuel de Falla and other artists who wished to preserve the genuine, folk *cante jondo,* which they felt was in danger of being forgotten, and to rescue it from further vulgarization at the hands of the professional performers of the *cante flamenco.* In his lengthy and detailed account of the *Concurso,* Eduardo Molina y Fajardo states that the original idea for the contest resulted from a conversation between Manuel de Falla and a colleague, Miguel Cerón, sometime during the latter months of 1921.[7] They decided that it should be held during the festival of Corpus Christi the following year in order to allow sufficient time to publicize the event and to take advantage of the fact that if it were included as part of these festivities, it would qualify for official support from the *Ayuntamiento* or municipal government. After subsequent discussions with his friends, Falla finally decided to make the appeal to the municipal authorities through the *Centro Artístico y Literario de Granada* to which some of the future promoters of the contest already belonged. Miguel Cerón drew up the petition which was then signed by the directors of the *Centro Artístico.*

This petition, dated December 31, 1921, stressed that the most culturally advanced countries in Europe had long ago undertaken an examitnation of the origins of their own music. In Spain a similar undertaking had revealed that an important part of the nation's musical heritage was to be found among the *cantos populares andaluces,* of which the *cante jondo* was of particular interest because it had greatly influenced French and Russian contemporary music. But in spite of the recognition accorded the *cante jondo* by foreign composers, the majority of the Spanish people were ignorant of its great cultural worth. Indeed, they contended that this musical treasure was presently in danger of dying out completely through neglect. The petition pointed out, furthermore, that the *cante jondo* did not lend itself to musical notation, and therefore it could not be written down for posterity. The document then concluded with an appeal for funds of not less than twelve thousand *pesetas* for the purpose of this contest. It was proposed that the *concurso* take place during the next festival of Corpus Christi and that it be held in San Nicolás Square, the decoration of which would be supervised by the painter Ignacio Zuloaga. Among the thirty-one signatures on the petition was that of Federico García Lorca who, within two months, was to play an important role in publicizing the forthcoming *Concurso del Cante Jondo.*

Don Antonio Ortega Molina, the president of the *Centro Artístico,* presented the petition to the municipal government on February 8, 1922, and it won initial approval. Several days later, however, the official chronicler of the province, Francisco de Paula Valladar, began a campaign against the contest via an article published in *La Alhambra* on February 15. This article, «Los cantos populares granadinos,» stated in part: «Soy entusiasta de la 'fiesta de los cantos populares granadinos,' pero dejémonos

[7] *Op. cit.,* p. 49.

44

de 'cante jondo.' Corremos, no lo olvide el Centro, el peligro gravísimo de que esa fiesta pueda convertirse en una 'españolada.'» [8] Valladar's attack was then taken up by some members of the *Ayuntamiento* who pointed to a possible budget deficit if the municipal government actually granted the amount requested by the *Centro Artístico.*

Four days later, on February 19, Federico García Lorca undertook the first major step in the campaign to publicize the forthcoming contest by means of a public lecture entitled «El cante jondo, primitivo cante andaluz,» given at the *Centro Artístico de Granada.* [9] This lecture began by stressing the need both to conserve the *cante jondo* from disappearance or further vulgarization and to combat the discredit into which it had fallen. Therefore, one of the aims of the proposed *Concurso del Cante Jondo* was to bring to public attention the present state of the *cante* and to emphasize its genuine artistic value. Lorca said:

> No es posible que las canciones más emocionantes y profundas de nuestra misteriosa alma estén tachadas de tabernarias y sucias; no es posible que el hilo que nos une con el Oriente impenetrable quieran amarrarlo en el mastil de la guitarra juerguista; no es posible que la parte más diamantina de nuestro canto quieran mancharla con el vino sombrío del chulo profesional.
>
> Ha llegado, pues, la hora en que las voces de músicos, poetas y artistas españoles se unan, por instinto de conservación, para definir y exaltar las claras bellezas y sugestiones de estos cantes.[10]

Lorca then proceeded to define the *cante jondo* and to differentiate it from the more widely known *cante flamenco,* which is derived from it. Next, he outlined the major historical and cultural influences on the development of the *cante jondo* and stressed, above all, the specific role played by the Gypsies. He repeated some of the statements made in the petition to the *Ayuntamiento* and pointed out that the *cante* had had a great influence on European music and had generally been held in greater esteem by foreigners than by Spaniards. He noted that the Russians Glinka and Rimsky Korsakov, as well as the French composer Debussy, had found a wealth of musical inspiration in this folk music of Andalusia.

In the second part of his lecture, Lorca discussed the poetic qualities of the *cante,* stating that the *cante jondo,* based on the dual theme of love and death, is insuperable in emotional depth. The *cante* is pure feeling, and, in contrast to the folk songs of other parts of Spain, it does not attempt to recreate a regional landscape. Its poetry evokes only the stary, night sky: «. . . el 'cante jondo' canta siempre en la noche. No tiene ni mañana ni tarde, ni montañas ni llanos. No tiene más que la noche, una noche ancha y profundamente estrellada. . . . Es un canto sin paisaje y, por lo tanto, concentrado en sí mismo y terrible en medio de la sombra.» [11]

---

[8] *Ibid.,* p. 70.
[9] MORA GUARNIDO, *op. cit.,* p. 161.
[10] GARCÍA LORCA, *Obras...,* pp. 1823-24.
[11] *Ibid.,* pp. 47-48.

In part three Lorca comments on the *cante's* pantheistic qualities, for all objects of nature enter into it and acquire individual personalities. He discusses the sentimental delicacy and beauty of these songs, and he laments the gross level to which they have been degraded by many urban performers.

In the fourth part Lorca compares the many affinities between the *cante jondo* and the oldest forms of oriental poetry. Persian and Arabic poems that treat the theme of tears, that praise wine, eternal love which is stronger than death, or the hair and eyes of a loved one, all find their counterparts in the lyrics of the Andalusian *cante jondo*. He concludes his lecture with a commentary on the role of the singer during the performance of the *cante* and with an evocation of the great *cantaores* of the past. He then asks his audience for their support in keeping alive this priceless treasure of Andalusian folk art: «Les suplico respetuosamente que no dejen morir las apreciables joyas vivas de la raza, el inmenso tesoro milenario que cubre la superficie espiritual de Andalucía y que mediten bajo la noche de Granada la trascendencia patriótica del proyecto que unos artistas españoles presentamos.» [12]

The first part of the lecture, in which Lorca discusses the origins and basic musical characteristics of the *cante,* is based to a great extent on the research of Manuel de Falla who had already drawn up a brochure concerning its origin, historical importance, and influence on European music. Since this brochure was later published anonymously as part of the propaganda campaign to elicit public interest in the forthcoming *Concurso,* there is some speculation among critics whether it was written entirely by Manuel de Falla or was composed by a group of friends using his notes. Of the latter opinion is Marie Laffranque who states: «Falla . . . confie à ses jeunes amis les notes qui leur permetront de rediger une brochure sur le 'cante' utilizée par Lorca dans sa conference.» [13] In the footnote following this statement, she explains the source of her information: «Déclarations orales à M. Laffranque de MM. José et Francisco García Carrillo, d'après leurs souvenirs et ceux de leurs amis rédacteurs de la brochure.» [14] Regardless of who the precise author or authors were, it is generally conceded that this booklet was used extensively by Lorca in the preparation of his lecture. A comparison between the pamphlet and the first part of Lorca's lecture reveals, in fact, that many passages, particularly those dealing with the origins of the *cante jondo,* are taken almost verbatim from the brochure.

Although it is probable that García Lorca had started writing the *Poema del Cante Jondo* in 1921 before becoming involved in the preparations for the contest, it was primarily the stimulus of the *Concurso* and other related events that induced him to undertake the task in earnest. [15] After this

---

[12] *Ibid.*, p. 56.
[13] *Les Idées...*, p. 96.
[14] *Ibid.*, p. 96.
[15] MOLINA FAJARDO, *op. cit.*, p. 65, and MARIE LAFFRANQUE, *Les Idées...*, p. 96.

lecture Lorca began to conceive of this book as his special contribution to the *Concurso* and to the effort to rehabilitate the *cante jondo*.

During the following month, the promoters of the contest tried to forestall any complications that might have arisen due to Francisco de Paula Valladar's comments of February 15, by publishing a counter article intended to assure the financial support of the *Ayuntamiento*. Thus, Miguel Cirón, using the pseudonym «Abelión,» published «La subvención para el concurso del Cante Jondo no altera el presunto general de nuestro ayuntamiento» in *El Defensor de Granada* on March 12.[16] The municipal government, however, decided to re-examine the proposed grant and announced a meeting for March 22. For this reason Manuel de Falla saw to it that another article, «La proposición del 'Cante Jondo',» was published the day before in *El Defensor de Granada*. It begins by reminding the public of the generally enthusiastic support given by the press to the proposed contest and regrets the apparent misconceptions that have arisen regarding its value. The author goes on to expose the erroneous opinions of those who oppose the project by pointing out the importance of the *cante jondo* as a living cultural link to the early civilizations of Andalusia and its relevance in the development of contemporary French and Russian music. Falla reiterates the warning that this part of Spain's cultural heritage will shortly disappear because of the popular vulgarization to which the *cante* has been subjected, unless adequate measures are taken to restore its original forms: «Pero no desesperemos; aún estamos a tiempo de corregir estos males, restituyendo a la canción andaluza toda su primitiva belleza; y éste es el fin que se proponen los organizadores del concurso de 'cante jondo', entre los que tengo el honor de encontrarme.»[17] In spite of a typesetter's error which inadvertently omitted fifty-six words, Manuel de Falla had the satisfaction of learning on the following day that the *Junta de Asociados,* reviewing the initial petition to the *Ayuntamiento,* decided to grant the full amount originally authorized.

This decision did not end the controversy, however, which now had reached Madrid where Eugenio Nöel began a journalistic campaign against the *cante jondo.*[18] Miguel Cerón answered his attack with an article «La música y el flamenquismo» which appeared in *El Defensor de Granada* on March 16.[19] The English painter Wyndham Tyron joined the controversy on the side of Cerón via the magazine *España* in which he published his commentary, «En favor del cante flamenco.»[20] Hermenegildo Giner de los Ríos also entered the debate, aiding Falla and Cerón with an article «El rey sabio y los cantos andaluces» in which he showed the historical importance of Andalusian folk music during the reign of Al-

---

[16] MOLINA FAJARDO, *op. cit.,* pp. 71-72.
[17] *Ibid.,* p. 174.
[18] *Ibid.,* p. 80. Unfortunately, MOLINA FAJARDO does not indicate the title of Eugenio Nöel's article nor when and where it was published.
[19] *Ibid.,* p. 80.
[20] *Ibid.,* p. 80. No indication is given of the date of this article.

fonso el Sabio.[21] In Madrid Manuel Chaves Nogales lent his support with an essay, «El Cante Jondo, serio y transcendente,» published in the *Heraldo de Madrid* on April 2.[22] At this time Ignacio Zuloaga wrote Falla from Paris describing the interest that the forthcoming contest was creating among artists and musicians there. Meanwhile, Falla was receiving enthusiastic letters from people in the arts all over Spain pledging their support for the proposed festivities. In spite of the overwhelming enthusiasm for the *Concurso* in other parts of the country, the journalistic battle between the two groups still continued unabated in Granada where those opposing the event were led by Francisco de Paula Valladar and Joaquín Corrales Ruiz who were writing in *La Alhambra* and *La Opinión,* respectively. The latter newspaper referred to the contest as «la fiesta del 'jipío' tabernario y del 'pingo' en tablado canalla.»[23]

In the meantime, invitations to the event were sent to the leading figures in the arts all over Europe. These invitations, written in French and English, explained the purpose of the contest and pointed out that its locality, the Plaza de San Nicolás, would be decorated by Granada's artists under the direction of Ignacio Zuloaga and that the decor would be in the Andalusian style of the 1830's and 40's.

On April 6, Manuel de Falla and two others attended a meeting of the *Comisión de Fiestas y Turismo* to announce the tentative plans for the contest. They explained that the individual prizes probably would be awarded in three areas: (1) *siguiriyas* and *martinetes*; (2) *carceleras, cañas, polos,* and *medios polos*; (3) *saetas, soleares* and *serranas*. The first evening, June 13, would begin with an introductory speech by Salvador Rueda. This would be followed by a group of selected performers, and, after an intermission, there would be a second group of singers. The second evening, June 14, named «Fiesta en honor del cante jondo,» would begin with an «Elogio del Cante Jondo,» again by Salvador Rueda. Following this, there would be a selection of *coplas* sung by those competing for the First Prize. After an intermission the second half of the evening would include a reading by García Lorca of his *Poema del Cante Jondo* and a performance of *coplas* by the celebrated Pastora Pavón, «La Niña de los Peines.» The last event would be a *baile a soleares,* which was to serve as a preview for the «Fiesta de la Danza Andaluza,» to be celebrated the following year. Falla went on to explain that the preliminary trials for the singers would take place in private sessions at the *Escuela de Cante Jondo* to be established shortly so that only those qualified for the final competition would perform on June 13 and 14.[24]

The final arrangements were made some weeks later and presented to the public in a brochure entitled «El 'Cante Jondo' canto primitivo anda-

---

[21] *Ibid.,* p. 80. MOLINA FAJARDO relates that before publication the article was corrected by Manuel de Falla, but, again, he gives no indication regarding the date or place of publication.

[22] *Ibid.,* p. 81.

[23] *Ibid.,* p. 85.

[24] *Ibid.,* pp. 92-93 and p. 228.

luz.» This pamphlet consisted of two parts. The first contained what is generally considered to be Falla's historical analysis of the *cante jondo,* a description of its oriental features, and its influence on modern European music.[25] This part of the brochure no doubt had been written some months earlier, since it was the source from which García Lorca borrowed much of his information on the *cante* when he prepared his lecture on that subject. The second part of the pamphlet, undoubtedly prepared much later —probably in April—, contained an entry blank for those wishing to enter the contest, along with a list of the rules governing participation.

The first regulation stated which songs could be considered true *cante jondo* for the purpose of the competition. It specified that only a limited group of songs would be acceptable and that this group did not include those known as *cantes flamencos.* The second rule divided the cante into three categories: (1) *siguiriyas gitanas*; (2) *serranas, polos, cañas* and *soleares*; (3) *martinetes, carceleras, tonás, livianas,* and *saetas viejas.*[26] Those songs in group three were to be sung without guitar accompaniment. This grouping, it will be noted, represents a slightly different arrangement from that suggested to the *Comisión de Fiestas y Turismo* on April 6. The third regulation stated that the contest was open to all non-professional performers over twenty-one, although professional singers under that age could enter. The fourth regulation defined «professional» to mean all those who sing in public for money. The fifth rule covered the procedure for entering the contest. The sixth listed the final day for entering as May 25, and the seventh stated that the guitarists who accompanied the singers would also be eligible for prizes. The eighth regulation gave the time and place of the contest and the preliminary eliminations, which were to begin on June 10, at 10 A.M. at the *Centro Artístico.* The ninth rule listed the prizes for each category of song, and the last regulation limited the number of prizes any one contestant could win.

Following these ten rules, the pamphlet outlined the procedure governing the preliminary eliminations. There were to be two series of them: one would serve as a *prueba de admisión* and the second would be a *prueba eliminatoria para premio.* Those wishing to qualify in the first category, the *siguiriya gitana,* would have to perform a simple *siguiriya* before a panel of judges, and those desiring to enter the second and third categories would be asked to perform one of the *cantes* listed under each heading. All contestants who passed the first preliminary selection would then proceed to the second round of eliminations. In the second series, those wanting to compete for the first category would be required to sing two *siguiriyas* of different styles. All who wished to participate in the second and third categories would be asked to sing two *coplas* from each of the different types of *cante.* Special preference would be given for

---

[25] See Chapter I for a complete discussion of its contents.

[26] This listing of the *cantes* differs slightly from that discussed in Chapter 1. Apparently, Falla chose not to include the *debla* in this contest, but instead substituted the *liviana,* a song which may not be a genuine part of the *cante jondo.*

4

the performance of those styles which «por su mayor antigüedad, están menos difundidos, puesto que el despertar interés hacia ellos es la principal finalidad del Concurso.» [27] The judges would then choose which of these contestants were to take part in the *Concurso* on June 13 and 14. The pamphlet closed with this observation:

> Debemos advertir con el mayor encarecimiento que serán preferidos los concursantes cuyo estilo popular de canto se ajuste a las viejas prácticas de los «cantaores» clásicos, evitando todo floreo abusivo y devolviendo al «cante jondo» aquella admirable sobriedad, desgraciadamente perdida, que constituía una de sus más grandes bellezas. . . .
> Recuérdese también que una gran extensión oral, es decir, una voz que abarque muchas notas, no sólo no es necesario para el «cante jondo,» sino que, si se hace un mal uso de esa propiedad, puede ser perjudicial al más puro estilo del mismo.[28]

In order to insure that all contestants were properly instructed in the correct singing styles, an effort was made to seek out two individuals to be in charge of the *Escuela de Cante Jondo* which began functioning on May 7. The search produced two men: Juan Crespo, a hat maker, and Rafael Gálvez, a fisherman, who excelled in the *soleares* and *siguiriyas,* respectively.[29] Not content with merely publishing the news about the forthcoming contest, its organizers —including García Lorca— took it upon themselves to search in the smaller Andalusian villages for those local singers who were reputed to excel in the various styles of the *cante* and to encourage their participation in the *concurso*.[30]

In the final two weeks before the contest, there occurred a series of important events in Granada that had a direct bearing on the planned festivities. The first was the arrival of Ignacio Zuloaga and Santiago Rusiñol from Paris on May 30, followed by a change of location for the *Concurso*. Zuloaga, who had charge of decorating the Plaza de San Nicolás where the event was to be held, decided that this initial choice was unwise, since it seemed too small to accommodate the large crowds expected. Consequently, he chose a new locality, the Plaza de los Aljibes. In addition, there were several preliminary cultural events scheduled for the first week in June which were part of the campaign to raise funds for the *Concurso,* since neither the 12,000 *pesetas* granted by the municipal government nor the donations of private individuals were enough to cover the expenses incurred.[31] The first of these events consisted of a series of four guitar concerts by Andrés Segovia in the theatre of the Alhambra Palace Hotel. The second was an exhibition of Zuloaga's oil paintings in the Museo de

---

[27] MANUEL DE FALLA, «El cante jondo, sus orígenes, sus valores, su influencia en el arte europeo,» in *Escritos sobre música y músicos* (Madrid: Espasa-Calpe, n. d.), p. 145.
[28] *Ibid.,* pp. 146-147.
[29] MOLINA FAJARDO, *op. cit.,* p. 98.
[30] MARCELLE AUCLAIR, *Enfances et Mort de García Lorca* (Paris: Éditions du Seuil, 1968), pp. 123-125.
[31] MORA GUARNIDO, *op. cit.,* p. 161.

Antigüedades de Meersmans. The third event took place the evening of June 7, at the theatre of the Alhambra Palace Hotel. On this occasion Antonio Gallego y Burín, vicepresident of the *Centro Artístico,* read Falla's essay on the *cante jondo* and Manuel Jofré performed examples of the *petenera* and the *siguiriya.* The principal attraction of the evening, however, was the first known public reading by García Lorca of this latest work, the *Poema del Cante Jondo.* The program concluded with the performance of a *soleares* by Andrés Segovia.[32]

In view of the fact that the *Poema del Cante Jondo* was not published until 1931, the immediate question concerning Lorca's reading that evening is which of the poems that now comprise the book were already written by that date? According to Marie Laffranque, who states that these poems were written especially for the occasion, the reading consisted of: the «Siguiriya» (later called «Poema de la siguiriya gitana»), «Baladilla de los tres ríos,» «Peteneras» (which was later renamed «Gráfico de la Petenera»), «Viñetas» (later, «Viñetas flamencas»), «Saeta» (lated called «Poema de la saeta»), and «Soleá» (later renamed «Poema de la soleá»). She uses as her source of information the *Gaceta del Sur* which described the recitation in its issue of June 8, 1922.[33]

The final days preceding the contest saw an influx of artists, musicians, writers, journalists, and *aficionados* of folk art and the *cante jondo,* not only from other parts of Andalusia and Spain, but from the rest of Europe and America as well. Among those arriving in Granada were Ursula Greville, the English soprano, Kurt Schindler of the *Schola Cantorum* of New York, John B. Trend, who, at that time, was a music critic for the *Times* of London, and writers like Ramón Gómez de la Serna, Ramón Pérez de Ayala, and Edgar Neville.[34]

Before the contest could take place, a panel of judges and special advisers had to be chosen to preside over the *Concurso* and to award the prizes. Curiously, there seems to be a diversity of opinions concerning who these judges and advisers were. According to Molina's account, the famous flamenco singer Antonio Chacón headed the panel, and the other judges were: Andrés Segovia, Antonio Ortego Molina (President of the *Centro Artístico*), Antonio Gallego Burín (Vice-President of the *Centro Artístico*), Amalio Cuenca, Gregorio Abril, and José López Ruiz.[35] This list differs substantially from other accounts. José Mora Guarnido states that the panel of judges was headed by Manuel de Falla rather than Antonio Chacón, who, he claims, served merely as a technical adviser.[36] Still a third account gives the additional names of Pastora Pavón, Manuel Torres («el Niño de Jerez»), and Manuel Jofré as advisers to the judges.[37]

One of the high points of the first evening of the *Concurso* was a per-

[32] Molina Fajardo, *op. cit.,* pp. 116-117, and Marcelle Auclair, *op. cit.,* p. 131.
[33] *Pour l'Étude...,* p. 339.
[34] *Ibid.,* pp. 119-120.
[35] *Ibid.,* pp. 132-133.
[36] *Op. cit.,* p. 162.
[37] Commentary by Rafael Jofré found in *Falla y Granada.*

formance of a *siguiriya* by Manuel Torres, to whom García Lorca years later would dedicate the «Viñetas flamencas» of his *Poema del Cante Jondo*. The second evening was an even greater success in spite of an unexpected rainstorm which forced the spectators to use their chairs as umbrellas.[38] Apparently, the second half of the evening of June 14 was devoted entirely to song, and García Lorca did not read selections from his *Poema del Cante Jondo* as planned.

The progress of the *Concurso* was closely followed by the national and international press, and in the days following the 13 and 14 of June, the controversy that had marked its inception began again. According to Molina:

> La ironía, la caricatura, la frase mordiente, se aliaron para rebajar el triunfo. Valladar, desde la Alhambra, escribía: «El Concurso de Cante Jondo ha sido una 'españolada' más, sin otros resultados que unas cuantas noches de brillantísima fiesta de mujeres muy bellas, bien vestidas y adornadas: unas cuantas noches de alegría, que buena falta nos hacen. . . .» En la prensa madrileña se comentaban los chaparrones del segundo día: «Muy grande ha sido el éxito del Concurso. Lo ocurrido supera todas las esperanzas. Que las canciones causasen impresión entre los mortales de la tierra era cosa que se tenía por descontada. Pero que tal emoción ocasionaran allá arriba, no podía suponerse. De ahí el gran efectazo: ¡Hicieron llorar hasta a las nubes!» [39]

In Seville one journalist protested in an article «El cante jondo no es 'pa eso'» that the *cante grande* should not be subjected to such public displays.[40] Another journalist, in an article published in *El Sol* of Madrid, claimed: «El concurso de 'cante jondo' de Granada ha causado sus estragos. . . . En Granada se celebró el entierro del 'cante jondo' . . . muerto recientemente en Granada a mano de los intelectuales.» [41] Although the majority of the press gave favorable coverage to the contest, the event did not prompt the restoration of the *cante jondo,* nor did it renew public interest in the preservation of the *cante* as its organizers had hoped.[42]

Whether those selections from the *Poema del Cante Jondo* read by García Lorca in the Teatro del Hotel Alhambra Palace are the same as the poems later published under the same titles is an open question. In any case, the first of the poems to appear in print was the «Baladilla de los tres ríos,» published in the review *Horizonte* the following year (1923).[34] Four more years were to pass before any of the others would appear, although it is known that several, notably «Adivinan-

[38] *Ibid.,* p. 140.
[39] *Ibid.,* p. 144.
[40] SOLLY AZOGURY, «El cante jondo no es 'pa eso'» *El Liberal,* Seville (June 1922); reported by EDUARDO MOLINA FAJARDO, *op. cit.,* p. 147.
[41] MOLINA FAJARDO, *op. cit.,* pp. 147-148.
[42] For a more detailed explanation of the relative success or failure of the *Concurso,* see EDWARD F. STANTON. «Federico García Lorca and Cante Jondo» (*Ann Arbor:* Univ. Microfilms, 1972), pp. 27-34.
[43] Reported by JACQUES COMINCIOLI, «En torno a García Lorca,» *Cuadernos Hispanoamericanos,* No. 139 (1961), p. 62.

za de la guitarra,» «Arqueros,» «Crótalo,» «La Lola,» «Muerte de
la Petenera,» «Las seis cuerdas,» and «Sorpresa,» had already been
written and circulated among Lorca's friends by 1923.[44] In 1926, however,
García Lorca read at Valladolid portions of several books in preparation.
According to Marie Laffranque, this reading consisted of parts of his *Suite,
Canciones, Poema del Conte Jondo,* and *Romancero Gitano.*[45] She gives no
information about the circumstances surrounding the reading, nor does
she specify which poems were recited.

The following year, 1927, saw the publication of the «Viñetas flamencas» in the review *Verso y Prosa,*[46] together with other poems which,
again according to Marie Laffranque, were all written in 1921 and were
incorporated later into his *Canciones* and *Primeras Canciones.*[47]. The «Viñetas flamencas,» dedicated to Antonio Luna, included the following poems:
«Adivinanza de la guitarra,» «Candil,» «Malagueña,» «Memento,» «Crótalo,» and «Baile.» Of these six, three, «Adivinanza de la guitarra,»
«Candil,» and «Crótalo,» were later to become part of the «Plano de la
Soleá» before being included finally in the «Seis caprichos,» the last section
of the future *Poema del Cante Jondo.* «Malagueña» and «Baile» would
later be incorporated into the «Tres ciudades.» Only one poem, «Memento,» remained in the «Viñetas flamencas.» Whether these were the same
six poems that were read on June 7, 1922, under the title «Viñetas» is
not known, nor is it known what changes, if any, may have been made
from 1922 to 1927.

Two years later, on December 16, 1929, García Lorca participated in
a celebration at Columbia University in honor of Antonia Mercé, «la Argentina.» On this occasion he read several poems from the *Poema del
Cante Jondo.*[48] Shortly thereafter, the brochure «Antonia Mercé, la Argentina,» written by Angel del Río, Gabriel G. Maroto, García Lorca, and
Federico de Onís, was printed in New York to commemorate the event.
This booklet contains the «Balada de los tres ríos,» «Gráfico de la petenera,» and «Plano de la soleá.»[49] We may assume that these were
the same poems which Lorca had read in December since the brochure
was published only a few months later. The «Gráfico de la petenera» consists of eight parts: «Clamor,» «Camino,» «La guitarra,»
«Danza,» «Muerte de la petenera,» «Falsete,» «Epitafio,» and «Clamor.»[50]
The «Plano de la soleá» is composed of nine segments. The first has no
separate title; the rest are called «Pueblo de la Soleá,» «Calle,» «Copla,»

[44] See JACQUES COMINCIOLI, *Federico García Lorca* (Lausanne: Editions Rencontre, 1970), pp. 37-38.
[45] *Pour l'Étude...*, p. 342.
[46] See *Verso y Prosa, Boletín de la Joven Literatura,* I, 4, (April 1927).
[47] *Pour l'Étude...*, p. 343.
[48] *Ibid.*, p. 349; and ORESTE MACRÌ, *Canti gitani e Andalusi* (Guanda: Collezione
Fenice, 1961), p. 58.
[49] ANGEL DEL RÍO, GABRIEL F. MAROTO, FEDERICO GARCÍA LORCA, FEDERICO DE
ONÍS, *Antonia Mercé, La Argentina* (New York: Instituto de las Españas en los
Estados Unidos, 1930).
[50] Note that the first and last parts bear the same title.

«La soleá,» «Adivinanza de la guitarra,» «Candil,» «Crótalo,» and «Madrugada.» It is, of course, impossible to determine if these are the same compositions that were read in 1922 under the titles «Peteneras» and «Soleá.» Curiously, the three poems «Adivinanza de la guitarra,» «Candil,» and «Crótalo,» which in 1927 were part of the «Viñetas flamencas,» are now included in the «Plano de la soleá.»

A comparison between the 1927 and 1930 texts of the «Adivinanza» reveals that, except for minor differences in punctuation, the two versions are identical until the last verse. The 1930 edition adds five additional verses to the last stanza:

1927	1930
Los sueños de ayer las buscan,	Los sueños de ayer las buscan,
pero las tiene abrazadas	pero las tiene abrazadas
un Polifemo de oro.	un Polifemo de oro:
La guitarra.	la guitarra,
	que baila
	con seis doncellas
	aprisionadas,
	tres de carne
	y tres de plata.

These additional lines reiterate the image found in the preceding strophe.

The two versions of «Candil» reveal even more striking changes. In 1927 the initial verses were: « ¡Oh qué grave mechita / la llama del candil! » In 1930 these two lines read: « ¡Oh qué grave medita / la llama del candil! » Since the use of «medita» seems more logical than «mechita,» and since all subsequent editions retain «medita,» we may assume that the earlier version could be an error caused by misreading the «d» as a «ch». Such an error would be particulary likely to occur if the original manuscript had been hand-written. Further variations occur in the ninth, tenth, twelfth, and thirteenth verses. Verse nine, which reads «a la sombra maciza,» becomes «a las sombras macizas,» giving the image a wider scope. The tenth verse in the 1927 version, «la llama del candil,» is discarded altogether in 1930, undoubtedly for being an unnecessary repetition adding little to the pom. Verses twelve and thirteen are completely altered:

1927	1930	
Y se asoma temblando	y se asoma temblando	11
por los ojos redondos	a los bordes azules	12
del gitanillo muerto.	agudos, sin cansancio,	13
	¡puros bordes del sur!	

In this case the change is of questionable merit, for it gives a *recherché*, Modernist feeling to the image. The original version is more forceful. It is curious that in 1930, when Lorca was already writing his highly surrealistic *Poeta en Nueva York,* he would alter the poem in the direction of a much earlier style he had already abandoned. Evidently he was dissatisfied with this change, for in 1931 he replaced these lines with others which, as we shall see, are almost identical to those of 1927.

The two versions of «Crótalo» are less strikingly different. In the 1927 edition the poem begins with the two-verse image «Escarabajo/sonoro.» In 1930 the words «crótalo/crótalo» precede these lines which are now written as one verse, «Escarabajo sonoro.» In the earlier version the poem concludes with «y te ahogas en su trino/de palo,» but in 1930 «crótalo/crótalo/crótalo/escarabajo sonoro» follow these lines, thereby repeating the opening image. The use of the onomatopoeic «crótalo» five times in the 1930 edition adds an auditory dimension to the poem that was missing in its original form. Furthermore, the verses are rearranged in such a way that they are reduced from four lines to two:

1927	1930
. . . . .	. . . . . .
En la araña	En la araña de la mano
de la mano	rizas el aire cálido
rizas al aire	. . . .
cálido,	
. . . .	

The first edition of the *Poema del Cante Jondo* appeared on May 23, 1931, published by the Editorial Ulises of Madrid.[51] A comparison between this first edition and the previous versions reveals several interesting changes. The introductory poem, «Baladilla de los trese ríos,» was originally entitled «Balada de los tres ríos» in 1930 and it had no dedication. En 1931 a dedication to Salvador Quintero appears beneath the title. The poem's double refrain was printed in regular type and on one line in 1930, but in 1931 it appears in italics and on two lines:

1930	1931
¡Ay amor que se fue y no vino!	¡Ay amor
... ...	que se fue y no vino!
¡Ay amor que se fue por el aire!	... ...
	¡Ay amor
	que se fue por el aire!

Furthermore, the thirteenth verse in the 1930 version reads: «Por las aguas de Granada,» whereas a year later it was changed to: «por el agua de Granada.» Finally, the twenty-first and twenty-second verses in the 1930 version, «Quién dirá que el agua lleva/un fuego fatuo de gritos,» are without exclamation marks, but these were added in the 1931 edition. Likewise,

---

[51] LAFFRANQUE, *Pour l'Étude...*, p. 350; and J. COMINCIOLI, *op. cit.*, p. 63.

lines twenty-four and twenty-five originally appeared with exclamation marks, but these were removed in the later edition. These changes in punctuation could be a correction of typographical errors or they could represent a change in emphasis.

«Gráfico de la petenera,» which appeared undedicated in 1930, is dedicated to Eugenio Montes in 1931. The first poem, «Clamor,» which was originally without a subtitle, has been renamed «Campana» and subtitled «Bordón,» a change that increases its auditory and musical suggestiveness. The only variation, aside from minor changes in punctuation, occurs in the last stanza which is reduced from three lines to two:

1930	1931
El viento con el polvo hace proras de plata.	El viento con el polvo hace proras de plata.

The next poem, «Camino,» shows only slight variations. In the 1930 edition the first verse read: «Cien jinetes andaluces.» This was changed to: «Cien jinetes enlutados,» which conveys a more sinister and mysterious image. The only other variation occurs in the word distribution of lines seven and eight. In the 1930 edition these verses read: «Ni a Granada / la que suspira por el mar»; in 1931 they where rearranged to: «ni a Granada la que suspira / por el mar.»

«La guitarra» later became «Las siete cuerdas.» In the 1930 edition the third verse was: «El perfil de las almas»; a year later «perfil» was replaced by the more audibly suggestive word «sollozo,» and the verse became: «El sollozo de las almas.» The other changes involve the division of two lines into four in the last image, thereby reducing two unusually long verses to a more conventional length, and discarding the last two verses which were a reiteration of the opening lines:

1930	1931
Y como la tarántula teje una gran estrella para cazar suspiros que flotan en su negro aljibe de madera. La guitarra hace llorar a los sueños.	Y como la tarántula teje una gran estrella para cazar suspiros, que flotan en su negro aljibe de madera.

The fourth poem, «Danza,» exhibits no textual variations between the two editions, except for the inclusion in 1931 of «En el huerto de la petenera» beneath the title. The poem's final word, «moradas,» was emphasized by the use of exclamation marks in the 1930 edition, but these were subsequently removed.

In the next poem, «Muerte de la petenera,» the refrain is printed in italics in 1931, though it was previously in regular type. There is also a change in the first two lines of the last stanza. In 1930 they appeared as:

«Sombra pura, ya sin cielo, / viene por el horizonte.» In the 1931 edition they become: «Largas sombras afiladas / vienen del turbio horizonte,» which creates a far less abstract and a more direct, awesome image.

The sixth part of «Gráfico,» entitled «Falsete» in 1930, later became «Falseta.» In addition, verses three and four were changed to reduce their length:

1930

Tu entierro no tuvo niñas buenas,
las que dan a Cristo muerto sus guedejas.

1931

Tu entierro no tuvo niñas
buenas.
Niñas que le dan a Cristo muerto
sus guedejas.

Verses nine and ten of the 1930 version were also shortened by dividing them into four lines:

1930	1931
gente con el corazón en la cabeza que te siguió llamando por las callejas.	Gente con el corazón en la cabeza, que te siguió llorando por las callejas.

The change from «llamando» to «llorando» is significant because the latter verb intensifies the emotional effectiveness of the image.

The next poem, «Epitafio,» becomes «De profundis,» but apart from this change in the title, it shows no other variation. The last poem, «Clamor,» is changed in several ways. Verses one and three are divided into two short verses each. Thus verse one: «En las torres amarillas,» becomes: «En las torres / amarillas,» and verse three: «Sobre los vientos amarillos,» is changed to: «Sobre los vientos / amarillos.» In line seven the figure of death is described as crowned by «arabescos marchitos.» This was then changed to «azahares marchitos.» The second version creates an image that is more effective emotionally, for the impression of horror is greater when death is portrayed wearing a bride's symbol rather than a crown of ornamental arabesques. At the same time, the later versions makes the image less precious, more traditional, and therefore in greater harmony with the general folk spirit of the book. Verses eight through eleven were altered considerably. In the 1930 edition they appear as:

canta y canta
una canción en su vihuela blanca.

57

> Muerte de ayer, fábula y brisa
> sin fin de luz que canta y canta.

In 1931 these verses are shortened as follows:

> Canta y canta
> una canción
> en su vihuela blanca,
> y canta y canta y canta.

The later version is an improvement in that it eliminates the more abstract, *recherché* lines and conveys an image that is completely musical, for it consists almost entirely of musically suggestive words like «canta,» «canción,» and «vihuela.» It is very likely that the 1930 version of this poem had been written years before, when García Lorca had not yet emancipated himself from his early literary influences. The verses «muerte de ayer, fábula y brisa / sin fin de luz . . .» reflect a coldly intellectualized poetic mold still influenced by Modernism; they suggest the poetic style of his earlier *Libro de Poemas* (1918). This version of «Clamor» was probably written in 1921 or 1922 and was not retouched until the first edition of the *Poema del Cante Jondo* in 1931. The fact that Lorca chose to eliminate these particular verses and to recast the image so that its musical qualities were foremost shows to what extent his own esthetic credo had changed. The image is now simpler, more direct, and much more in accord with the general intention of recreating the spirit of a musical folk art.

«Plano de la soleá,» which in the 1930 edition followed the «Gráfico de la petenera,» is placed before it in the later edition. Furthermore, in 1931 its title is changed to «Poema de la soleá,» and it is dedicated to Jorge Zalamea. The first poem of «Plano,» untitled in both editions, shows a number of variations, particularly in its opening lines:

1930	1931
Tierra	Tierra seca,
quieta.	tierra quieta
Tierra	de noches
seca	inmensas.
de noches abiertas.	

In 1930 the image is divided into two statements, each conveying a separate concept: «tierra quieta» and «tierra seca.» The words «de noches abiertas» seem to refer only to the «tierra seca.» In 1931 the two phrases are separated only by a comma, thus making it clear that «de noches inmensas» modifies both statements about the land. Hence the continuity and poetic quality of the image are improved by a change in the punctuation which fuses two separate impressions into a single concept. In addition, the image becomes more concise by reducing it from five lines to four, and its meter conforms more closely to that of traditional folk poetry. Also, the change in the word order which places «seca» before «quieta» results in a change in the order of sense perceptions. We now perceive the image first in terms of the tactile sensation it conveys and then in auditory terms, rather than viceversa. This shift in sequence is important in that «de noches inmensas,» which conveys an auditory impression of vast stillness, reinforces the auditory sensation of silence inherent in the «tierra quieta» that immediately precedes it. Thus there is a greater continuity of sensations than in the previous version which had «de noches abiertas» (auditory) follow «tierra seca» (tactile). Furthermore, the substitution of «inmensas» for «abiertas» expands the image's physical or psychic dimensions, for the former word creates an impression of spacial distance that is not suggested so concretely by «abiertas.» The next variation between the two texts is minor. Line seven, «viento en las sierras,» becomes, «viento en la sierra.» The following verses show several changes, however:

1930	1931
Tierra	Tierra
del candil y la pena.	vieja
Tierra de las hondas cisternas.	del candil
Tierra	y la pena.
de la muerte sin ojos	Tierra
y la sabiduría de la fecha.	de las hondas cisternas.
	Tierra
	de la muerte sin ojos
	y las flechas.

«Vieja» has been added after «tierra» to create an eternal, timeless impression. The second and third verses have been shortened by dividing them into four lines, thereby creating a greater continuity in the over-all verse length. In the last line, the more abstract phrase, «la sabiduría de la flecha,» has been simplified to the more direct «la flecha.» The poem's final two verses: Viento por los caminos. / Viento ¡sí! viento sólo por la arena» were changed to: «(Viento por los caminos. / Brisa en las alamedas.)» The use of parentheses creates the impression of a subdued, minor tone and serves to make these lines, in the words of Roberto Yahni: «una acotación de tipo teatral» whose presence «convierte a ese paisaje —al dramatizarlo—en algo más dinámico.» [52] The change in the last verse, in which «viento» is replaced by «brisa,» has the effect of diminishing the psychic force of the image even more, for a *brisa* is obviously a diminutive form of *viento*. These changes in the last line do not, however, appreciably decrease the sensation of desolation implicit in its original form.

The next poem, «Pueblo de la soleá,» is shortened to «Pueblo» in the 1931 edition. The first two verses: «Sobre el monte redondo / un cal-

---

[52] «Algunos rasgos formales en la lírica de García Lorca: función del paréntesis,» *Bulletin Hispanique*, LXVI, 1-2 (1964), p. 110.

vario» become: «Sobre el monte pelado / un calvorio.», which gives a tree-
less, desolate impression not necessarily conveyed by the former version
that emphasized the shape of the mountain.   Furthermore, the period that
follows «calvario» separates the image from the one following instead of
making it an integral part of it.   Lines five through eight are rearranged
slightly and have one word change:

1930	1931
En las callejas hombres embozados y en las torres veletas girando	Por las callejas hombres embozados y en las torres veletas girando.

The change in verse length regularizes the meter, and the period after
«girando» gives the impression that this image cluster is a complete unit,
separate from the verses that follow it.   The word change from «En» to
«Por» creates an implied sensation of movement, as the reader's eyes seem
to traverse the length of the streets.   In the 1931 edition, «Pueblo»
is followed by «Puñal,» which does not appear in the earlier publication.

The next poem, «Calle,» becomes «Encrucijada» in 1931.   The change
is symbolically significant, for an *encrucijada* is a symbol of fate or death,[53]
a meaning not usually associated with *calle*.   The first line of the poem,
«Calle sin sueño,» is changed to «Viento del Este,» which creates a more
forceful image, since a *viento* can have associations of strength, power,
even violence and death.   The rest of the poem is identical except for a
change in lines five through seven:

1930	1931
La calle tiene un temblor de cuerda en tensión	La calle tiene un temblor de cuerda en tensión

In 1931 this poem is followed by « ¡Ay!,» which does not appear in the
1930 edition.

The next composition, called «Copla» in 1930, is given a more descriptive title in 1931, «Sorpresa.»   In its later form, line four is surrounded
by exclamation marks, giving it greater emphasis; line five is followed by
a period instead of a comma; and, lines six and seven are also surrounded
by emphatic exclamation marks.   The most important variations, however,
occur in lines eight through ten:

1930	1931
Era madrugada, alguien pudo asomarse a sus ojos quebrados ya por el aire.	Era madrugada. Nadie pudo asomarse a sus ojos abiertos al duro aire.

[53] GUSTAVO CORREA, *La poesía mítica de Federico García Lorca* (Eugene: Univ.
of Oregon Press, 1957), p. 9.

In the earlier version the comma after «madrugada» makes the setting more an integral part of the scene, whereas in the later edition the period sets it apart, creating a break in the description. The use of «nadie» instead of «alguien» conveys an impression of finality due to its essentially negative connotation. The change in line ten, in which the dead man's eyes are seen to be «open,» creates a greater sense of terror than in the previous version in which the eyes are merely «broken» or defunct. Furthermore, the use of «duro aire» conveys a strong tactile sensation which is lacking in the former edition.

The following poem, «La soleá,» incorporates several changes in its 1931 form. The refrain, «Vestida con mantos negros,» is in italics. But the most important change involves the third stanza which originally read: «Y siente que su deseo, / dura sierpe de retama, / se le ha enroscado en el cuello.» These verses are deleted from the 1931 edition, possibly because the poet felt that they added nothing essential. They are an expression of disillusionment, which may have detracted from the stoic mood conveyed by the rest of the poem. The word order is altered somewhat in the final stanza and there is a change in a verb tense:

1930	1931
Se dejó el balcón abierto	Se dejó el balcón abierto
y al alba desembocaba	y al alba por el balcón
por el balcón todo el cielo.	desembocó todo el cielo.

In both versions the precondition for the action is given in the first line: «se dejó el balcón abierto.» From then on, in the 1930 edition, the following sequence is established: time when («al alba»), action portrayed («desembocaba»), place where («por el balcón»), and subject performing the action («todo el cielo»). In the later edition this sequence is altered to time when, place where, action portrayed, and subject doing the acting. It is significant that the two elements principally responsible for the poetic effectivenes of the image —the action («desembocó») and the subject («todo el cielo»)— are presented last, with the others merely forming a prelude. In the first version the sequential unity of action-subject («desembocaba-cielo») is interrupted by the place-where element which, by being positioned between them, decreases the final poetic effect. Furthermore, the change from the imperfect to the preterite tense in 1931 has the effect of speeding the flow of the action to make it occur in an instant, which intensifies the poetic sensation conveyed. In the 1930 version this third stanza is followed by the words: «Vestida con mantos negros / ¡Ay yayayay / que vestida con mantos negros! » In the later edition the first line is eliminated, undoubtedly for being overly repetitious, and the last two verses are put in italics and surrounded by exclamation marks to intensify their emotional effect.

In the 1931 edition «La soleá» is followed by «Cueva» and «Encuentro» which do not appear in 1930. Instead, this earlier version includes «Adivinanza de la guitarra,» «Candil,» and «Crótalo» which were part of the «Viñetas flamencas» in 1927. In the 1931 edition, these poems are more correctly placed among the «Seis caprichos» with which the *Poema del Cante Jondo* ends. A comparison between the 1930 and 1931 versions of these poems reveals some interesting changes. «Adivinanza de la guitarra» remains almost the same, except that the final five lines: («que baila / con seis doncellas / aprisionadas, / tres de carne / y tres de plata») are eliminated, thereby restoring the poem to its earlier, 1927 form. This revision may indicate that the poet considered these final lines superfluous and repetitious. With the elimination of the extra verses, the poem ends with the words « ¡La guitarra! » which are now surrounded by exclamation marks to emphasize their importance as the answer to the riddle posed by the *adivinanza* form.

«Candil» shows little change from 1930 to 1931 except for the last two verses: «a los bordes azules, / agudos, sin cansancio, ¡puros bordes del Sur! » These are replaced by: a los ojos redondos / del gitanillo muerto» which are almost identical to the words used in 1927. The only difference between the 1927 and 1931 versions is that «a» in the first of these two lines was previously «por». This restoration of the original ending within one year shows that the poet must have realized that the 1930 variation was not in harmony with the rest of the poem. As we suggested earlier in another context, the 1930 version seems to represent a momentary return to his earlier period, when he was still under the partial influence of Modernism whose esthetic credo is hardly appropriate for a work attempting to capture the essence of a folk art whose qualities include directness and an emphasis on basic emotions.

«Crótalo» shows some differences between the 1930 and 1931 versions. In its earlier form the poem's opening lines are «Crótalo / crótalo / escarabajo sonoro.» These are modified to: «Crótalo. / Crótalo. / Crótalo. / Escarabajo sonoro.» This third repetition of the word, as well as the following periods, create a separation or pause that allows the reader to absorb more fully the onomatopoeic affect of the sounds. An additional change occurs in verses four and five, which now form broken lines as follows:

1930	1931
En la araña de la mano rizas el aire cálido.	En la araña de la mano rizas el aire cálido,

This rearrangement, followed by a comma after «cálido,» is actually a restoration of the 1927 form. The shortening of the lines may be due to a desire to have them correspond more closely to the first three verses. Finally, the exclamation marks surrounding the last verse in the 1930 version were removed as unnecessary.

The last poem in «Plano de la soleá,» entitled «Madrugada,» was changed to «Alba» in 1931.   Other changes include the division of line six, containing an unwieldy fourteen syllables—«que lloran a la tierra Soleá enlutada,»—to a more manageable two lines of seven syllables each.   The punctuation is improved by replacing the commas following lines six and nine with periods which divide the image cluster into separate image concepts.   Furthermore, line eleven, contining twelve syllables («de pie menudo y temblorosa falda»), is reduced to two lines of five and seven syllables each, and the singular «falda» is given a plural form: «de pie menudo / y temblorosas faldas.» In the final stanza:

> ¡Oh campanas de Córdoba
> en la madrugada.
> Y campanas de amanecer
> en Granada!
>
> (1930)

the later edition co-ordinates the two concepts more closely by replacing the period after «madrugada» with a comma, thereby eliminating the implied stop, and by including «oh» after «y» in line three.   This change makes the third verse closely parallel to the first:

> ¡Oh campanas de Córdoba
> en la madrugada,
> Y oh campanas de amanecer
> en Granada!
>
> (1931)

In comparing the 1927 text of «Memento» with the 1931 variation, we find that there are only three changes. Line five of the earlier edition reads: «por el naranjo loco.» In the later version this was replaced by «entre los naranjos,» a more direct, less abstract verse.   In line six the words «hierba buena» become «hierbabuena,» giving it a more logical meaning. Since this latter form has been retained in all subsequent editions, it is very likely that the earlier version was a misprint. Finally, in the 1931 edition the last line, «cuando yo me muera,» is emphasized by exclamation marks.

«Malagueña» and «Baile that were part of the «Viñetas flamencas» in 1927 were transferred to the «Tres ciudades» in 1931. In comparing the two versions of «Malagueña,» we find that in 1927 line six read: «por la métrica lluvia» and that subsequently it was changed to: «por los hondos caminos.» An examination of the context indicates that the change is an improvement:

1930	1931
Pasan caballos negros	Pasan caballos negros
y gente siniestra	y gente siniestra
por la métrica lluvia	por los hondos caminos
de la guitarra.	de la guitarra.

The original version seems a bit forced and artificial. In addition, lines eight and nine in 1927 were: «Y olores de sal / y muslo rendido.» By 1931 these verses were changed to: «Y hay un olor a sal / y a sangre de hembra.» The first line is not substantially different in content, but in the second verse an obvious sexual image has been replaced by one that implies violence more than sexuality. The last change involves the addition of five extra lines after the eigth and final verse of the 1927 edition. These additional lines are a reprise that repeats the opening verses, but in such a way as to create the impression of a guitar being strummed:

> La muerte
> entra y sale,
> y sale y entra
> la muerte
> de la taberna.

«Baile» reveals several changes. Three of the four lines in the first stanza are substantially altered:

1930	1931
La Carmen está bailando	La Carmen está bailando
en la calle de Sevilla,	por las calles de Sevilla.
dolor de rama dorado	Tiene blancos los cabellos
en primavera fingida.	y brillantes las pupilas.

The use of a plural in line two broadens the scope of the image. Verses three and four, which are highly abstract in the original version, are replaced by more directly descriptive words that treat the woman's physical appearance rather than her psychic state. The latter version eliminates the *cultista* impression conveyed before. The next two lines, repeated as a refrain after each succeeding stanza, are surrounded by exclamation marks in the 1931 edition. In the following stanza, the third and fourth verses are replaced as follows:

1927	1931
En su cabeza se enrosca	En su cabeza se enrosca
una serpiente amarilla.	una serpiente amarilla,
Exceso de ayer maduro	y va soñando en el baile
y vieja sabiduría.	con galanes de otros días.

The earlier version implies a sense of regret and suggests a wisdom that came late. The 1931 edition, which is less abstract, implies quite the opposite: a feeling of contentment with her past life that seems close to pride. Hence the entire concept of the image is changed. The only other variation is a minor one. Line fourteen in 1927 read: «En los fondos se adivinan.» This subsequently became: «y en los fondos se adivinan.»

The other two major editions of the *Poema del Cante Jondo* are those published by Losada of Buenos Aires and Aguilar of Madrid. In both there is little variance from the 1931 first edition. Most of the changes that do occur are primarily matters of minor punctuation. The following variations, however, are worth mentioning: The *Edición Ulises* (1931) divides the seventh line of «La guitarra» into two verses: «Es inútil / callarla,» whereas both Losada and Aguilar print it as a single verse. The Aguilar edition omits the accent mark over «sólo» in lines four, nine, and fourteen of «Y después»: «solo queda / el desierto,» thereby changing the meaning of the word from «only» to «alone.» Losada uses the first line of the «Poema de la soleá,» «Tierra seca,» as a title for the first section, which is without a specific title in the other two editions. In «La soleá,» Aguilar omits the word «y» in line six, although it is present in the other versions which read: «Y el grito, desaparecen.» In the same poem the *Edición Ulises* and Aguilar show line ten as «y al alba por el balcón.» The Losada edition, however, writes the tenth verse as «y el alba por el balcón.» This discrepancy is apt to be misleading, for it seems to make «alba» the subject of «desembocó,» which then changes the meaning of the image. In our opinion, the other editions which make «alba» part of an adverbial clause and «cielo» the subject of «desembocó» are more likely correct.

Losada	Ulises and Aguilar
Se dejó el balcón abierto	Se dejó el balcón abierto
y el alba por el balcón	y al alba por el balcón
desembocó todo el cielo.	desembocó todo el cielo.

In «Paso» Losada omits the word «la» from line two, which in the other publications is: «virgen de la Soledad.» In «Falseta,» the Losada version capitalizes the «m» of «muerto» in verse five: «Niñas que le dan a Cristo Muerto.» In the Aguilar edition line nine of «Lamentación de la muerte» divides «adónde» into two words: «Quise llegar a dónde,» whereas it remains a single word in the other two publiactions. Finally, in the second verse of «Conjuro,» the Aguilar edition fails to capitalize the «m» in «Medusa.»

Although there is no indication of the order in which the various sections of the *Poema del Cante Jondo* were written, José Mora Guarnido believes that «Candil,» «Crótalo,» and «Chumbera» were among the last compositions to be completed, for they seem to him to be little more than brief sketches having no relation to the theme of the *cante jondo*: «. . . por lo menos algunos de los romances estaban ya terminados al mismo tiempo que Lorca agregaba los últimos trozos al 'Poema,' esos que más bien parecen como brochazos finales, simples recuerdos a elementos decorativos y externos del cante: 'Candil', 'Crótalo', 'Chumbera.'» [54] Such an argument seems unconvincing on several grounds. «Candil,» which depicts a Gypsy wake, and «Crótalo,» a fantasy based on the sound of a flamenco dancer's castanets, are hardly foreign to the Gypsy world

[54] *Op. cit.*, p. 193.

5

of the *cante jondo*. Furthermore, if «Chumbera,» describing a cactus, is to be considered a late composition because it lacks a direct connection to the *cante,* then «Pita» and «Cruz» which describe, respectively, another variety of cactus and a cross above an irrigation ditch, should also be so categorized. In addition, these same criteria of judgement could be applied to other poems like «Baladilla de los tres ríos,» «Pueblo,» «Noche,» as well as «Campana,» «De profundis,» and «Clamor.» These six poems, however, are known to have been written by June 1922 and cannot be considered later additions.[55]

It is well known that García Lorca was also working on two other books of poetry during the years 1922-1927—the *Canciones* and the *Romancero Gitano*. Carl W. Cobb believes that there was a possible confusion in Lorca's mind concerning which poems were to be part of the *Poema del Cante Jondo* and which were better suited for the *Canciones*. Consequently, he believes that most of the «Seis caprichos» should have been included in the *Canciones,* while some of the poems from «Andaluzas» in the latter work more properly belong in the *Poema del Cante Jondo*.[56] Although he does not specify which poems he is referring to, it is very likely he feels that «Chumbera,» «Pita,» and «Cruz» should be part of the «Andaluzas», while the two poems entitled «Canción del jinete» are closer in spirit to the *Poema del Cante Jondo*.

When the *Poema del Cante Jondo* was finally published in 1931, it consisted of eight sections: the introductory «Baladilla de los tres ríos,» followed by «Poema de la siguiriya gitana,» «Poema de la soleá,» «Poema de la saeta,» «Gráfico de la petenera,» «Dos muchachas,» «Viñetas flamencas,» «Tres ciudades,» and «Seis caprichos.» The *Editorial Ulises* also included two dramatic sketches: «Escena del teniente coronel de la guardia civil» (followed by the «Canción del gitano apaleado») and «Diálogo del Amargo» (which included, as a conclusion, «Canción de la madre del Amargo»). According to *don* Francisco García Lorca, these two dialogues and their poems were never intended to be a part of the *Poema del Cante Jondo,* but were merely included by the original publisher as added material to fill out a relatively short volume of poetry.[57] However, all subsequent publishers have assumed that these additional compositions were an integral part of the *Poema* and have continued to publish them as such. The majority of the critics have perpetuated the same error, although some recognize that these compositions were probably written long after the rest of the book. Jean-Louis Schonberg, for example, refers to them as «. . . deux saynettes d'une écriture très postérieure au reste.» [58]

---

[55] MELCHOR FERNÁNDEZ ALMAGRO cites some verses from «Crótalo» in his article «El mundo lírico de García Lorca» published in *Esaña,* n. 391, Madrid, October 13, 1923, pp. 7-8, proving that this particular poem could not have been an «último trozo» as MORA GUARNIDO states.

[56] *Federico García Lorca* (New York: Twayne, 1967), p. 46.

[57] An observation made during a conversation with *don* Francisco García Lorca, brother of the poet and Professor Emeritus, Columbia University.

[58] *A la Recherche de Lorca* (Neuchâtel: Éditions de la Baconnière, 1966), p. 180.

Carl Cobb claims that the «Escena del teniente coronel de la guardia civil» and the «Diálogo del Amargo» were both written about 1925 and that the former may have been based on Valle-Inclan's «Los cuernos de don Friolera.» [59]   Marie Laffranque dates the «Canción del gitano apaleado» as March 1926. [60]

A final question to be raised is why García Lorca waited so long to publish a work that was probably completed long before 1931. Doubtlessly, he had become more preoccupied with other projects in the intervening years, such as the *Romancero Gitano,* to which the *Poema del Cante Jondo* is in many ways a prelude, and the *Poeta en Nueva York,* not to mention his growing interest in the theatre, as well as his own insistence on artistic perfection, an insistence that caused him to revise his poems continuously and which made him reluctant to submit them for publication. [61]

[59] *Op. cit.,* p. 50.
[60] *Pour l'Étude...,* p. 341.
[61] See GUILLERMO DE TORRE's comments in *Tríptico del sacrificio* (Buenos Aires: Losada, 1960), p. 64.

CHAPTER III

CONTENT AND STRUCTURE

In its final form, the 1931 edition, the *Poema del Cante Jondo* consists of fifty-one poems grouped into eight sections within which each poem has its own individual function. These eight sections are divided into two divisions. The first contains an introductory poem, «Baladilla de los tres ríos,» and four sections, each concerned with the poetic expression of one song or musical style of the *cante jondo*: the *siguiriya, soleá, saeta,* and *petenera.* Each of these four songs consists of a varying number of poems that reveal different phases of the poet's subjective reaction to the music or spirit of the particular *cante.* The second division is made up of a series of sketches that illustrate various facets of Andalusia: its people, landscape, cities, or different aspects of the world of the *cante jondo* with its singers, dancers, and flamenco cafes.

«Baladilla de los tres ríos» has been interpreted in a variety of ways. One writer, for example, feels that this poem «presents all the elements which will be found throughout the entire *Poema,*» and that, through the symbols of the orange and olive trees, it gives «a panorama of Andalusia as well as an introduction to the poet's themes to be developed in his recreation of the 'cante.'»[1] Albert Henry, on the other hand, affirms that this poem has no thematic connection to the rest of the book, that it is like a great chorus dedicated solely to the Andalusian cities Seville and Granada: «Cette ouverture n'a en commun avec le 'Poema' ni les thèmes, ni la qualité particulière de l'émotion et du lyrisme, ni la structure, ni le schéma prosodique. C'est un fragment du grand choeur, épars dans toute l'ouvre de Lorca, consacré aux villes andalouses. . . .»[2] Still another critic, J. M. Flys, sees the poem as more than a song of praise for Seville and Granada. To him it is an attempt to define their essential character: «Acaso pudiéramos considerar simbólica la primera composición 'Baladilla de los tres ríos.' Todo el poema define de una manera intuitiva las dos ciudades: Sevilla y Granada.»[3] Edward F. Stanton regards the poem as a statement of Lorca's attitude towards Andalusia—a region he regarded as divisible into two contrasting parts: the dry, parched, essentially tragic hinterland, represented by Granada, and the gayer, freer seacoast, exemplified by Seville.[4]

---

[1] CELIA LICHTMAN, «Federico García Lorca: A study in Three Mythologies,» Diss. New York University, 1965, pp. 213, 159.
[2] «Les Grands Poèmes Andalous de Federico García Lorca,» *Romanica Gandensia,* VI (1958), p. 101.
[3] *El lenguaje poético de Federico García Lorca* (Madrid: Gredos, 1955), p. 175.
[4] «Federico García Lorca and 'cante jondo',» Diss. University of California, Los Angeles, 1972, pp. 84, 96-99.

«Baladilla de los tres ríos» is divided into four-line quatrains linked by a light refrain composed of contrasting couplets. Ostensibly, these four-verse strophes compare and contrast the Guadalquivir of Seville with the smaller rivers, the Darro and Genil, associated with Granada, but in the process, the poetic character of the two cities and their respective regions are also contrasted. Seville, with its high tower and wind in the orange groves, is the antithesis of Granada, with its small towers «muertas sobre los estanques.» In the course of this double comparison, the main features of the Andalusian countryside, its traditional landscape of orange blossoms, olive trees, snow, wheat, water, and wind, are infused with the feelings of tragedy, grief, sadness, and death that are typical of both the *cante jondo* and the Andalusians themselves. Thus, this initial poem may indeed be considered an introduction, not only to the world of the *cante jondo,* but to Andalusia and its inhabitants, the Gypsies.

THE SONGS

Given the importance of the *siguiriya* as the prototype from which Lorca and Falla believed that all other types of the *cante jondo* were derived, it is not surprising to find that this work begins with the «Poema de la siguiriya gitana.» This recreation of the *siguiriya* does not attempt to utilize the classic four-line stanza of 6-6-11-6 syllables which corresponds to its musical form. Each of the seven individual poems that constitute the «Poema» illustrates the poet's subjective reaction to one aspect of this *cante,* and each tries to convey the emotional content of the song at every stage. Albert Henry has remarked: «Et c'est précisément ce qu'il a voulu recréer par son chant: faire avec des mots, des rythmes et des images ce qui était déjà vivant et bouleversant par les mots, la guitarre et la mélodie. Il ne s'agit pas d'un art qui imite un autre art dans ses moyens extérieurs, mais qui, avec d'autres ressources, essaie d'attendre la même essence et des effects de même ordre.» [5]

There is, however, an attempt to structure the «Poema de la siguiriya gitana» in such a way that its various movements follow the same sequence as the musical *siguiriya.* As we noted in Chapter I, the *siguiriya gitana* normally begins with the strumming of the guitar which establishes the basic rhythmic patterns for the song. The guitar introduction is followed by the strident cry of the *cantaor* who, with his *grito,* creates the dramatic tension that the actual verses of the song will later develop. This cry is usually followed by an almost audible silence that absorbs the lingering reverberations of sound. The *cantaor* then begins the *siguiriya*'s second phase, the lyrics of the song itself, which slowly increase in affective tension as the music develops. The *siguiriya* finally ends as the singer's voice gradually diminishes, thereby reducing the emotional tension created by the music. In his lecture on the «Arquitectura del cante jondo» in 1931, which was

[5] *Op. cit.,* p. 104.

an amplification of his earlier lecture, «El cante jondo (primitivo canto andaluz)» of February 1922, García Lorca modified his description of the *siguiriya*'s musical structure as follows:

> La «siguiriya» gitana comienza por un grito terrible. Un grito que divide el paisaje en dos hemisferios iguales; después la voz se detiene para dejar paso a un silencio impresionante y medido. Un silencio en el cual fulgura el rostro de lirio caliente que ha dejado la voz por el cielo. Después comienza la melodía ondulante e inacabable en sentido distinto de Bach. La melodía infinita de Bach es redonda, la frase podría repetirse eternamente en un sentido circular; pero la melodía de la «siguiriya» se pierde en el sentido horizontal, se nos escapa de las manos, y la vemos alejarse hacia un punto de aspiración común y pasión perfecta donde el alma no logra desembarcar.[6]

The degree to which he has followed the structural sequence outlined above will be apparent in the course of our commentary.

The first poem in the «Poema de la siguiriya gitana,» entitled «Paisaje,» creates an atmosphere of mystery and suspense that will be further developed in each successive part. The night and a starry coldness predominate as a series of strange phenomena and physical sensations emanate from the countryside to give a foreboding of impending tragedy. In his lecture on the *cante jondo* in 1922, Lorca had stated: «. . . el 'cante jondo' canta siempre en la noche. No tiene ni mañana ni tarde, ni montañas ni llanos. No tiene más que la noche, una noche ancha y estrellada.»[7] And so it is here: the grove of olive trees opens and closes like a fan; the gray air curls, and the trees are weighed down by cries as a band of captive birds move their long tails in the darkness. Each new verse increases the feelings of fear and dread, for these olive groves, symbols of human destiny,[8] and the cries create a landscape that is more spiritual than real; it is an Andalusian landscape whose geographical features are symbolic of the tragic destiny of its Gypsy inhabitants.[9] The sound of these cries, metamorphosed into visual form, prepares the way for the *grito* of the *cantaor*.

The «Siguiriya gitana» actually begins with the next poem, «La guitarra,» which creates a poetic, guitar introduction that continues to build upon the emotions of fear and impending tragedy established in «Paisaje.» These feelings are now imbued with music in verses whose rhythmic pattern consciously reproduces the guitarist's reiterated strumming of a single chord:

> Es inútil callarla.
> Es imposible
> callarla.
> Llora monótona

[6] «Arquitectura del cante jondo,» in *Obras completas* (Madrid: Aguilar, 1963), p. 57.
[7] «El cante jondo,» in *Obras completas*, pp. 47-48.
[8] LILIA V. BOSCÁN, «La muerte en la poesía de Lorca,» *AFZ*, IV, Núm. 4 (1965), p. 290.
[9] FLYS, *op. cit.*, p. 121.

como llora el agua
como llora el viento
sobre la nevada.

The critic J. L. Flecniakoska has commented: «Certaines pièces atteignent à la parfaite imitation du chant et de son accompagnement par la traditionelle guitare. C'est ce que nous pouvons étudier en particulier dans la poésie intitute «Guitare»: début lent et grave du chant qui s'amplifie et s'assourdit, puis diminue pour reprendre avec plus d'inténsité, grâce à un mot accentué sur l'antepénultième et qui se prolonge au delà du terme des autres vers.» [10]

The opening lines, «Empieza el llanto / de la guitarra,» form the basis for the entire composition whose subsequent verses will explain, by means of metaphor and symbol, the various forms the weeping of the guitar will talle. For García Lorca the verb *llorar* seemed to express more precisely than any other the spirit of the *siguiriya gitana,* which he called a «perfecto poema de las lágrimas» in which «llora la melodía como lloran los versos.» [11] In response to the guitar's lament, the goblets of early dawn (of light and life) shatter, plunging us once again into a spiritual night. The weeping continues; it is impossible to silence it because it is beyond consolation.[12] The weeping of the guitar is likened to the falling of water or to the wind over new fallen snow, images chosen to suggest the music's loneliness and desolation. It weeps for «cosas lejanas» and the word *lejano,* a common lorquian symbol for the ideal that is unattainable,[13] is followed by a series of enigmatic terms that obscure rather than clarify the nature of these «faraway things.» Each of these enigmas is both a metaphorical definition of the guitar's weeping and an ambiguous, symbolic statement about the human condition, and in the end they only increase the poem's sense of mystery. Its weeping is said to be like the sand of the warm South which asks for white camelias, a comparison that has been explained to mean: «. . . gentes apasionadas del sur, que, corroídas de inseguridad, anticipan y preguntan el fin de su jornada,» [14] but which may simply refer to a more general, frustrated human longing for things that will never be.[15] It is also like an arrow without a target, which may represent «el curso de la vida humana sin explicación ni rumbo,» [16] or a life without any discernible goal or purpose. It is an afternoon without a morning (human life cut off from its past) or the first dead bird upon the branch, which may symbolize «la ilusión primera, muerta sin desplegar su

---

[10] *L'Univers Poètique de Federico García Lorca* (Paris: Éditions Bière, 1952), p. 94.
[11] «El cante jondo,» p. 50.
[12] CARLOS RAMOS-GIL, *Ecos antiguos, estructuras nuevas, y mundo primario en la lírica de Lorca* (Bahía Blanca, Arg.: Cuadernos del Sur, 1967), p. 43.
[13] GUSTAVO CORREA, *La poesía mítica de Federico García Lorca* (Eugene: Univ. of Oregon Publications, 1957), p. 13.
[14] RAMOS-GIL, *op. cit.,* p. 43.
[15] EDWARD F. STANTON, *op. cit.,* p. 61.
[16] CORREA, *op. cit.,* p. 13.

vuelo,»[17] but which may also represent the primordial beginning in time or the essential nature of the song itself, since *primero* is symbolically identified with essence or beginnings.[18] In the final verses the guitar is compared to a heart badly wounded by five swords, an image that may well be the dramatic high point of the poem. These five swords have been interpreted variously as the five fingers of the guitarist,[15] the five wounds of Christ,[20] or human grief in general.[21]

Just as in the musical *siguiriya gitana,* the strumming of the guitar is suddenly broken off by the violent cry of the *cantaor* which appears in the form of the next poem, «El grito,» and creates a new dramatic tension:

> La elipse de un grito
> va de monte
> a monte.

The singer's elliptical cry unleashes a feeling of cosmic terror that is continually augmented by the death symbols found in each successive image. The geometric shape of the cry may be suggested by the vibrating strings of the guitar itself—a possibility that would then establish a thematic connection between this poem and the preceding one, «La guitarra.»

«El grito» presents a series of transformations. The ellipse of a cry, perceived in the first image as movement and sound, becomes a black rainbow spanning the blue night.   Black, symbolizing death, forms an emotional contrast with the placid blue of the sky.[22] The «Ay,» which acts as the poem's refrain, is placed between the strophes and therefore has the double function of both separating the images and emphasizing the emotional drama that unites them. Finally, the cry becomes a viola bow that causes the strings of the wind to vibrate, meaning that the cry animates or unleashes sinister forces since the wind is often a death symbol.[23] The use of vibrating cords establishes a connection between this image and the first, for the original, elliptical shape of the cry may have been suggested by the vibrations of the guitar's strings. The poem, therefore, seems to have an essentially circular thematic structure, returning to the point at which it began. The final two verses in which the Gypsies peer from their caves, holding up their lanterns to see what has happened, are like an epilogue to the preceding drama. These lines are put in pa-

---

[17] *Ibid.*

[18] JUAN EDUARDO CIRLOT, *Diccionario de símbolos* (Barcelona: Editorial Labor, 1969), p. 341.

[19] CORREA, *op. cit.,* p. 18.

[20] RAMÓN XIRAU, «La relación metal-muerte en los poemas de García Lorca,» *NRFH,* VII (1953), p. 365.

[21] CONCHA ZARDOYA, «La técnica metafórica de Federico García Lorca,» in *Poesía española contemporánea* (Madrid: Ediciones Guadarrama, 1961), p. 351.

[22] CARLOS EDMUNDO DE ORY, *Federico García Lorca* (Paris: Éditions Universitaires, 1967), p. 72.

[23] LICHTMAN, *op. cit.,* p. 201.

rentheses, either to create an impression of subdued gravity and stillness,[24] or to indicate that they are a commentary by the poet who wishes to show the affects of the cry on the inhabitants of the region. In either case, they increase the sense of mystery by raising the unanswered question of what these people see.

Just as the singer's cry is followed by an awesome silence in the musical *siguiriya gitana*, so it is in this poem whose next phase is called «El silencio.» This silence is a living, undulating silence that transforms as it prolongs the image of the wind's vibrating strings. The resonant vibrations of the cry are projected on a seemingly endless horizontal plane: «Oye, hijo mío, el silencio. / Es un silencio ondulado,» but this horizontal direction of movement is immediately checked by an essentially vertical, downward movement conveyed by the image «un silencio / . . . / que inclina las frentes / hacia el suelo.» This poem, based as it is on a contradictory concept («silencio ondulado») and on opposite geometric planes (horizontal and vertical), captivates the reader and holds him in a state of suspended fascination that is a preparation for the next phase.

With «El paso de la siguiriya» begins the second phase of the song, that which normally corresponds to the actual lyrics of the *siguiriya gitana*. In Lorca's poem, however, there is no attempt to model the «Paso» on traditional *siguiriya* lyrics. Instead, he has chosen to create a poem whose various elements allude to and seek to define, through symbol and metaphor, the essential spirit and sentimental content of these lyrics. The «Paso,» therefore, is the high point of the entire composition. Its verses are introduced into the preceding silence by means of images whose function is to transform it into rhythm and sound. This is accomplished by presenting the *seguiriya* as a personified «muchacha morena» who, amidst black butterflies, is accompanied by a white serpent of fog and is chained to the trembling of a rhythm that never arrives. The use of rolling fog, trembling rhythm, butterflies, and a slithering serpent suggests an undulating movement that ties this poem to the preceding one. In addition, black butterflies and a snake are ominous portents of the essentially tragic nature of the *siguiriya*.

In the next stanza the song is said to have a «corazón de plata,» perhaps indicating insensivity to human fate,[25] and a «puñal en la diestra,» a symbol of tragedy and death. It is equally possible, however, as J. M. Flys believes, that these two symbols, as well as the «dolor de cal y adelfa» in the following verses, may represent certain characteristics of the song itself: «. . . cada término de la descripción del canto personificado coincide con las características del canto mismo (en una serie de imágenes de tipo metafórico o simbólica). Así, 'temblor,' 'corazón de plata'

---

[24] See TOMÁS NAVARRO TOMÁS, *Manual de la entonación española* (New York: Hispanic Institute, 1944), p. 114, where he states: «La entonación del paréntesis se caracteriza por su nivel grave respecto al de las unidades inmediatas . . . La línea melódica del paréntesis se desenvuelve de ordinario a unos seis o siete semitonos por debajo de la altura media de la frase en que se halla intercalado.»

[25] HENRY, *op. cit.*, p. 105.

(=voz argentina), 'puñal' (=gudeza), 'dolor de cal y adelfa' (=emblema de la tristeza y amargura) definen la 'siguiriya' . . .» [26]

The «Paso» ends with a double question: «¿Adónde vas, siguiriya, / con un ritmo sin cabeza?» (suggesting an enigmatic, endless, spiritual wandering) and «¿Qué luna recogerá / tu dolor de cal y adelfa?» In Lorca's poetry the moon is often a death symbol or the enigmatic repository of love or grief, and in this image it has been interpreted specifically as a symbolic tomb for lost love.[27] In fact, one critic's mythological interpretation states that we are dealing with a woman whose quest for love will end with her becoming the bride of the moon: «Como mujer que ha perdido la cabeza en locura de amor, la 'siguiriya' marcha a ciegas por el horizonte llevando un anuncio de muerte (dolor de cal y adelfa) y en su destino final irá a conjugarse con la luna.» [28] J. L. Schonberg has suggested that the words quicklime and rose-bay imply that the grief expressed by the *siguiriya* has a burning and a poisonous quality, for these are the very properties inherent in «cal y adelfa.» [29] Still another interpretation, that of A. Henry, is that the purpose of the image is to: «rendre sensible l'irrémédiable brúlure» and «fixer, en même temps, le contenue sentimental de la siguiriya gitane.» [30]

The next poem, «Después de pasar,» arises as a response to the passing of the *siguiriya*. The events described are a dramatic commentary on the song's aftermath. The endless melody has now become lost in the horizon, and a group of unidentified children follow it with fascinated gaze up to «un punto lejano,» which Gustavo Correa has interpreted as a symbol for: «. . . un reino mágico que se pierde en las distancias de lo inalcanzable. Es como un final de plenitud que está vedado al hombre que ve sorpresivamente truncado su destino a lo largo del camino.» [31] This poem immediately calls to mind García Lorca's lecture on the *cante jondo* in which he remarked: «. . . la melodía de la 'siguiriya' se pierde en el sentido horizontal, se nos escapa de las manos y la vemos alejarse hacia un punto de aspiración común y pasión perfecta donde el alma no logra desembarcar.» [32] In the following verses the lamps go out unexplainably; some blind girls question the moon, and through the air spirals of weeping ascend as the mountains, like the children in the first image, also gaze at the same faraway point. Thus the circle is closed and the poem returns to its point of departure.

A sense of mystery pervades the entire composition and forms the basis for its affective qualities. What new hope or cause for despair lies at this faraway point; what has caused the lamps to be suddenly extinguished;

[26] *Op. cit.*, p. 232.
[27] CORREA, «El simbolismo de la luna en la poesía de Federico García Lorca,» *PMLA*, LXXII, No. 5 (1957), p. 1066.
[28] GUSTAVO CORREA, *La Poesía mítica*, p. 7.
[29] *Federico García Lorca, el hombre; la obra* (México: Compañía General de Ediciones, 1959), p. 189.
[30] *Op. cit.*, p. 116.
[31] *La poesía mítica...*, p. 13.
[32] «Arquitectura...» p. 57.

what question was asked of the moon; and what new tragedy has made the blind girls weep? The questions are inevitable, but no answer is given. In speaking of the *cante jondo*'s poetry, Lorca referred to this use of mysterious, unanswered questions as one of its essential characteristics: «En el fondo de todos los poemas late la pregunta, pero la terrible pregunta que no tiene contestación.» [33] Perhaps, as J. M. Flys suggests, these spirals of weeping are simply another attempt to define and give concrete form to the song's rhythm which is slowly receding into the distance [34] —a view shared by Gustavo Correa who regards the spiral as a geometric representation of rhythm in an ascensional stage. [35]

This poem bears a structural resemblance to «El silencio» because of its brevity (the two are the shortest poems in this section) and because of its obvious use of horizontal versus vertical directions of movement. The first and final images emphasize a horizontal plane, as the children and the mountains stare at the same faraway point, while the verses in between depict a vertical direction when the girls question the moon and their weeping ascends skyward.

As in many of Lorca's poems, the features of the landscape take an active part in the drama and become co-participants with the human figures. Hence the childen and the mountains are equated insofar as they perform the same act. In his 1922 lecture Lorca noted that this tendency towards pantheism was another typical characteristic of the *cante*: «Todos los poemas del 'cante jondo' son de un magnífico panteísmo, . . . Todos los objetos exteriores toman una aguda personalidad y llegan a plasmarse hasta tomar parte activa en la acción lírica.» [36]

The enigmatic question of what lies at the mysterious *punto lejano* is partially answered in the next and final poem, «Y después.» There are only the dual symbols of the labyrinth and the empty desert. This closing phase of the *siguiriya* may be construed as a series of random mental reflections arising in response to the music and the emotions evoked by the previous six parts and by the final dying of the song. In the opening verses, the labyrinth, the archetypal symbol for an enigma, appears in the form of «los laberintos / que crea el tiempo.» These labyrinths symbolize not only the enigmatic mysteries of life, [37] but more specifically, they represent the musical labyrinths formed by the rhythm of the *siguiriya*. [38] Since this rhythm is fading away, the labyrinths are said to disappear, and the poem's refrain, «Solo queda / el desierto,» may be understood to mean that only the final emptiness of a vast, silent desert of complete spiritual desolation and loneliness is left. This refrain is put in parentheses to indicate a subdued tone, for these two verses provide a spiritual undercurrent for the emotions conveyed in each successive image. In the

---

[33] «El cante jondo,» p. 46.
[34] *Op. cit.*, p. 123.
[35] *La poesía mítica...*, p. 19.
[36] «El cante jondo,» p. 49.
[37] SCHONBERG, *op. cit.*, p. 189.
[38] CORREA, *La poesía mítica...*, p. 10.

75

succeeding stanzas, the heart, a symbol of love, and the dawn, representing hope, also disappear. Each new statement is followed by the refrain whose constant, obsessive repetition implies a fatal discovery without recourse. In the closing lines these verses, now written without parentheses, becomes the dominating image, as the desert is converted into a final death symbol that provides a tomb for the music whose undulating rhythms are now a part of the *ondulado desierto*.[39]

The structure of the «Poema de la siguiriya gitana» may be summarized in the following way: The first part, «Paisaje,» establishes a scenic and affective background for the poem. The second, «La guitarra,» begins the music of the *siguiriya*, which is abruptly interrupted by the cry of the third phase, «El grito,» and by the ensuing, undulating silence depicted in the fourth part, «El silencio.» The actual song of the *siguiriya* begins with part five, «El paso de la siguiriya,» only to be followed, not by a cry as in the previous instance, but by another type of sound, that of weeping, in the sixth poem, «Después de pasar.» In part seven, «Y después,» the «Poema» is brought to a close as all sound gradually diminishes, and the previous, undulating silence again imposes itself, this time in the form of a silent, undulating desert. It is now obvious that after part one, the introduction, part two corresponds to part five in that they both represent the music of the *siguiriya*; part three complements part six, for they follow the music and introduce a new phenomenon of sound; and part four corresponds to part seven because both arise as emotional responses to the silence that follows, and they use the same geometric figure of horizontal undulation. The seven parts or phases of this composition can be represented graphically as follows:

1
«Paisaje»
(Introduction)

2		5
«La guitarra»	———————	«El paso de la siguiriya»
(music)		(music)
3		6
«El grito»	———————	«Después de pasar»
(sound)		(sound)
4		7
«El silencio»	———————	«Y después»
(silence)		(silence)

The second section of this work presents the poet's vision of the *soleá*. The ten parts of the «Poema de la soleá» are also a series of fantasies suggested by the ever-changing mood of this *cante*. As we shall see, this

[39] *Ibid.*

poem is not so well structured as the preceding one, and there is little attempt, except in one of its parts, to convey the formal pattern of the musical *soleá*.

The opening phase, «Tierra seca,» acts as the first half of the introduction. It is a stylized evocation of the Andalusian earth, though its features are not so much those of the concrete region of southern Spain, but are instead an affective interpretation of this landscape—a psychic, intuitive landscape of the mind whose purpose is to depict the ageless grief of the Gypsies.[40]   Instead of a fertile grove of olive trees, we are introduced to a land of dry, sterile earth and immense nights. There is a conspicuous absence of human figures, but the landscape is filled with man-made objects, such as oil lamps, cisterns, and arrows, symbolizing death, grief, or pain.   A telluric sadness pervades this introductory poem which seems to be structured around two opposing groups of symbols. The first and most numerous group includes the words «tierra seca,» «quieta,» «vieja,» «noches inmensas,» «candil,» «pena,» «hondas cisternas,» «muerte sin ojos,» and «flechas,» all of which suggest stagnation, annihilation or death.   The second group includes «viento,» «olivar,» «sierra,» «caminos,» «brisa,» and «alamedas,» representing life, freedom, and fulfillment.[41]   Although these two sets of symbols are opposite in meaning and they seem to point to a dramatic struggle within the Andalusian countryside, the emotional effect each series conveys is almost identical.   The four verses containing the positive symbols: («Viento en el olivar / viento en la sierra)» and «(Viento por los caminos / Brisa en las alamedas)» are as emotionally negative in their feeling of emptiness and desolation as those verses expressing the more obvious negative symbols.   So there is, in fact, no real affective contrast behween the two groups, and the poem presents a series of emotional reactions to the landscape that is entirely consistent.

The next part, «Pueblo,» introduces human figures into this landscape and completes the introductory evocation.   The foreboding silhouette of a cross on a mountain top is complemented by misterious «hombres embozados» moving along the streets as the «veletas,» the symbol of man's changing destiny,[42] continue their eternal gyrations.   The foreboding of tragedy increases as the poem concludes with the cry: « ¡Oh, pueblo perdido / en la Andalucía del llanto! »   This personal comment by the poet becomes a key note for the four-part drama that follows.

The separate phases of this drama are united through their sense of intense tragedy and anguish.   Death without hope and the poet's horrified reaction to it are the predominant themes.   In Schonberg's opinion, the images found in Part One, «Puñal,» seem to be the direct result of the sinister «hombres embozados» of the previous poem.[43]   «Puñal» is centered

---

[40] HOWARD T. YOUNG, «Lorca and the Deep Song,» *Claremont Quarterly*, II, 2 (1964), p. 9.

[41] CORREA, *La poesía mítica...*, pp. 13-14.

[42] *Ibid.*, p. 12.

[43] *Op. cit.*, p. 191.

around the theme of the dagger, which in all of Lorca's poetry is imbued with a desire to pierce the flesh.[44] Its appearance here marks the first mention of it in this work. According to another critic, the dagger is the first of two great themes in the «Poema de la soleá,» with the *soleá* itself as the second.[45] In «Puñal» the knife is seen to enter the human heart and is compared, in a series of similes, to a plowshare and a ray of sunlight which pierce the earth. Thus, the world of man and the world of nature are equated in their vulnerability to pain and death. The poem's refrain:

No.
No me lo claves.
No.

is the poet's personal cry of angush, a cry which, according to Daniel Devoto, is taken directly from popular folk songs.[46] Even the typographical arrangement of this refrain is such that it too forms a dagger or possibly a cross. Throughout the «Poema de la soleá,» there seems to be an unmistakable affinity between the two as they are both death symbols. In fact, the cross, in the form of a *calvario,* was a prominent feature of the landscape in the preceding «Pueblo.»

The sense of physical, even visceral pain that characterizes every image In fact the cross, in the form of a *calvario,* was a prominent feature of descriptions of intense, at times morbid, physical suffering. The *cante* deals with dramatic, extreme situations usually involving plenitude and fulfillment or death. As García Lorca stated: «Una de las características más notables de los textos del 'cante jondo' consiste en la ausencia casi absoluta del 'medio tono'. . . El andaluz o grita a las estrellas o besa el polvo rojizo de sus caminos. El medio tono no existe para él.»[47]

Just as «Puñal» was based on the dagger symbol, the next poem, «Encrucijada,» is based on that of the crossroads. In Lorca's poetry the crossroads is usually a negative symbol associated with a cross, labyrinth, cemetery, and therefore with death itself.[48] The *encrucijada* has been described as the: «punto de convergencia de caminos y en ella se encuentran vidas humanas en tensión ante la presencia del puñal.»[49] Here the metaphoric *encrucijada* is a point of convergence for the sinister «viento del Este,» «farol,» and «puñal,» all of which symbolize impending annihilation. In the presence of these three ominous symbols, the street seems to tremble in fear, like a cord under tension or an enormous fly. This image of the trembling street is probably a metaphoric description of the effect of the

[44] LICHTMAN, *op. cit.,* p. 81.
[45] HENRY states: «Bréf, le 'Poema de la Soleá' est une composition heurtée où se mêlent sans se fondre deux thèmes, 'puñal' et 'soleá.'» *Op. cit.,* p. 106.
[46] «Notes sobre el elemento tradicional en la obra de García Lorca,» *Filología,* año II, núm. 3 (1950), p. 318.
[47] «El cante jondo,» p. 46.
[48] CORREA, «El simbolismo religioso en la poesía de Federico García Lorca,» *Hispania,* XXXIX, 1 (1956), p. 44.
[49] CORREA, *La poesía mítica,* p. 9.

East wind, and as such it is in keeping with another characteristic of the *cante jondo:* the strange materialization of the wind which takes an active role in shaping or distorting the features of the landscape as well as the lives and destinies of its inhabitants.[50] «Encrucijada,» like the preceding «Puñal,» closes with a fearful, personal commentary by the poet who exclaims:

> Por todas partes
> yo
> veo el puñal
> en el corazón.

Thus, in both this and the preceding poem, the theme of the dagger in the heart becomes a symbol for total tragedy which is magnified until it obscures all else.

Just as in the «Poema de la siguiriya gitana,» part three of this drama, the poem « ¡Ay! », utilizes the cry as its central theme. This time, however, the unexpected cry acts as a cathartic release for the emotional tension built up in the two preceding parts. The opening image fuses sensations of sight, movement, and sound, as the cry leaves the shadow of a cypress tree in the wind. The audible sound acquires a material, visual form suggesting mystery and approaching disaster, for both the cypress tree [51] and the shadow [52] are traditional death symbols. The refrain that follows, «(Dejadme en este campo / llorando.),» is the poet's personal comment to the reader, and it is a statement that rejects all hope of consolation. As one critic has pointed out, this direct statement in parentheses gives the poem a bipartite structure; it establishes a two-plane dialogue so that the poem becomes: «Una verdadera poesía a dos voces en la que aparecen quizá los 'dos yo' del poeta. . . que dialoga a veces consigo mismo.» [53] One of these two voices consists of the verse couplets that are the strophes while the second voice corresponds to the refrain in parentheses. In contrast to the cry of the first stanza, the theme of the second is silence, which is the replaced in the third strophe by the image of a lightless horizon bitten by bonfires that create an impression of extreme pain and anguish.

The last poem in this four-part drama, «Sorpresa,» presents the concrete actualization of the death motif which pervaded the previous three parts in abstract form. Here violent death by the dagger is no longer merely a potential threat; the poem opens with a dead man lying in the street, a dagger in his chest. It is a vision of anonymous, solitary death, with only a trembling street lamp as a witness to the tragedy. The dead

---

[50] FEDERICO GARCÍA LORCA, «El cante jondo,» pp. 49-50.
[51] CORREA, «El simbolismo del sol en la poesía de Federico García Lorca,» *NRFH*, XIV, 1-2 (1960), p. 44.
[52] *La poesía mítica,* p. 17.
[53] ALBERTO YAHNI, «Algunos rasgos formales en la lírica de García Lorca: función del paréntesis,» *Bulletin Hispanique*, XLVI, 3-4 (1964), p. 112.

man's open, unseeing eyes stare at the indifferent «duro aire,» and the poem concludes with the somewhat bitter comment: «y que no lo conocía nadie,» which is in keeping with the generally pessimistic attitude towards life that frequently characterizes the musical *soleá*.[54]

The next poem, «La soleá,» introduces what may be the second major theme, the song itself, personified as a woman dressed in mourning. This poetic device is frequent in the lyrics of the *cante jondo* where pain and suffering are often transformed into the figure of a dark and tragic woman. The poem seems to be a response to the preceding drama and, in particular, to the death scene depicted in «Sorpresa.» This composition is one of the few in the *Poema del Cante Jondo* which attempts to reproduce not only the spirit and emotional atmosphere of the *cante* (the *soleá* is known for its contemplative melancholy, stoic resignation, and philosophical tone), but its actual metrical form as well—octosyllabic tercets rhyming in assonance. As we shall see in greater detail in Chapter V, the entire composition is based on a series of skillfully contrived contrasts. The first tercet: «Vestida con mantos negros / piensa que el mundo es chiquito / y el corazón es inmenso,» establishes a stoic attitude within which the indifference of the world or of life itself is contrasted to the immensity of an individual's suffering. This stoic attitude is increased in the second tercet which seems to imply that all sadness, even grief, will pass away with time. And finally, the poem closes with the animated sky flowing into the room at dawn, which provokes a final cry of anguish from the poet or singer.

The composition «Cueva» has been interpreted in many different ways. J. M. Flys regards it as a poem based on a series of chromatic emblems which define a Gypsy's song. In his opinion the opening verses: «De la cueva salen / largos sollozos» indicate that the Gypsy is singing a *soleá* and that the «sollozos» are a metaphor representing the song's emotional content.[55] Concha Zardoya points to the difficulties in interpreting this poem and suggests that the colors may be no more than an esthetic game similar to certain tendencies found in modern painting: «El color tiene una significación poco determinable en poemas casi por completo cromáticos y que son estudios, juegos y manchas de color semejantes a los de la pintura contemporánea.»[56] Schonberg, however, views it as a play of antithetical colors which are universal symbols for the tragic existence of the Gypsy race.[57] Still another critic, Roberto Yahni, emphasizes the poet's use of color as the principal means for creating the emotional atmosphere: «En 'Cueva' la acotación de color ambienta la acción poética, con la base del rojo (pasión).»[58] Unquestionably, the most nearly com-

---

[54] In the opinion of DANIEL DEVOTO, this composition is «casi un hecho folklórico,» incorporating several characteristics of Spanish folk poetry. *Op. cit.*, pp. 317, 318,
[55] *Op. cit.*, p. 162.
[56] *Op. cit.*, p. 381.
[57] *Op. cit.*, p. 189.
[58] *Op. cit.*, p. 113.

plete attempt to interpret this poem is that of Celia S. Lichtman whose commentary we quote in full:

> The gypsy living in the cave is singing a «soleá» telling of love and resulting in death. Use of the chromatic pattern emphasizes the various parts of the poem; the pain of the knife wound «lo cárdeno / sobre lo rojo,» which caused the death «lo negro / sobre lo rojo,» of which the singer tells from the whitewashed cave «lo blanco / sobre lo rojo.» The death theme is further reiterated by the various elements in addition to the red-black color pattern. These are the white lime, the deep sobs of the singer which, in addition to being the «ayes» of the «cante,» are also the cries of the dead men as well as their grief-stricken relatives; his hesitating voice which sings the broken rhythm of the «coplas» but whose adjectival description «entre*cortado*» also is indicative of the knife wound and the unseeing eyes of the dead.[59]

In our opinion, this composition is primarily an experiment in structure and color. Its structure, like that of «¡Ay!,» is essentially bipartite: it develops on two levels simultaneously. In this case one of these is anecdotal, the other symbolic. The verses not in parentheses relate events in a narrative fashion, whereas those in parentheses are always symbolic restatements or further elaborations of the same event. Thus, the initial lines telling that the sound of sobbing is coming from a cave are restated symbolically by the two verses that follow: «(Lo cárdeno / sobre lo rojo).» «Cárdeno,» the color of flesh, may be a symbol for a human being, the Gypsy living in the cave. «Rojo,» a traditional symbol for blood or violence, implies that he has experienced a personal tragedy. In the following lines, the Gypsy evokes mysterious, far off countries. The same theme is then elaborated further by the verses: «(Torres altas y hombres / misteriosos»)» which metaphorically describe these faraway lands. The next lines tell us that his eyes portray the same intense suffering as his sobbing voice. This statement is then followed by: «(Lo negro / sobre lo rojo).» In addition to the obvious death symbolism represented by «black,» it is likely that the word also refers to the color of the Gypsy's eyes—eyes which are witnessing death's presence. «Red» is a symbolic reminder of the violence or tragedy that caused the death which the Gypsy is mourning. The next two verses describe the physical surroundings of this scene: a whitewashed cave that shimmers in the golden sunlight. This is then expressed by chomatic emblems: «(Lo blanco / sobre lo rojo).» «White» refers to both the cave and to the intense sunlight, and «red» again represents the human tragedy that has taken place within this whitewashed cave.[60]

The next poem, «Encuentro,» which presumably describes the encounter of two people at a crossroads where one of them, the poet, confesses that

---

[59] *Op. cit.,* p. 209.
[60] Schonberg offers an alternate interpretation for these lines with his suggestion that the sunlight is a positive symbol whose purpose is to scatter the shadows cast by the mood of the *cante jondo*: «Ce filet d'or filtrant de la tanière du troglodyte entre'oeuvre la seule échappée de lumière qui égaie les ténèbres du *Cante Jondo*.» *A la Recherche de Lorca* (Neuchâtel, Suisse: Éditions de la Baconnière, 1966), p. 187.

he has been martyred for love and that, therefore, they will no longer be able to meet, seems, at first glance, to be curiously out of place in the «Poema de la soleá.» Its theme and the religious analogy between the poet's suffering and Christ's crucifixion: «(En las manos / tengo los agujeros / de los clavos)» has little apparent connection to the rest of this section. It may be, however, that the poem is a metaphoric dramatization of a particular *soleá* with which Lorca was familiar, since the use of religious allusions (San Cayetano is also mentioned) is a common occurrence in folk poetry. Schonberg suggests, moreover, that this image indicates nothing more than that in the world of the *cante jondo* even love is a martyred god: «l'amour lui-même, ce dieu de la jeunesse, dans le Cante jondo, est un dieu percé de clous.» [61] The «encounter» referred to in the title presumably occurs at a crossroads—a sinister place of death or suffering [62]—and the poet, like most male figures in Lorca's writings, becomes the victim in a blood sacrifice, crucified by his passions: [63] «¿No ves cómo me estoy / desangrando?»

«Alba» brings the «Poema de la soleá» to its conclusion on a more positive note. This final poem is, in part, a return to the introduction in that it also evokes the countryside and the people of Andalusia. Yet this time the sinister omens and portents of imminent tragedy, so much an integral part of the introductory poems, have been purged by the intervening drama. [64] Gustavo Correa, on the other hand, does not believe that the poem is necessarily optimistic. He points out that the ringing of the bells in the first verses may well be «anuncios funerarios que acompañan a la 'soleá enlutada.'» The crossroads are still present, though they are being filled with lights brought by «Las niñas de España / de pie menudo / y temblorosas faldas.» But even this seemingly positive act is not without sinister overtones, for, according to Correa, it is precisely at the crossroads that love is converted into dramatic tension and potential violence. [65] Another opinion, that of Lichtman, draws particular attention to the sexual implications of the poem, for she sees in the symbol of the crossroads «the road into womanhood which the young girls who have not yet known love must traverse.» [66]

The «Poema de la soleá» is not so well structured as the preceding «Poema de la siguiriya gitana.» The two part introduction presenting the Andalusian landscape and its people is not essential to the four part drama that follows. Furthermore, this drama is composed of four independent,

---

[61] *Ibid.*, p. 188.
[62] CORREA, *La poesía mítica*, p. 9.
[63] LICHTMAN, *op. cit.*, p. 219.
[64] Acording to ALBERT HENRY, the poem's melancholy tone is in keeping with the true spirit of the *soleá*: «Seule, 'Alba' est bien dans la tonalité mineure de la vraie soleá, la 'tierna soleá enlutada,' et l'on y retrouve la mélancholie, mais aussi la vivacité et la grâce de cette pure descendante du lyrisme moresque, comme on retrouve dans 'La soleá' l'harmonie légère et la tristesse souriante de la danse au même nom,» *op. cit.*, p. 106.
[65] *La poesía mítica*, pp. 8, 9.
[66] *Op. cit.*, p. 218.

autonomous poems that are related only by the general theme of death and (in the case of three of them) by the symbol of the ubiquitous knife. Structurally, their only similarity is in the use of the poet's direct commentary to the reader. The next three poems abandon the theme of the *puñal* and seem to concentrate on the *soleá*. But even this tentative thematic bond is uncertain. In the second of the three, «Cueva,» Lorca seems to be more interested in experimenting with a bipartite structure and color symbolism than in developing further the *soleá* theme. The third poem, «Encuentro,» has a quasi religious motif and deals with amorous disappointment. The final part brings the «Poema de la soleá» to a close amidst an atmosphere of ringing bells whose significance is ambiguous.

This general looseness of structure may be accounted for in part by an examination of the 1930, pre-original version called «Plano de la soleá.» As we noted in Chapter II, the «Plano» contained three poems which were later transferred to the «Seis caprichos,» and it did not include «Puñal,» « ¡Ay! ,» «Cueva,» and «Encuentro,» all of which were added before the first edition of the book in 1931. In the 1930 «Plano,» the first two poems, «Tierra seca» and «Pueblo de la soleá,» had the same function as in the first edition a year later: that of establishing the geographical setting and introducing sinister human figures into the landscape. The next poem, «Calle,» (later called «Encrucijada») was related to the preceding by a common theme, the street. Two verses from «Pueblo de la soleá»: «En las callejas hombres / embozados,» provided the thematic background for «Calle» which told what was happening in these «callejas.» The two central images, the trembling street and a dagger in the heart, formed a prelude to «Copla,» later renamed «Sorpresa.» Here a man lay dead in the street with a dagger in his heart, and the street's trembling motion was now transferred to the «farol.» In the 1930 version, both «Calle» and «Copla» were emotional preludes for «La soleá,» the mourning widow dressed in black; they were not the last two parts of a separate drama. This tightly woven structure, within which each poem led into the next, was weakened substantially in the first edition by the inclusion of the other four compositions mentioned above. The first of these, «Puñal,» was placed between «Pueblo de la soleá» and «Calle,» thereby interrupting the natural transition from one to the other. Furthermore, the change in the title from «Calle» to «Encrucijada,» as well as the replacement of the first verse, «Calle sin sueño» by «Viento del Este,» inevitably lessened the thematic link between it and «Pueblo.» The second interpolated poem, « ¡Ay! », placed between «Encrucijada» and «Sorpresa,» also interrupted the continuity of development and obscured the fact that «Sorpresa» was the logical outcome of «Encrucijada.» The other additional poems, «Cueva» and «Encuentro,» which the first edition of 1931 were included after «La soleá,» created the impression that the three formed a separate thematic unit. This impression conceals the fact that «La soleá» is the inevitable result of «Sorpresa.» However, it is important to note, as Albert Henry has done, that the four interpolated poems not only change the structure of the entire *Poema,* but they alter its content in the direction of greater dramatic pathos.[67]

The third major section, «Poema de la saeta,» consists of eight parts and presents a series of dramatic, picturesque scenes that depict the celebration of Holy Week in Seville. In many of these poems, *saetas* means both an arrow and the songs telling of the Passion of Christ and the sufferings of the Virgin, which are traditionally sung during these festivities.

The first poem, «Arqueros,» is the first half of a prelude whose function is to establish the dramatic mood for the scenes that follow. The archers gather in the pre-dawn darkness outside Seville. It is they who will «shoot» their *saetas* of song at the floats in the passing religious procession. Their somber appearance is described in threatening terms, for they are dark archers with wide gray hats and long slow capes who come from the remote lands of grief and go a labyrinth of love, glass, and stone.

This image of the mysterious, enigmatic labyrinth has been the subject of several critical interpretations. For Gustavo Correa the labyrinth, as well as the *piedra,* are simply death symbols, and the image means nothing more than that the archers are going to their deaths: «El laberinto es símbolo de términos sin salida donde la vida humana y el amor encuentran la dureza de la piedra (tumba). Los 'arqueros oscuros' que se acercan a Sevilla y que 'vienen de los remotos / países de la pena,' van directamente al final de su trayectoria; 'Y van a un laberinto.' / Amor, cristal y piedra.»[68] Another writer believes that the labyrinth refers to the winding streets and alleys of the city through which they will be moving.[69] To Howard T. Young, the labyrinth expresses the very essence or «heart of the 'cante jondo',» and it is a symbol of the *cante's* mysterious, echanting power.[70] Celia S. Lichtman, on the other hand, considers the labyrinth to be symbolic of «the entanglements of the sentiments» in which the archers will become lost. Its component elements, love, glass, and stone, are symbols for «passion, illusion and death.»[71] Another interpretation, that of Alfredo de la Guardia, compares the *arqueros* to the *saetas's* musical notes, and it is these notes that become lost in a labyrinth of passion, illusion, and grief: «Llegan los sombríos peregrinos desde una lontananza umbría y dolorosa como las notas del 'cante' surgen desde el fondo de un alma atormentada por la pena. Y se pierden entre la maraña de los sentimientos, de la pasión, de la ilusión, del dolor.»[72] It is also possible that this culminating image may refer to the content of the *saeta* itself whose verses sing of the labyrinth or enigma of man's fate.

---

[67] *Op. cit.,* p. 106.
[68] *La poesía mítica,* p. 10.
[69] EDWARD F. STANTON, *op. cit.,* p. 159.
[70] «The Magic of Reality,» in *The Victorious Expression* (Madison: Univ. of Wisconsin Press, 1966), p. 159.
[71] *Op. cit.,* p. 217.
[72] *García Lorca, persona y creación* (Buenos Aires: Editorial Schopire, 1952), p. 149.

The labyrinth's three elements—«amor,» «cristal,» «piedra,»—would then represent the three principal stages of our human life cycle: birth, life (the fragile crystal), and death («piedra» suggests a tomb). Man is fated to be born, to live, and to die, to repeat over and over his pre-ordained destiny. It is also possible to interpret the labyrinth's three component elements to mean that the enigma of the *saeta* is one of love, the spirit (*cristal's* traditional symbolic meaning),[73] and death, an interpretation that seems more likely, since these are typical Christian themes frequently found in the religious *saetas*.

The next poem, «Noche,» completes the prelude as we witness the start of the religious procession from a distance. As it moves along in the early dawn, the lights from the candles and lanterns carried by the processioners or placed upon the religious floats join with the lights from the street lamps and glow worms to form the four-starred «constelación de la saeta.» These distant points of light are reflected in the windows of the houses the processioners pass, and the crosses they carry sway with their steps. This second half of the prelude is more picturesque than dramatic, although Gustavo Correa sees an undercurrent of drama in the description. The fact that the windows are said to «tremble» connotes not only movement, but fear, and the marchers' «cruces superpuestas» become a «visión metafórica del cementerio cuajado de cruces.» [74] In another work this same critic explains the image «Ventanitas de oro / tiemblan» as a transference to the windows of the trembling in the human voices singing *saetas*.[75] It seems more likely, however, that the «trembling» is caused not by sound, but by the quivering reflection of light either from the dawn's first rays or from the lights carried by the marchers passing beneath the windows.

The next part, «Sevilla,» is a dramatic composition in which the sinister *arqueros* now shoot their arrows, symbolic of life and communication as well as death,[76] from a tower that is at once the Giralda and a symbol for human fate.[77]

> Sevilla es una torre
> llena de arqueros finos.
>
> Sevilla, para herir.
> Córdoba, para morir.

The implications are clear: Seville, like Cordova, is a universal symbol for tragic human destiny presided over by the archers, the fates, and because Seville is dominated by them, it is no longer a city of festive gaiety,[78] but rather:

---

[73] CIRLOT, *op. cit.*, p. 160.

[74] «El simbolismo religioso,» p. 44.

[75] *La poesía mítica*, p. 19.

[76] YOUNG, «The Magic of Reality,» p. 157; and GUSTAVO CORREA, *La poesía mítica*, p. 20.

[77] *Ibid.*, pp. 20, 21.

[78] M. IGLESIAS RAMÍREZ, *Federico García Lorca, el poeta universal* (Barcelona: Dux, 1963), p. 214; G. DÍAZ-PLAJA, *Federico García Lorca* (Madrid: Espasa-Calpe, 1961), p. 40.

Una ciudad que acecha
largos ritmos,
y los enrosca
como laberintos.
Como tallos de parra
encendidos.

These «ritmos» are symbolic of the trajectory of human life,[79] and in Seville their final destiny is the inevitable labyrinth of death. The sinister humanization of the city continues in the next stanza in which Seville is identified with the archers themselves, and, in an image that utilizes both meanings of *saeta,* the city is said to: «dispara la constante / saeta de su río.» The final verses describe Seville's character as a mixture of Don Juanesque bitterness and Dionysian perfection.

With this description the setting is now complete, and the main part of the «Poema de la saeta,» a four-part depiction of the religious procession and the general street scene in which it takes place, is ready to begin. The obscure, mysterious figures whose approaching lights were seen at a distance in the prelude are now close and in full view of the reader-spectator.

In «Procesión» the dark archers become robed penitents whose tall, pointed hoods make them look like mythological unicorns, medieval astronomers, fastastic Merlines, the Ecce Homo, Durandarte, and Roland. There seems to be a definite progression in this description which goes from mythological animals to a collective group of human beings and then to historico-legendary figures.

The scene then shifts to two floats depicted in «Paso» and «Saeta.» Each deals with one of the two central figures around whom the Easter celebrations revolve: the Virgin and Jesus. The first opens with a picturesque image of a statue of the Virgin dressed like a nineteenth-century woman in a crinoline skirt that resembles an immense tulip. The humanization of a divine figure is, of course, a common occurrence in the folk *saetas* that this section of the *Poema del Cante Jondo* celebrates.[80] The statue is carried on a wooden platform illuminated by candles or lanterns, and it is transformed metaphorically into a «barco de luces.» This metaphor then initiates a series of nautical images, for the ship of lights is said to float amidst the multitude of processioners and spectators who become «la alta marea / de la ciudad.» It is carried «por el río de la calle, / hasta el mar» among turbid «saetas» and «estrellas de cristal.» These «estrellas» may be the lights from the street lamps, lanterns, and candles mentioned in the prelude. They now acquire a shimmering, crystalline look, since they are reflected in the water suggested by both the street-river metaphor and by the fact that the procession is gradually approaching the Guadalquivir.

---

[79] CORREA, *La poesía mítica,* p. 9.
[80] GINO L. RIZZO, «Poesía de Federico García Lorca y poesía popular,» *Clavileño,* VI, 36 (1955), p. 49.

«Saeta,» describes a second float in the procession. This one carries a statue of the crucified Christ, a Gypsy «Cristo moreno» who is said to change from the lily of Judea to the carnation of Spain. These two flowers, whose multiple symbolic meanings are discussed fully in Chapter V, frequently appear in many folk *saetas*. The refrain « ¡Miradlo por donde viene! » is a traditional *saeta* verse. Its use here lends a musical character to the composition and signifies the approach of Christ's statue, described at the conclusion of the poem. The next group of verses seeks to define Spain by depicting its landscape in both realistic and symbolic terms. The «cielo limpio,» which represents life and hope, is also «oscuro»; it is darkened by the omnipresent threat of death. This ambiguous situation is also true of the earth, for the «tierra» (fertility, life, womb) is a «tierra tostada» (sterile, without life.) Even the «agua,» the life force, moves slowly and barely performs its function. The final image returns to the theme of the first stanza, but now it describes Christ's statue directly, in realistic detail. Its dark color, jutting cheekbones, and flashing eyes seem to be modeled on the features of the Andalusian Gypsy race.

«Balcón,» the final poem in this central part of the «Poema,» is a vignette which acts as an aftermath to the preceding «Saeta.» It shifts the focus of attention from the procession itself to the street scene, and specifically to a balcony where a girl, la Lola, is singing *saetas*. As she sings:

> Los toreritos
> la rodean,
> y el barberillo
> desde su puerta
> sigue los ritmos
> con la cabeza.

These brief, realistic details contribute much to the «Poema de la saeta's» picturesque, *costumbrista* atmosphere. The light-hearted, ingenuous charm of the opening lines is continued in the following verses that utilize a joyous succession of vowel sounds in «a.»

> Entre la albahaca
> y la hierbabuena
> la Lola canta
> saetas.

This over-all gay impression is, of course, in marked contrast to the majority of poems in the book, but, according to Carlos Ramos-Gil, even this relative gaiety is partially nullified by the closing lines: «'La Lola aquella—que se miraba—tanto en la alberca', con lo que se desvanece la ilusión de felicidad, implícita en lo anterior. Esa Lola, que canta saetas desde un balcón florido, debe tener una pena muy honda, y tal vez pensará ahogarla en las aguas de la alberca.»[81] This interpretation, suggesting contemplated suicide, would imply

[81] *Op. cit.,* p. 70.

a complete reversal in the emotional content of the poem. It seems more likely, therefore, that these final lines are merely a mildly humorous allusion to the fact that Lola, who obviously enjoys being the center of attention, is somewhat narcissistic.

The last poem, «Madrugada,» represents a return to the beginning. The archers reappear and the time of day, early dawn, is the same as that of the prelude. But this poem, unlike «Arqueros,» is far less dramatic, and it reflects a more positive emotional atmosphere. The *saeteros* are now associated with love, and their songs «leave traces of a warm lily,» the Easter flower traditionally associated with resurrection and triumph. The words «lirio caliente» are taken directly from Lorca's lecture on the «Arquitectura del cante jondo» in which he described the silence following the cry of the *siguiriya* as: «un silencio en el cual fulgura el rostro del lirio caliente que ha dejado la voz por el cielo.» [82] In this case «la voz» is not that of the *siguiriyero,* but of the *saeteros* mentioned in the preceding verses. In the concluding stanza a pleasing chromatic effect is created as the yellow crescent moon, like the keel of a ship, breaks through the purple clouds while the archers' quivers fill with dew.

Structurally, the «Poema de la saeta» is the least complex of the four sections devoted to four types of the *cante jondo.* The first two poems form a nocturnal prelude. «Arqueros» introduces the sinister archers and the enigma of the labyrinth. «Noche» depicts the start of the religious procession at a distance. The next poem, «Sevilla,» provides a dramatic description of the city where the central part of the «Poema» will be enacted. The next four compositions form a central unit within the «Poema.» The first, «Procesión,» returns to the theme of the religious parade, which is now quite close, and it describes the costumes of the various penitents. Next follow the two major floats which, in «Paso» and «Saeta,» describe the Virgin and Christ, the two figures most celebrated in the *saetas.* Part four concentrates on another aspect of the street scene and draws attention to a balcony where la Lola is singing *saetas.* The «Poema» then closes with a return to the beginning. The mysterious archers reappear, but now they are described as blind, indicating that the enigma of the labyrinth, posed at the beginning, is still unresolved. It is important to note that none of these eight separate poems attempts to reproduce the form or content of an actual *saeta.* Even the poem by that name is, in reality, a description of the statue of Christ rather than of the *saeta* sung to him.

The final section of this first division is the «Gráfico de la petenera,» an eight-part choreographic composition in which music and dance often seem to predominate. Each one of its parts is a separate creation with its own internal drama and atmosphere, but each corresponds to or complements at least two other parts in such a way that the entire poem displays a tightly woven structure.

[82] *Op. cit.,* p. 57.

The «Gráfico de la petenera» begins with «Campana» whose initial stanzas convert auditory sensations into visual imagery:

> En la torre
> amarilla
> dobla una campana.
>
> Sobre el viento
> amarillo
> se abren las campanadas.

These opening lines are reminiscent of the traditional verses of the musical *petenera*:

> Si oyes doblar las campanas,
> no preguntes quién ha muerto,
> porque a ti te lo dirá
> porque a ti te lo dirá
> tu mismo remordimiento.

From the very beginning, the funeral tolling of a bell in a tower (the *torre* is a frequent Lorquian symbol for human destiny) [83] creates a foreboding of impending tragedy that will dominate every part of the first half of the «Gráfico.» In the second image, the bell transfers its chromatic tonality to the wind. The ringing then ceases abruptly, thereby creating a mysterious void in which only the desolate wind is left to carve an enigma in the sand: «El viento con el polvo / hace proras de plata.» This introductory poem, whose subtitle is «Bordón,» acts as a bass chord for the entire composition,[84] but its primary function is to provide an essentially auditory and affective prelude for the next poem, «Camino,» whose content is mainly visual and symbolic.
It begins:

> Cien jinetes enlutados
> ¿dónde irán
> por el cielo yacente
> del naranjal?

In «Camino» the relentless rushing of life towards death is symbolized by one hundred horsemen in mourning who, in a swirling course of movement suggestive of the Apocalpse, travel through the Andalusian sky on their way to the labyrinth of crosses, the cemetery where both the song of the *petenera* and life itself will end. C. B. Morris has pointed out that the poem's metric structure, in which a strong stress is placed on the final syllable of every other line, creates a consistent rhythmic pattern that reinforces the seeming inevitability of their journey: «In 'Camino' the alter-

---

[83] CORREA, *La poesía mítica*, p. 11.
[84] HENRY, *op. cit.*, p. 108.

nation of long and short lines, and the strong stress placed, as in many popular poems, on the final syllable of every even line, create a purposeful, regular rhythm which emphasizes that nothing will deflect these riders from their course.»[85] The *jinete,* a frequent death symbol,[86] forms an affective contrast to the *naranjal,* symbolic of love and life.[87] The dramatic tension between these two opposing forces is carried over into the next verses in which Cordova, a melancholy city of tragedy,[88] «le nid de la mort,»[89] is contrasted with Seville, resplendent with life and gaiety.[90] The horses, described as «caballos soñolientos,» possibly to create a nocturnal, nightmarish impression, are themselves a forewarning of misfortune and death.[91] They will bring their riders to mourn the *petenera* whose death we shall witness in part five. The poem closes with the question:

> Con siete ayes clavados,
> ¿dónde irán
> los cien jinetes andaluces
> del naranjal?

Even the numbers *siete* and *cien* have significance in this poem rich in symbolism. In Andalusian folk superstitions, *siete* is symbolic of human passion: «Un campo singolare d'innervazione espressiva è quello dei numeri, nell'uso dei quali le ragioni occulte, pitagoriche, della scelta si mescolano con gli estri dell'arbitrio e della superstizione andalusa . . . Il 'siete,' per esempio, è impiegato all' acme della passione.»[92] This number frequently occurs in oral ballads where human lives are regulated by the number seven, and heroes wander for seven years through seven kingdoms or die of seven wounds.[93] J. E. Cirlot mentions that seven is also a symbol for grief,[94] which would explain why there are seven «ayes» associated with these horsemen. *Cien* or *ciento* is often used to indicate an unlimited amount rather than a specific quantity.[95] Hence, the «cien jinetes» of this poem may be understood to mean a vast and unlimited number of death figures. However, Oreste Macri also points out that one hundred is a mystic number signifying both love and death: «Il 'cien' è impiegato con accento mitico di amore e di morte . . . »[96] Both meanings are applicable

---

[85] *A Generation of Spanish Poets: 1920-1936* (Cambridge: Cambridge Univ. Press, 1969), p. 46.

[86] BOSCÁN, *op. cit.,* p. 284.

[87] FLECNIAKOSKA, *op. cit.,* p. 45.

[88] DÍAZ-PLAJA, *op. cit.,* pp. 43, 44.

[89] SCHONBERG, *A la Recherche de Lorca,* p. 183.

[90] DÍAZ-PLAJA, *op. cit.,* p. 37; IGLESIAS RAMÍREZ, p. 214; MODESTO RIVERA, «Federico García Lorca, motivos naturales, Sevilla, Córdoba, Granada,» *Brújula,* II, 3-4 (1936), p. 32.

[91] BOSCÁN, *op. cit.,* p. 284.

[92] ORESTE MACRÌ, *Canti Gitani e Andalusi* (Guanda: Collezione Fenice, 1961), p. 24.

[93] MORRIS, *op. cit.,* p. 66.

[94] *Op. cit.,* p. 342.

[95] CORREA, «El simbolismo de la luna,» p. 1081.

[96] *Op. cit.,* p. 24.

in the «Gráfico,» for these one hundred horsemen are later to become the one hundred lovers in the poem «De profundis.»

The sensations of fear and dread are continued in the third part, «Las seis cuerdas.» Here our attention is focused primarily on the guitar whose moving strings weave the melody of the *petenera*. A nightmare scene is evoked in which the music acquires a sinister animation and is converted into a tarantula that ensnares the sighs of lost souls floating in a dark pool of wood, the mouth of the guitar. Like part one, «Campana,» this poem is a visual representation of sound, as the dreams and emotions suggested by the song itself are converted into weeping. «Las seis cuerdas» is, in fact, a musical prelude to the following «Danza,» and the two, like the preceding «Campana» and «Camino,» form an auditory-visual unit within the «Gráfico de la petenera.»

«Danza,» whose opening verses are:

> En la noche del huerto
> seis gitanas,
> vestidas de blanco,
> bailan

has been described as an attempt to synthesize poetry and dance in a fusion of the arts: «A ello habría que añadir la abundancia de efectos plásticos o de movimiento rítmico sugerido por el baile expresado magníficamente en la 'danza' de las seis gitanas vestidas de blanco, cuyas sombras se alargan hasta llegar al cielo en el nocturno encantado del 'Huerto de la petenera'. No se trata tanto de buscar equivalencias como en los simbolistas, sino de un intento de síntesis de las varias artes, quizá inconsciente, que si no nos engañamos es uno de los rasgos fundamentales en la estética de Lorca.»[97]

The poem's four stanzas, written in a repeated rhythmic pattern resembling a dancer's measured steps, depict a quiet, moonlight scene across which the moving white figures of the six dancing girls form a pleasing color contrast to the surrounding darkness. This poem is not, however, the «danse légère, vive, blanche et sereine, toute harmonieuse . . . calme tourbillon de pas mésurés qui tourne et qui renaît sans heurt» that one critic has interpreted it to be.[98] Its seemingly peaceful contrast with or respite from the preceding scenes of terror is misleading, for these six girls in white may be the six gleaming strings of the guitar whose sinister qualities were explored in the preceding poem.[99] The number six is in itself symbolic of the human soul,[100] and these dancing figures have a ghost-like appearance

---

[97] ANGEL DEL RÍO, *Federico García Lorca* (1899-1936) (New York: Hispanic Institute, 1941), p. 35.

[98] HENRY, *op. cit.*, p. 108.

[99] CORREA, *La poesía mítica*, p. 8; MACRÌ, *op. cit.*, p. 12.

[100] CIRLOT, *op. cit.*, p. 342. Cirlot states that six represents an: «unión de los dos triángulos (fuego y agua) y por ello símbolo del alma humana. . . . También se ha establecido relación del seis con la virginidad y con la balanza.» Generally, both meanings (human souls and virginity) are implied whenever this number ocurs in the *Poema del Cante Jondo*.

as they glide through the surrounding darkness. In any event, the sense of apparent calm lasts only through the first two stanzas where we learn that the dancers are «coronadas / con rosas de papel / y biznagas,» the symbols of false love and disillusionment. Thus, the impression of calm serenity begins to dissipate. In the next two strophes there is a marked change in the description, and a new feeling of foreboding begins to assert itself in preparation for the death scene we are to witness in part five. We learn that «sus dientes de nácar / escriben la sombra / quemada» and that «sus sombras se alargan / y llegan hasta el cielo / moradas.» Thus «Danza» closes with a definite emphasis on somber words like *sombras, quemada, moradas,* all of which have connotations of fatality or pain.[101]

The next four poems, beginning with «Muerte de la petenera,» form the second half of the «Gráfico.» The omens of impending tragedy and destruction which permeated the first half now become a concrete reality. Hence «Muerte de la petenera» begins with the announcement: «En la casa blanca muere / la perdición de los hombres» whose second line is taken from a traditional *copla* of the *petenera*:

> Quien te puso petenera
> no te supo poner nombre,
> que debió de haberte puesto
> la perdición de los hombres.[102]

In the introductory verses, the *petenera* is personified as a woman who will be the central figure in a dramatic and tragic episode.

Following the two line introduction is the refrain: «Cien jacas caracolean. / Sus jinetes están muertos.» The reappearance of the one hundred riders who have come to witness the *petenera*'s death establishes a direct link to «Camino» and answers the question with which it closed: «¿dónde irán / los cien jinetes andaluces / del naranjal?» The nervous prancing of the horses, suggestive of musical rhythm and dance, is then transferred in the next stanza to the quivering lamp flames and the trembling dress of the woman as she lies dying. The words *estremecidas* and *tiembla,* also suggestive of the vibrating strings of the guitar or a singer's voice, enhance the musical qualities of this poem. Such is the opinion of Gustavo Correa who states: «En forma más genérica, las vibraciones procedentes de la guitarra o de la voz humana se hacen explícitas en un estremecimiento de 'temblor' que se comunica a todo el universo animado a large number of the *lora* or *loree* singers with them. The melodies and tiembla la falda de la petenera.» [103]

The dramatic high point occurs in the final image:

> Largas sombras afiladas
> vienen del turbio horizonte,
> y el bordón de una guitarra
> se rompe.

---

[101] CORREA, *La poesía mítica,* p. 8; FLYS, *op. cit.,* p. 223.
[102] PEMARTÍN, *op. cit.,* p. 129.
[103] *La poesía mítica,* p. 19.

These shadows are converted metaphorically into knives that cut not only the bass string of the guitar, but the life of the *petenera* herself, thereby bringing both the music and the poem to an abrupt end. The moment of death occurs at the precise instant at which these shadows fall across the guitar, for the *petenera,* though personified, is in reality only a song that dies when the guitar ceases to be played.

With «Falseta» the guitar begins again. The poem is, in fact, the commentary of this instrument on the preceding death scene, a commentary that describes the funeral of the *petenera.* The opening verses: « ¡Ay, petenera gitana! / ¡Yayay, petenera! », are reminiscent of the singer's cry that is an integral part of the musical *petenera.* From a thematic point of view, we may also interpret this opening cry as the response of the mourners who will accompany the dead woman to her grave. The rest of the poem is divided into two stanzas of six verses each that form a direct thematic contrast with one another. We learn that her burial was not attended by «niñas buenas,» of the kind who adorn the statues of Christ during religious celebrations or who wear the virginal white *mantillas* to the *ferias.* Her burial, rather, was assisted by a cortege of: «gente / siniestra / Gente con el corazón / en la cabeza» who seem to define the character of the *petenera.* «Falseta» then closes with a reprise of the cry: « ¡Ay, petenera gitana! / ¡Yayay, petnera! » This composition is related to the third poem, «Las seis cuerdas,» in two ways: Both are commentaries of the guitar, and the «negro / aljibe de madera» of the latter suggests the grave in which the *petenera* is buried.

The seventh poem in the «Gráfico,» «De profundis,» has been described as a «poema epitáfico» in relation to the preceding themes of death and burial.[104] However, «De profundis» does not deal directly with the *petenera,* but with «cien enamorados» who lie sleeping beneath the dry earth. Once again *cien* is used for its mythological significance of love and death.[105] The next verses:

> Andalucía tiene
> largos caminos rojos.
> Córdoba, olivos verdes
> donde poner cien cruces,
> que los recuerden

contain a cluster of symbols that complement the notion of death. *Camino* is a symbol for the trajectory of human life, and as such it leads to the grave.[106] *Rojo,* the color of spilled blood, is an obvious death symbol. Cordova, traditionally a city of tragedy,[107] is frequently associated with

---

[104] CORREA, *La poesía mítica,* p. 9.
[105] MACRÍ, *op. cit.,* p. 24.
[106] CORREA, *La poesía mítica,* pp. 9, 16.
[107] DÍAZ-PLAJA, *op. cit.,* p. 44.

annihilation.[108] The *olivo* is often utilized by Lorca as a symbol for tragic human destiny,[109] and its color *verde* can be symbolic of mystery,[110] danger,[111] the desperation of human life,[112] bitter fatality,[113] and death.[114] The *cruces* are, of course, obvious symbols for a cemetery.[115] The poem then closes with the same two verses used at the beginning: «Los cien enamorados / duermen para siempre.»

Althought the burial theme unites this poem to «Falseta,» it is significant that the individual tragedy which was the subject of the two preceding compositions is converted in «De profundis» into a more general, human, and above all, Andalusian theme. Furthermore, this poem is also related to the second composition, «Camino,» in three ways: The one hundred horsemen in the former have now become the one hundred lovers. Secondly, they both use cemetery crosses in their imagery («el laberinto de las cruces» in «Camino» and the «cien cruces que los recuerdan» in «De profundis»). Thirdly, both utilize the Andalusian countryside as their scenario.

The final part of the «Gráfico de la petenera,» «Clamor,» is related to the preceding «De profundis» by its theme of death pervading the Andalusian countryside, but it is even more closely joined to the introductory «Camapana.» «Clamor» is, in fact, essentially the same poem as «Campana» except for two differences: In «Clamor,» the tower, bell, and wind are presented in plural form instead in the singular, and there is an additional seven verse strophe interpolated after the second stanza.   The use of the plural may be because the bells are now tolling for the one hundred buried lovers of «De profundis,» whereas in «Campana» the bell was ringing for only one person, the *petenera*.   Although death was always an implied element in «Campana,» it is physically present in the interpolated verses of «Clamor»:

> Por un camino va
> la muerte, coronada
> de azahares marchitos.
> Canta y canta
> una canción
> en su vihuela blanca,
> y canta y canta y canta.

[108] SCHONBERG, *A la Recherche de Lorca*, p. 183.
[109] BOSCÁN, *op. cit.*, p. 290.
[110] ZARDOYA, *op. cit.*, p. 387.
[111] J. M. AGUIRRE, «El sonambulismo de Federico García Lorca,» *Bulletin of Hispanic Studies*, XLIV, 4 (1967), p. 271.
[112] *Ibid.*, p. 273.
[113] FLECNIAKOSKA, *op. cit.*, p. 50.
[114] XIRAU, *op. cit.*, p. 367.
[115] JOSÉ FRANCISCO CIRRE, «El caballo y el toro en la poesía de García Lorca,» *Cuadernos Americanos*, XI, 6 (1952), p. 239.

The road, described by Gustavo Correa as a «cauce natural a la presencia de la muerte,» [116] is one of the fatal «largos caminos rojos» referred to in the preceding «De profundis.» Death now appears ironically as a bride crowned with the traditional wreath of orange blossoms, a symbol of love. But these blossoms are withered, indicating the end of love and of the *petenera* herself. The lifeless, monotonous song of death is represented by the obsessive repetition of the same words: «Y canta y canta y canta.» This poem, like «Campana,» closes on a note of solitude as the bells abruptly cease tolling, and the wind blows dust swirls in the sand.

The structure of the «Gráfico de la petenera» is far more complex than most critics have recognized. Albert Henry has observed that each of its eight parts corresponds to one other part with the whole composition revolving around the two central poems, «Danza» and «Muerte de la petenera,» in such a way that they form a ballet scenario: «Tous ces 'tableaux', si délibérément personnels, s'appellent cependant. Ils se succèdent en un déroulement qui s'enverse autour des figures centrales: à 'Campana' (1) correspond 'Clamor' (8); à 'Camino' (2), 'De profundis' (7); à 'Las seis cuerdas' (3), 'Falseta' (6), les deux 'peteneras' centrales faisant pivoter le tout, de sorte que, géométrie vivante, les figures qui se correspondent se font finalement face:

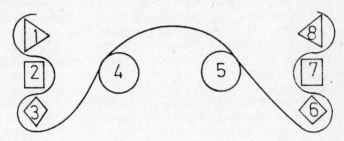

Bien mieux, un scénario de ballet est inscrit en filigrane au long du poème.» [117]

The Italian critic Oreste Macrì uses Henry's analysis as the starting point for his own. He accepts Henry's basic concept, but he points out that the first four parts, those on the left side of Henry's illustration, share a common theme: the anticipation of tragedy and death, whereas those figures on the right, the last four poems, have a different theme: the fulfillment or actualization of what was formally presentiment and expectation. Death finally appears in part five and dominates the rest of the composition. In Macrì's words:

> Possiamo aggiungere che la parte sinistra (1-4), guardando, sta nella zona del sospiro, pianto, interrogazione, attesa, la parte destra (5-8) nella zona della morte, celebrazione funebre. Infatti, «Clamor» (8) è una variante di «Campana» (1), in più la morte incoronata; il labirinto delle croci, intravvisto nella

[116] *La poesía mítica*, p. 16.
[117] *Op. cit.*, p. 109.

cosa dei cento ginnetti in «Camino» (2), è una realtà in «De profundis», dormendo i cento innamorati per sempre; «Falseta» (6) è, appunto, una variazione de «Las seis cuerdas» (3), il cui «negro / aljibe de madera» è presentimento del funerale della Petenera; con la «Danza» (4) delle «seis gitanas» si chiude la parte sinistra, cui risponde l'inizio della destra con «Muerte de la petenera» (5). Si osservi però che la stessa «Danza» (4) si collega con «Las seis cuerdas» (3), che si identificano con le «seis gitanas»; mentre «Muerte de la petenera» (5) anticipa il «De profundis» (7) nella sorte dei cento cavalieri.[118]

Although we accept the general interpretation of both Henry and Macrì, we believe that the question of structure needs further analysis. Part one does correspond to part eight, part two to seven, and part three to six, as Henry suggests, but we do not accept his statement that the entire «Gráfico» centers around parts four and five as the two pivotal poems. Macrì is perhaps more perceptive in stating that the «Gráfico» is actually divided into two main sections, poems one through four, and five through eight, with the first section acting as a preparation for the second. However, further analysis reveals that each of these two sections has its own structure, a possibility not mentioned by either critic. Parts one, «Campana,» and two, «Camino,» form a unit in that «Campana» is an auditory prologue or preparation for «Camino» whose images are primarily visual. Similarly, part three, «Las seis cuerdas,» in which auditory sensations are foremost, forms a dramatic prologue to part four, «Danza,» in which the visual impressions predominate. Thus, the two units, 1-2, 3-4, are interrelated in that 2 and 3 are characterized by a predominance of auditory phenomena, and 2 and 4 are primarily visual in nature. However, this alternating pattern of sound-sight, sound-sight is not continued in the next section of the «Gráfico.» In poems five through eight, auditory and visual sensations are more closely fused, so that neither may be said to be a dominant factor in any one composition. Nevertheless, the second section can also be divided structurally into two units. Poems five and six, «Muerte de la penetera» and «Falseta,» form a natural unit in that they describe the death and burial of the personified *petenera*. Similarly, seven and eight, «De profundis» and «Clamor,» are a unit in themselves, since they both expand the death theme into a total Andalusian setting. These two basic units are not completely separate from each other, however, because poems six, «Falseta,» and seven, «De profundis,» are interrelated by their common theme of burial.

It is curious that neither Henry nor Macrì recognizes an interrelationship between poems four, «Danza,» and five, «Muerte de la petenera,» beyond the rather vague statement that they are pivotal points for the «Gráfico's» ballet scenario, an affirmation that is never really explained. We believe there are three ways in which these two compositions are similar: Both are written in a flowing, dance-like, musical harmony of balanced verses in which the dancing girls of the former correspond to the prancing

[118] *Op. cit.,* p. 12.

horses of the latter. Both poems also utilize an ever changing color contrast between black and white:

«Danza»	«Muerte de la petenera»
En la noche del huerto, seis gitanas vestidas de blanco bailan	En la casa blanca muere la perdición de los hombres ... ... Largas sombras afiladas vienen del turbio horizonte

And finally, both make use of a vertical direction of movement, which in the case of «Danza» is from the earth towards the night sky («sus sombras se alargan / y llegan hasta el cielo / moradas»), and in «Muerte de la petenera» it is in the opposite direction, from the night sky towards the earth («Largas sombras afiladas / vienen del turbio horizonte»). This interconnection between parts four and five establishes a closer relationship between both halves of the «Gráfico.» In order to depict these various interrelationships between the eight parts of the composition, we would change the previous illustration to the following in which the interconnections mentioned by Henry are indicated by the lines at the bottom while Macrì's observation appears as a solid vertical line separating both halves of the composition. Those additional interrelationships we have pointed out appear as vertical dashed lines and as solid horizontal lines appearing at the top of the drawing:

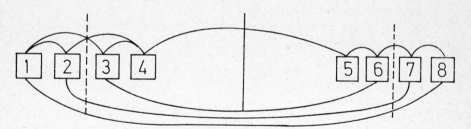

Thus, the eight part «Gráfico de la petenera» displays a highly intricate structure which can be divided into two main parts (poems 1-4 and 5-8) and then subdivided into units of two poems each (poems 1-2, 3-4; 5-6, 7-8). Such divisions could easily lead to a fragmentation of the composition were it not for the fact that a system of symmetrical counterbalancing is employed as a primary unifying principal. Each poem in the first half of the «Gráfico» has a counterpart in the second half to which it corresponds either in theme, setting, poetic figures, or symbols.

This careful balancing of poems creates a harmonious, symmetrical unity that is then reinforced by other, secondary interconnections that join the various phases of the composition even more closely. Hence, not only does the first poem correspond to the last, but it is also related

97

7

to the second and the third. Likewise, the second poem has the seventh as its counterpart, and it is fruther integrated into the total composition by its conection with the first and fourth. Poem three corresponds to six, but it is also related to one and four. Poem four relates principally to five and secondarily to two and three. In a similar fashion, poem five corresponds to four and six. Poem six is a counterpat to three, but it is also related to five and seven. Poem seven corresponds to two, and it is also connected to six and eight. Likewise, the last poem is related to the first and seventh. The result is a structurally well integrated poetic composition whose essential unity is maintained throughout in spite of the fact that each constituent part of the total «Gráfico de la petenera» is a complete poetic creation in itself.

ILLUSTRATIONS AND SKETCHES

The second and final division of the *Poema del Cante Jondo* contains a series of sketches illustrating various aspects of Andalusia and the world of the *cante*. The first section, «Dos muchachas,» consists of two poems, «La Lola» and «Amparo,» which contrast the lives of two Andalusian girls who, as we shall see, represent two universal feminine types. These poems have been characterized as a joyful interlude, a respite from the scenes of tragedy and fatality which predominated in the previous four sections and which will be reasserted in the «Viñetas flamencas» that follow. While this interpretation may be correct in the case of «La Lola,» it is somewhat questionable when applied to «Amparo.»

The first poem depicts a young woman, Lola, washing diapers under a flowering orange tree:

Bajo el naranjo lava
pañales de algodón.

Tiene verdes los ojos
y violeta la voz.

¡Ay, amor,
bajo el naranjo en flor!

This orange tree, a symbol of «el florecimiento de la pasión amorosa,» [119] also represents Lola herself. The fact that she is washing diapers suggests, as Andrew P. Debicki has pointed out, that love for her is an elemental passion with procreation as its goal.[120] The poem's refrain, surrounded by exclamation marks suggesting vitality and enthusiasm, is prob-

[119] CORREA, «El simbolismo del sol,» p. 112.
[120] *Op. cit.,* p. 209.

ably an imitation of a popular *estribillo* if not an actual folk refrain.[121]
The next stanza continues the same kind of associations as the opening
verses:

> El agua de la acequia
> iba llena de sol,
> en el olivarito
> cantaba un gorrión.

All of the objects named, «acequia,» «sol,» «olivarito,» and «gorrión,»
are commonplace features of the Andalusian countryside, and they suggest
life and vitality. The poet creates a feeling of harmony between Lola and
the world of nature, and he continually reinforces it by the repetition of
the *estribillo*, « ¡Ay, amor / bajo el naranjo en flor! »

The second poem, «Amparo,» is in many ways a complete contrast to
the preceding. Whereas Lola was washing diapers in the open countryside
beneath a flowering orange tree, Amparo is cloistered within the confines
of her patio.

> Amparo,
> ¡qué sola estás en tu casa
> vestida de blanco!

Her white dress is a symbol of virginity and erotic passivity. In this poem
the exclamation marks are used with verses denoting isolation and an absence of love, rather than enthusiasm and amorous fulfillment.

In the following strophe:

> Oyes los maravillosos
> surtidores de tu patio,
> y el débil trino amarillo
> del canario

the carefully controlled water of the fountains and the weak, joyless trilling
of the caged canary, symbolic of Amparo herself, are in marked contrast
to the more freely flowing water of the *acequia* and the happy singing
of the *gorrión* in «La Lola.» Furthermore, the water of the *acequia* has
a practical function, that of sustaining life, whereas the fountains' water
is purely ornamental.

The sense of solitude becomes even stronger in the next stanza as sinister
signs begin to appear that predict the unhappy future awaiting Amparo.
The trees in her sheltered patio are not the *olivos,* a word that has many
symbolic meanings, including fecundity [122] and «firmeza en la fuerza y el
trabajo,» [123]—both meanings are associated with Lola—but *cipreses,* symbolic

---

[121] M. V. D. FERRIS, «Federico García Lorca: A Study of the Popular and
Traditional Inspiration of his Poetry,» an unpublished Master's thesis, Columbia Univ.,
1941, p. 174.

[122] WILLIAM ROSE BENET, *The Reader's Encyclopedia,* 2nd. ed. (New York: Thomas Y. Crowell Co., 1965), p. 735.

[123] FLYS, *op. cit.,* p. 58.

of approaching old age [124] and death.[125] The trees are trembling under the weight of a group of unidentified birds, a traditionally sinister omen.[126] Thus, the sense of basic harmony between nature and the heroine, implicit in «La Lola,» is absent in this poem. Meanwhile Amparo, seemingly unaware of the foreboding signs gathering about her, sits passively embroidering letters on a canvas, not realizing that the surrounding phenomena are symbols of her empty future. The poem closes with a reiteration of the opening verses, but this time her white dress acquires an added symbolic meaning, that of the shroud in which she will be buried. The poet then adds his own commentary: («¡Y qué difícil decirte / yo te amo!») emphasizing his dismay at her isolation and inaccessibility.

It is obvious that the two poems' symbols represent the different social status as well as the contrasting ways of life of the two girls. The *naranjo, pañales, acequia, olivarito, gorrión,* and *lavar* are indicative of the humble social background of Lola, whereas the delicate *jazmín, surtidores, canario,* and *bordar* all denote the more refined but restrictive social milieu of Amparo who may never know love or maternity.

Although both girls are intended to be symbolic social types, there is evidence that «Amparo» is based on a historic individual, Amparo Medina, with whom the García Lorca family was acquainted. José Mora Guarnido recounts that the story of Amparo Medina was essentially that of the heroine in Lorca's poem:

> Cada vez que Lorca venía a mi casa de Pinos Puente, visitábamos a María Sánchez y esperábamos a la tarde para pasar frente a la casa de Amparo Medina y verla de codos en la ventana adornada y esperando a su novio. . . . Morena de tez rosa y ojos ahondados por la espera inútil, los cabellos negrísimos retorcidos en dos gemelos rodetes a cada lado de la cabeza, un hondo descote al que asomaban las cándidas morbideces de un seno insatisfecho. Amparo sufría el brutal desamparo de un noviazgo inerte, un enamorado indeciso y egoísta que todos los años aplazaba para el siguiente la boda con vanos pretextos, y así la tenía engañada y esperanzada desde la ya lejana mocedad.[127]

The next section of the book, «Viñetas flamencas,» plunges us once more into the drama of the *cante jondo,* for its six poems are sketches of various aspects of the flamenco-Andalusian world. The two initial compositions evoke memories of two famous singers of the *cante,* Silverio Franconetti and Juan Breva. The third recreates the spirit of the *cafés cantantes* and recalls the singer Dolores Parrala, while the fourth poem is possibly a recreation of the content of one of Juan Breva's songs. The

---

[124] FLECNIAKOSKA, *op. cit.,* p. 58.
[125] CORREA, «El simbolismo del sol,» p. 112.
[126] J. E. CIRLOT relates that in a flock, birds become a sinister omen, for any multiple is usually symbolically negative: «. . . los pájaros, sobre todo en bandada —pues lo múltiple es siempre de signo negativo—, pueden revestir significado maligno.» *Op. cit.,* p. 364.
[127] *Federico García Lorca y su mundo* (Buenos Aires: Losada, 1958), pp. 168-169.

fifth describes the movements of a flamenco dancer's hand, and the last poem evokes the Andalusian earth.

This part of the *Poema del Cante Jondo* is dedicated «A Manuel Torres, 'Niño de Jerez', que tiene el tronco de Faraón.» In his day Manuel Torres was considered to be one of the greatest singers of the *siguiriya*. Rafael Alberti recounts how Lorca's dedicatory phrase originated in a remark made to the poet by Manuel Torres himself when they were guests at the home of Ignacio Sánchez Mejías:

> Una de aquellas noches, Sánchez Mejías organizó una fiesta en su casa —Pino Montano—de las afueras de Sevilla. . . . Gran emoción y alegría fue para García Lorca al ver aparecer a Manuel Torres, el «Niño de Jerez», aquel gitano y «cantaor» genial que había conocido en Granada cuando el «Certamen del Cante Jondo,» organizado por él y don Manuel de Falla. Después de unas cuantas rondas de manzanilla, el gitano comenzó a cantar. Parecía un bronco animal herido, un terrible pozo de angustia.
> —¿De dónde sacas esas coplas?—se le preguntó.
> —Unas me las invento, otras las busco.
> Manuel Torres no sabía leer ni escribir. Pero eso sí, su conciencia de «cantaor» era perfecta. Aquella noche se le oyó decir, con seguridad y sabiduría iguales a las que un Góngora o un Mallarmé hubieran demostrado al hablar de su estética:
> —En el cante jondo lo que hay que buscar siempre, hasta encontrarlo, es el tronco negro de Faraón.
> ¡El tronco negro de Faraón! Como era natural, de todos los ahí presentes, fue García Lorca el que celebró con mayor entusiasmo la inquietante expresión empleada por el «cantaor» jerezano.[128]

The first poem of the «Viñetas,» «Retrato de Silverio Franconetti,» is more a portrait of Silverio's singing than of the man himself.[129] The historic Silverio Franconetti, who was known as: «el sumo pontífice del cante flamenco . . . el primer gran cantaor no gitano que conoce la historia flamenca,» [130] was renowned as the most accomplished flamenco singer of his time, for he had mastered all the existent forms of the *cante flamenco*. He was born in Seville of an Italian father and a Spanish mother, a fact alluded to in the first verses of the «Retrato»:

> Entre italiano
> y flamenco,
> ¿Cómo cantaría
> aquel Silverio?

The double nature of his parentage is transferred metaphorically to his song which is said to consist of «La densa miel de Italia,» alluding perhaps to the melodic and operatic qualities of his singing, and «el limón nues-

---

[128] *Los hombres de la Historia: García Lorca*, núm. 14 (Buenos Aires: Centro Editor de América Latina, 1968), p. 156.
[129] HENRY, *op. cit.*, p. 115.
[130] RICARDO MOLINA and ANTONIO MAIRENA, *Mundo y forma del cante flamenco* (Madrid: Revista de Occidente, 1963), p. 200.

tro,» a reference to its sharp, piercing quality. Both are said to be combined «en el hondo llanto / del siguiriyero.»

The next two images present a graphic illustration of the power behind his «hondo llanto»:

> Su grito fue terrible.
> Los viejos
> dicen que se erizaban
> los cabellos
> y se abría el azogue
> de los espejos.

This second image also appears in Lorca's lecture «El cante jondo (primitivo cante andaluz)» where he celebrates the past masters of the *siguiriya*: «Quiero recordar también a los maestros de la 'siguiriya', Curro Pablos el Curro, Manuel Molina, y el portentoso Silverio Franconetti, que cantó como nadie el cante de los cantes y cuyo grito hacía abrirse el azogue de los espejos.»[131] According to Molina and Mairena, this image may be based on a traditional *siguiriya copla* which states: «Yo no sé por donde / al espejito donde me miraba / se le fue el azogue.»[132]

The poem closes with the statements that Silverio was a *creador* and a *jardinero,* a creator of bowers for silence, and that now his song sleeps with the final echoes. These concluding lines have been interpreted by Debicki to indicate a desire to: «ligar lo humano perecedero con lo natural perenne, y . . . salvarse así del tiempo y de la muerte.» This attitude is part of the poet's search to find significance and meaning for Man within the realm of Art. In the case of Silverio, his song is now preserved by becoming part of the world of nature and by the fact that it is also remembered through Lorca's poem. Debicki concludes, saying: «El arte pasado del 'cantaor' ha suscitado y se ha entablado con el arte presente del poeta; los valores de su canto y de su visión no se han perdido por completo. Este poema indica, por lo tanto, las posibilidades del arte para preservar los valores humanos, y sugiere un tema que aparecerá frecuentemente en la obra posterior de Lorca.»[133]

The second poem, «Juan Breva,» begins as a portrait of the singer whose corpulent size («cuerpo de gigante») is contrasted with the delicacy of his voice («voz de niña»); but, as in the preceding poem, it quickly changes into a description of his song. An extremely popular artist in his day, Antonio Ortega, the real name of Juan Breva, specialized in singing the *malagueñas.*[134] To Lorca his style: «Era la misma / pena cantando / detrás de una sonrisa,» and his song: «Evoca los limonares / de Málaga la dormida.» This description of the content of the song closely parallels Lorca's statement about Juan Breva and other singers in his lecture

---

[131] «El cante jondo,» p. 55.
[132] *Op. cit.,* p. 76.
[133] *Op. cit.,* pp. 220-221.
[134] MOLINA and MAIRENA, *op. cit.,* p. 300.

in which he exclaims: «Quiero recordar a Romerillo, al espiritual loco Mateo, a Antonia la de San Roque, a Anita la de Ronda, a Dolores la Parrala y a Juan Breva, que . . . evocaron a la virgen pena en los limonares de Málaga o bajo las noches marinas del Puerto.»[135]   In the poem he then amplifies his description of this singer's voice by saying: «y hay en su llanto dejos / de sal marina.»   Lorca tells us that like Homer, Juan Breva sang blind, a comment that is also reminiscent of another of the poet's statements concerning the *cante jondo*:   «el 'cante jondo' canta como un ruiseñor sin ojos, canta ciego. . . .»[136]

He then concludes, indicating that Juan Breva's voice had something of a sea without light and of a squeezed-out orange.   These last two images have been given various interpretations. Lichtman considers the expression «naranja exprimida» to be a visual representation of the singer's «deep dark tones.»[137]   Schonberg, on the other hand, states that the «mar sin luz» and «naranja exprimida» refer to a voice that is «tenebrosa y dulzona.»[138]   Debicki, however, assigns a much broader artistic purpose to these images.   Accordingly, the metaphor which equates the singer to the pain of his song, and the simile comparing him to Homer are devices whose purpose is to make us view Juan Breva not as a specific individual, but as a general symbol for art and the artist.

The next poem, «Café cantante,» evokes the memory of the cafes where the *cante flamenco* achieved a tremendous popularity during the final decades of the past century, and it is also a memorial to Dolores Parrala, a renowned nineteenth century singer of great beauty.[139]   The poem's initial verses: «Lámparas de cristal / y espejos verdes,» describe the atmosphere of one of these cafes.[140]   This image synthetizes the impressions conveyed by the cafe's furnishings and by the spirit of the music sung there, for *verde* suggests not only the color of the room, but it also emphasizes the sinister content of La Parrala's song.[141]   The rest of the poem, except for the three concluding verses, describes her singing as a monologue in which she tries, in vain, to summon death.   The cafe's atmosphere becomes tense as the listeners breathe in the sobbing expressed by her voice.   The poem then closes with a partial return to the initial lines:

> Y en los espejos verdes
> largas colas de seda
> se mueven.

These mirrors, which are witnesses to her attempt to converse with death, reflect the train of La Parrala's green silk dress whose movements

---

[135] «El canto jondo,» p. 55.
[136] *Ibid.,* p. 47.
[137] *Op. cit.,* p. 135.
[138] FEDERICO GARCÍA LORCA, p. 189.
[139] PEMARTÍN, *op. cit.,* p. 206.
[140] ZARDOYA, «La técnica metafórica,» p. 392.
[141] «Los espejos de Federico García Lorca,» in *Poesía española del 98 y del 27* (Madrid: Gredos, 1968), p. 262.

suggest the slithering of serpents as she moves about the stage. But on a symbolic level, these reflected images imply the first stirrings or materialization of a sinister, ominous force, perhaps the beginning of death's reply. The poem ends without further explanation thereby creating the same sense of mystery that we found so often in the sections dealing with four styles of the *cante jondo*.

Special mention should be made of the important role played by the mirrors in developing the emotional atmosphere of this poem. They do not merely reflect the material reality of the cafe; they infuse it with a new meaning. The mirrors seem to be a repository for the spiritual content of La Parrala's song. It is these mirrors and their symbolic reflections that act as a gateway through which we are able to perceive a deeper, more transcendental reality, that of the *cante jondo* for which the physical cafe is only an outward symbol. Concha Zardoya, recognizing the importance of the mirror in García Lorca's poetry, has written: «Como todo gran poeta, sintió, sin duda, la atracción de los espejos, la silenciosa llamada de sus aguas profundas, el azaroso instinto de la aventura en los oscuros y luminosos azogues sin fondo. Los espejos lorquianos reflejan—según veremos—no sólo realidades vividas y contempladas, sino que dan a éstas nueva vida y nueva forma, al dotarlas de un aliento poético y de un espíritu en muchas ocasiones trascendente. Instintos, afectos, percepciones, sentimientos, recuerdos, sueños, en oculto proceso, penetran el espejo y, en síntesis simbólica, devienen su propia alma.» [142]

The fourth poem, «Lamentación de la muerte,» begins with the verses: «Sobre el cielo negro / culebrinas amarillas» which establish the emotional tone and prepare for the implied death scene and lament that follow. As in many of Lorca's images, sinister overtones are conveyed not only by nouns like *culebrinas* that suggest a serpentine movement, but by adjectives like «black» (symbolic of death) [143] and «yellow» (betrayal, disillusionment, or misfortune). [144]

The first stanza, abounding in death symbols, begins the lament:

> Vine a este mundo con ojos
> y me voy sin ellos.
> ¡Señor del mayor dolor!
> y luego,
> un velón y una manta
> en el suelo.

The eyes are symbols of comunication and therefore of life itself. Consequently, to be *sin ojos* is to be lifeless. [145] The interjection « ¡Señor del mayor dolor! » in the middle of the strophe reinforces the idea of suffering, and, according to Devoto, it is probably a phrase taken from folk poetry,

[142] *Ibid.*, pp. 256-257.
[143] ALFONSO SOLA GONZÁLEZ, «La adjetivación en la poesía de Federico García Lorca,» *Cántico, Poesía y Poetas*, núm. 1 (1940), p. 35.
[144] BENÉT, *op. cit.*, p. 1109, and FLECNIAKOSKA, *op. cit.*, p. 48.
[145] CORREA, *La poesía mítica*, pp. 12-13.

possibly from a *saeta*.[146] The *velón* and the *manta* on the ground may be considered death symbols since they are traditionally present at a wake.[147] It is customary among the poor to lay the cadaver on the ground wrapped in a blanket and to place one or more lanterns at his head.[148] The second stanza seems to imply a quasi-religious motif in its opening verses: «Quise llegar adonde / llegaron los buenos. / ¡Y he llegado, Dios mío! . . .,» but it then concludes with a repetition of the *velón-manta* motif. As in the preceding strophe, there is an interjection after the first two lines which serves as the poet's or singer's personal commentary. The third and final stanza:

> Limoncito amarillo,
> limonero.
> Echad los limoncitos
> al viento.
>
> ¡Ya lo sabéis! ... Porque luego,
> luego,
> un velón y una manta
> en el suelo

contrasts the lemon and the lemon trees (in this poem symbols of life, beauty, happiness) [149] with the death symbols *velón-manta* in verses suggesting the language of popular poetry. The poem then closes, repeating the two introductory lines.

There have been several interpretations offered for this poem. Schonberg believes that it has a religious motif and that it is a lamentation based on the Book of Job.[150] Another critic feels that the last strophe indicates a lament on the brevity of life and the certainty of death.[151] Still a third view holds that it has essentially a *carpe diem* theme.[152] The most comprehensive analysis is that of Celia Lichtman who believes that the poem is about a dying man who «sings of his despair and the love he once knew.» The verses of the second stanza: «Quise llegar adonde / llegaron los buenos» indicate to her that «this man wishes to find love and he did, but all ends in death.» With regard to the lines: «Limoncito amarillo, / limonero. / Echad los limoncitos / al viento,» Lichtman notes that «the color of the fruit is the same as the snakes the dying man sees reflected against the black sky,» and therefore she concludes that the image

[146] *Op. cit.*, p. 318.
[147] CORREA, *La poesía mítica*, p. 15.
[148] A. BASAVE FERNÁNDEZ DEL VALLE, «Sentido de la muerte en Andalucía,» *VUM* (25 oct. 1964).
[149] ARTURO BAREA, *Lorca, the Poet and his People* (London: Faber & Faber, 1944), p. 88.
[150] *Federico García Lorca*, p. 192.
[151] MONELISA LINA PÉREZ MARCHAND, «La inquietud existencial en la poesía de Federico García Lorca,» *Asomante*, IV, 3 (1949), pp. 78-79.
[152] ENRIQUE MARTÍNEZ LÓPEZ, «Aljibe y surtidor o la Granada de Federico García Lorca,» *La Torre*, X, 40 (1962), p. 23.

depicts the death of love, as the trees' withered and dead fruit is carried away by the wind.[153]

There is another possible interpretation which seems to have been overlooked by all of the critics. The poem may represent the lyrics of a song or of a particular singer's style. The two verses: «Vine a este mundo con ojos / y me voy sin ellos» refer not only to a death theme, but to the fact that during those moments of intense concentration, the *cantaor* may be singing with his eyes closed. The exclamatory verse « ¡Señor del mayor dolor! » is typical of the kind of phrase interjected into a *copla* in order to increase the emotional intensity of its lyrics. In addition, the play on words in the verses: «Limoncito amarillo, / limonero» is suggestive of the kind of verbal repetitions frequently found in the *cante*'s folk *coplas*. Lorca, however, may have had more in mind than just a general representation of musical lyrics; the poem may be a specific portrayal of Juan Breva or of one of his songs. The statement: «Vine a mundo con ojos / y me voy sin ellos» is reminiscent of Juan Breva's manner of singing which García Lorca had described as: «Como Homero cantó / ciego ...» Secondly, the phrase: «Y luego, / un velón y una manta / en el suelo,» repeated after each strophe like an *estribillo*, was part of a comment overheard by García Lorca during a conversation between Juan Breva and the poet's uncle.[154]

«Conjuro,» the fifth poem, is generally interpreted as a depiction of witchcraft or Gypsy magic. The first stanza describes a sinister hand, resembling a Medusa, snuffing out the flame of a lamp:

> La mano crispada
> como una Medusa
> ciega el ojo doliente
> del candil.

The *candil*, like the *velón*, is a death symbol.[155] The hand blinding or extinguishing its eye reinforces the idea of death, since the eye, as we observed previously, is a symbol of communication and life. The first image thus dramatizes a theme that will be used in each succeeding stanza: the opposition between life and death. In this case, the latter has momentarily overcome the former.

The refrain that follows: «As de bastos. / Tijeras en cruz,» has intrigued many critics who generally regard it as a double death symbol. Without elaborating on its meaning, Flecniakoska speaks of the image as representing «les mystères de la magie,» [156] and Umbral regards these verses as an indication of Lorca's interest in the satanic.[157] In one of his books, Correa

---

[153] *Op. cit.,* pp. 83, 125, 131-132, 199.
[154] This detail was mentioned during a conversation with *don* Francisco García Lorca, brother of the poet and Professor Emeritus, Columbia University.
[155] CORREA, *La poesía mítica,* pp. 14-15.
[156] *Op. cit.,* p. 93.
[157] FRANCISCO UMBRAL, *Lorca, poeta maldito* (Madrid: Biblioteca Nueva, 1968), p. 61.

describes the «tijeras en cruz» as part of a «conjuro siniestro,» [158] and in another work he states: «En el azar de las figuras de naipes, al mismo tiempo que señala el final de sangre, sugiere el instrumento que ha de efectuar la tragedia (tijeras).» [159] Still another critic, Ramón Xirau, generally regards cards as death symbols throughout Lorca's poetry.[160] Lichtman, who interprets the entire poem as depicting the hand of a Gypsy witch conjuring a spell of love and death, states: «Death is also present in the ace of clubs of the tarot cards which the gypsy uses in fortune telling and in the crossed scissors. Both are folk symbols for impending disaster.» [161] Although it is true that the «tijeras en cruz» are considered a negative sign in Andalusian folk superstition, the Tarot card *as de bastos,* which is more properly translated as Ace of Wands rather than Ace of Clubs, is certainly not a death symbol. According to Eden Gray, the card has a positive significance: «Aces signify beginnings; Wands, animation and enterprise.   Therefore, something of a creative nature is being offered to the Querent.   Divinatory Meaning: Beginning of an enterprise, invention, or the beginning of a family.   Perhaps the beginning of a journey, an adventure, an escapade.» [162]   The refrain would seem, then, to represent a contrast between positive and negative symbols, between life and death.

The next stanza describes the Gypsy's hand as having the qualities of a mole and an indecisive butterfly as it moves above the white incense smoke.   This image is also based on a contrast, this time between the earthbound mole,[163] possibly symbolizing death, and the light, graceful butterfly, representing life.[164]   The poem's final image:

> Aprieta un corazón
> invisible, ¿la veis?
> Un corazón
> reflejado en el viento

has been interpreted by Schonberg to indicate a cry carried by the wind.[165] Lichtman, however, explains the image as follows: «The magic charms which conjure love pinch the invisible heart the old gypsy is invoking. It is the heart of a man she is seeking as is seen in the wind, a Lorquian masculine symbol.» [166]   The dramatic conflict between the forces of life and death, which we saw symbolized in all the preceding strophes, remains

---

[158] *La poesía mítica,* p. 10.
[159] «El simbolismo religioso,» p. 45.
[160] *Op. cit.,* p. 368.
[161] *Op. cit.,* p. 49.
[162] *A Complete Guide to the Tarot* (New York: Crown Publishers, 1970), p. 48.
[163] Although the mole's supposed blindness seems to establish a thematic link between this strophe and the preceding one in which the lamp's flame is «blinded» by the Gypsy's hand, this theme is not continued in the final image, which inclines us to believe that this apparent connection between the first two stanzas is of scant importance.
[164] CIRLOT, *op. cit.,* pp. 310-311.
[165] *Federico García Lorca,* p. 189.
[166] *Op. cit.,* p. 49.

unresolved in this final stanza, since the vulnerable heart, a traditional symbol for life, seems to be at the mercy of the wind whose meaning is ambiguous. Many critics consider the wind to be both a positive life force, representing virility and fertility, and, simultaneously, a death symbol, a cause of destruction and annihilation.[167] It is difficult to determine which meaning is intended here, and the ambiguity may be intentional in order to imply the lack of an affective solution to the eternal struggle between life and death.

There is still a question, however, whether this poem is really concerned with witchcraft and Gypsy magic as many of the critics have indicated. Certainly the title «Conjuro» and the use of the «As de bastos. / Tijeras en cruz» suggest such an atmosphere. But at the same time, this theme would not be entirely consonant with those of the other poems in the «Viñetas flamencas» which have dealt with the songs and singing styles of several famous *cantaores*. Therefore, we suggest that the actions depicted in this poem are in reality part of a dance performed by a flamenco dancer whose expressive hand movements are weaving a *conjuro* as her dance acts out the dramatic conflict between life and death, a recurrent theme throughout the *cante jondo*. Such an interpretation is entirely consistent with the imagery of the poem. The «mano crispada,» suggesting a dance position, extinguishes the lamp's flame in the sense that the dancer's hand moves in front of the light, momentarily obstructing it from view. The refrain «As de bastos. / Tijeras en cruz» is, according to Devoto, a common, popular expression in Andalusian speech.[168] We feel, therefore, that the refrain is used not to convey the specific implication of witchcraft, but as another expression of the life-death conflict symbolized by its two objects. The final two strophes are, of course, further descriptions of the hand's movement as the Gypsy dances.

The next composition, «Memento,» the last of the «Viñetas flamencas,» is pessimistic in tone as it deals with the triumph of death. Its initial strophe seems to express a sad, stoic acceptance of this fact:

> Cuando yo me muera,
> enterradme con mi guitarra
> bajo la arena.

The critics have interpreted the poem in a variety of ways. Devoto stresses its importance in providing an example of how Lorca utilizes a traditional motif in a skillful working of fantasy: «Partiendo de la tradición—las tantas coplas en las que el cantor pide sepultura 'en el campo verde' (línea que va del romancero tradicional hasta el *Santos Vega* de Obligado, y más allá) o en una viña, 'para chupar del sarmiento'—el poeta la sobrepasa, sin abandonarla del todo, con el ágil vuelo de su fantasía.» [169] Debicki

---

[167] See MARIA TERESA BABIN, *García Lorca, vida y obra* (New York: Las Américas Pblg. Co., 1955), p. 69; CORREA, *La poesía mítica*, p. 12; LICHTMAN, *op. cit.*, pp. 181, 198-199, 201).

[168] *Op. cit.*, p. 317.

[169] *Ibid.*, pp. 318-319.

views the poem as: «el deseo del hombre de salvarse de una existencia temporal limitada, y de formar parte de lo natural perenne.» [170] Lichtman regards it as the request of a dying Gypsy,[171] and Stanton views these verses as a Gypsy's last will and testament. He then notes that the practice of burial with a guitar is a folk custom among certain Gypsies.[172] Schonberg believes that the poet is thinking of his own fate and that the composition is therefore an ironic commentary.[173] Pérez Marchand also believes that far from expressing a stoic acceptance of death, the poem actually implies «un gesto de indiferencia y desprecio socarrón» towards life.[174]

The same attitude of wishing to become a part of nature is continued in the second stanza:

Cuando yo me muera,
entre los naranjos
y la hierbabuena.

Here the poet uses two emblems, *naranjos* and *hierbabuena*, both of which may represent life, as a contrast to death. In the final image, he requests that he be buried in a weathervane, often regarded as a symbol for man's fate.[175] The poem then concludes its evocation of Andalusia with a repetiton of the verse «Cuando yo me muera.»

The next section of the book, «Tres ciudades,» is a lyric description of three Andalusian cities: Malaga, Cordova, and Seville. The first poem, «Malagueña,» is a poetic transcription of the spirit of the *malagueña*, which, as we saw in Chapter I, is a type of flamenco music originating in Malaga and whose lyrics often contain references to the sea and to those whose livelihoods depend on it.[176]

Unquestionably, the best analysis of this composition is that of Andrew Debicki. In his opinion it depicts events taking place within the *malagueña* as it is being played and sung by a guitarist in a tavern, rather than portraying actual events occuring in the world of reality. The point that Lorca is making, according to Debicki, is that the reality of art, of the song, is superior to and of more transcendence than anecdotal reality, and that what we usually assume to be real is, in fact, not so true as artistic reality, normally regarded as fictional. The initial verses:

La muerte
entra y sale
de la taberna

[170] *Op. cit.,* p. 218.
[171] *Op. cit.,* p. 215.
[172] *Op. cit.,* p. 66.
[173] *Federico García Lorca,* p. 193.
[174] *Op. cit.,* p. 79.
[175] CORREA, *La poesía mítica,* p. 12.
[176] DOMINGO MANFREDI CANO, *Geografía del cante jondo* (Madrid: Colección «El Grifón,» 1955), p. 164.

do not refer to an actual death in a tavern, but to the fact that the guitarist starts and stops his playing of the *malagueña* whose lyrics sing of tragedy.[177]

Other critics have generally tended to interpret the poem on a more literal level. Alfredo de la Guardia believes that this first image refers to an actual fight occuring within a tavern: «Y es que los mozos enamorados y borrachos se encelan y riñen.» [178] Stanton also subscribes to this view and comments: «This poem with a Malagan setting has a sordid, visceral quality. Lorca seems to be interpreting the seamy side of flamenco life, the dark underworld of vice and crime that became associated with Andalusian music in the last part of the nineteenth century, and led to its loss of prestige.» [179] Gustavo Correa believes that the image conveys the idea that death enters the tavern in the guise of a customer: «La atmósfera de las tabernas viene cargada de trágicos presentimientos y en ellas entra la muerte como uno de los parroquianos cotidianos.» [180] Pedro Salinas has stated that the tavern is a symbol for human life and that it is Lorca's intention to show that death waits for man in even the most unexpected localities.[181] Another critic, Edwing Honig, feels that this image, especially the form in which it is repeated at the end of the poem, represents the monotonous, rhythmic motion of a tavern door swinging back and forth.[182]

The next strophe clarifies the scene depicted in the preceding verses, for we learn that these events occur «por los hondos caminos / de la guitarra.» In other words, everything is taking place within the song of the *malagueña*. The following stanza:

> Y hay un olor a sal
> y a sangre de hembra
> en los nardos febriles
> de la marina

may be a characterization of Malaga itself with the salt and blood as emblems for its bitterness and passion.[183] It is more likely, however, that these verses again refer to events happening within the song. The *sal* (bitterness), *sangre de hembra* (death of a woman), *nardos* (eroticism and death) seem to imply that the *malagueña* describes an encounter, possibly motivated by jealousy, that ends in a woman's death. The final strophe reiterates the initial verses with a slight variation suggestive of a guitar's repeated strumming or the modulations of the *malagueña*'s melody.

The second poem, «Barrio de Córdoba.» subtitled «Tópico nocturno,» depicts a wake held for a dead child. The starry night, reminiscent of

[177] *Op. cit.*, pp. 203-204.
[178] *Op. cit.*, p. 168.
[179] *Op. cit.*, pp. 115-116.
[180] *La poesía mítica*, p. 16.
[181] «García Lorca y la cultura de la muerte,» in *Ensayos de Literatura Hispánica* (Madrid: Aguilar, 1966), p. 389.
[182] *García Lorca* (Norfolk: New Directions, 1963), p. 55; HENRY, *op. cit.*, p. 114.
[183] FLYS, *op. cit.*, p. 176.

Lorca's statement about the *cante jondo*'s true setting: «En cambio, el 'cante jondo' canta siempre en la noche . . . No tiene más que la noche, una noche ancha y profundamente estrellada,» [184] is converted into a threatening being against which the inhabitants of the house must defend themselves:

> En la casa se defienden
> de las estrellas.
> La noche se derrumba.

The stars, often symbols of the mysterious, the enigmatic,[185] seem to be sinister objects, perhaps the conveyers of death. Schonberg, however, believes that these three verses mean nothing more than that the inhabitants of the house are overcome by sadness.[186] The dead child wears a flesh-colored rose, symbolic of life and the love she will never know,[187] and six nightingales, converted into mourners, weep for her at the window. These six weeping nightingales suggest the six strings of a guitar playing a lament, or they could be symbols for the dead child herself, since the number stands for both the human soul and virginity.[188] The poem then closes with the verses: «Las gentes van suspirando / con las guitarras abiertas,» meaning that the lament of the guitar has ceased, and it has been replaced by human sights.

«Baile,» the last poem, deals with Seville and has as its protagonist the legendary Carmen. In this composition, however, Seville is not a city of gaiety and charm, nor is Carmen the beautiful, romantic heroine of literature. She has become a hideous old woman with white hair and flashing eyes, a grotesque parody of her former self as she dances through the streets. The refrain, «Niñas, / ¡corred las cortinas!», acts as a warning and as the poet's personal reaction to this Medusa-like creature who, we are told, has a yellow serpent symbolizing betrayal, disillusionment, or misfortune coiled on her head. Schonberg has suggested that the warning is given because «se desprende de ella un poder perverso.» [189] As she dances she is: «soñando en el baile / con galanes de otros días,» a desire to reject old age and to recapture her youth.

The last section of the *Poema del Cante Jondo,* «Seis caprichos,» is a group of six poems that are fantasies of the imagination based on random associations suggested by various objects common to the Gypsy-flamenco world or the Andalusian countryside. It is apparent that in some of these compositions, the somber, tragic mood of the preceding poems is considerably lessened. These *caprichos,* often mirthful in spirit, have been characterized by Cesco Vian as: «sei 'caprici' o puittosto stampe che fissano

---

[184] «El cante jondo,» p. 48.
[185] FLYS, *op. cit.,* p. 169.
[186] *Federico García Lorca,* p. 189.
[187] LICHTMAN, *op. cit.,* p. 40.
[188] CIRLOT, *op. cit.,* p. 342.
[189] *Federico García Lorca,* p. 189.

in gesti barocchi taluni particolari del paesaggio dell'Alta Andalusia.»[190] In fact, all of these poems, with the possible exception of the last one, seem to reflect a direct influence of Luis de Góngora's baroque style in that they all contain highly decorative, often dazzling images and metaphors whose imaginative conception is reminiscent of the seventeenth century Cordovan poet for whom García Lorca, as well as most members of his literary generation, were known to have a profound respect. It is of interest to note that three of these six poems, «Adivinanza de la guitarra,» «Candil,» and «Crótalo,» were first published in 1927, the year of the tricentenary celebration in honor of Góngora.

The first composition, «Adivinanza de la guitarra,» imitates a traditional *adivinanza* or riddle. This kind of folk poem has no specific metrical form, and it is concerned solely with the idea presented.[191] The words are intended to create a puzzle which the listener must solve. In Lorca's poem six girls, «Tres de carne / y tres de plata,» dance at a crossroads. The dreams of the past search for them, but a golden Polyphemus, the guitar, holds them in his embrace. The six girls are, of course, the humanized guitar strings, three of gut («carne») and three of metal («plata»). The crossroads on which they dance refers to the place where the strings encounter or come into contact with the hand of the guitarist. However much the music played in the past («los sueños de ayer») seeks them, they are held by the guitar whose round opening or eye is reminiscent of the cyclops Polyphemus. Since the guitar's wood apparently has a golden hue, the instrument becomes a «Polifemo de oro.» At first glance, the poem seems to be a fanciful, light-hearted, decorative composition whose highly imaginative, esthetically pleasing images are suggestive of Góngora's «Fábula de Polifemo y Galatea,» in which Polyphemus unsuccessfully pursues another *doncella,* the nymph Galatea.[192] But this initial impression may be misleading, for the sinister implications found in most of Lorca's poetry are present even here. These girls have already been seized in the cyclops' hideous embrace at an *encrucijada,* a symbol for malign fate or death.[193]

The second poem, «Candil,» also makes use of images suggestive of Góngora's influence on Lorca. This composition describes the meditation of a lamp's flame during a wake for a Gypsy boy. The critics have interpreted this poem in many ways. J. Mora Guarnido dismisses it rather abruptly, saying that all the poems in the «Seis caprichos» are extraneous to the theme of the *cante jondo*: «. . . más bien parecen como brochazos finales, simples recuerdos o elementos decorativos y externos del cante.»[194]

[190] *Federico García Lorca, Poeta e Drammaturgo* (Milano: La Goliardica, Edizione Universitarie, n. d.), p. 93.

[191] FERRIS, *op. cit.,* p. 174.

[192] This poem may well be, in fact, an excellent example of Lorca's ability to combine within a single composition elements from both the popular and learned or *culto* traditions of Spanish poetry.

[193] CORREA, *La poesía mítica,* pp. 8-9; LICHTMAN, *op. cit.,* pp. 216, 218-219.

[194] *Op. cit.,* p. 193.

Schonberg has chosen to analyze it in Freudian terms: «Et cette flame de chaleil que le chevalier du 'Dialogue de l'Amargo' fait briller au bout de son couteau d'or (dont on connait le sens), comme elle rappelle la même flame du chaleil comparée dans 'Candil' à une cigogue incandescente qui tremble sur les 'oeufs' gonflés du petit Gitan mort, et qui ne peut représenter que le pénis dressé.» [195] Probably the most accurate commentary is that of María Teresa Babín who suggests that the lamp's flame is a pervasive symbol of man's effort to see within himself and to know who he is: «La llama del candil en el *Poema del Cante Jondo* es ya un símbolo de este esfuerzo del hombre por verse por dentro, por desentrañar su incógnita y conocerse.» [196] However, this lamp is also a death simbol. In Correa's terms it is a «compañero solitario de los que acaban de morir,» [197] whose silent meditation creates an atmosphere of both suspense and calm.

The first stanza compares the flame, a symbol of life,[198] to an Indian faquir:

> Como un faquir indio
> mira su entraña de oro
> y se eclipsa soñando
> atmósferas sin viento.

The flame's «entraña de oro» simbolizes its own inner being or spiritual essence, and the «atmósferas sin viento» represent a transcendent sphere of perfect calm. The second half of the strophe seems to be the logical result of the inward contemplation suggested in the first half. These two verses infer a stage of mystic progression in which the meditating flame has transcended («se eclipsa») the material, physical world and contemplates a realm of eternal perfection. The fact that it is «sin viento,» a noun which often symbolizes a disruptive, destructive force, or even death, adds to the implication of permanence, for within this spiritual realm, no wind will ever threaten to extinguish the flame of life.

Finally, the flame is transformed into an incandescent stork that pecks at the massive shadows and peers out, trembling, at the round eyes of the dead Gypsy boy. In this image the poem returns from the plane of mystical abstraction to that of physical, everyday reality which was its starting point. The two key words, «gitanillo muerto,» are reserved for the very end, and it is here that we are given an explanation for the events in the preceding verses. We now learn the reason not only for the flame's fearful trembling, but for its pensive meditation, its desire to reach the mystical realm symbolized by «atmósferas sin viento.» The poem implies a desire to affirm life, even in the face of death.

---

[195] *A la Recherche de Lorca*, p. 190.
[196] *García Lorca, vida y obra*, p. 89.
[197] *La poesía mítica*, p. 15.
[198] CIRLOT, *op. cit.*, p. 299.

«Crótalo» presents a light-hearted, almost frivolous characterization of another aspect of the Gypsy-flamenco world. J. L. Flys claims that the poem lacks a theme and that it is based on a single image.[199] This assertation seem to be an over-simplification, since the composition has four separte movements, described by Albert Henry as follows: «Son unique matière, ce sont les claquements en cascade du crotale (genre de castagnettes); mais le poète passe par plusieurs champs de sensibilité: sur un effet d'harmonie imitative, il greffe une image mixte ('escarabajo sonoro'), propose ensuite une transposition visuelle ('rizas'), puis une transposition synesthésique ('ahogas'), pour clore enfin par une reprise.» [200]

Its opening verses: «Crótalo. / Crótalo. / Crótalo. / Escarabajo sonoro» describe the sound of a flamenco dancer's castanets in an image that presents a perfect fusion of visual and auditory impressions. «Crótalo» is not only the Greek word for a castanet, but, as Carl Cobb points out, it is also an onomatopoeic word for the sound made by a beetle.[201]

The next six verses:

> En la araña
> de la mano
> rizas el aire
> cálido
> y te ahogas en tu trino
> de palo

present a Gongoristic image cluster in which either the dancer's hand and moving fingers, or the castanets held against the web of lines formed by the palm of the hand, is metaphorically compared to a spider. As the castanet-spider moves about this web, the visual impression it creates is combined with other physical sensations that further illustrate the quality of its sound, which is said to curl the warm air and to drown in its own wooden trilling. The poem then closes with a reprise of the initial image.

«Chumbera» also reflects a baroque, Gongoristic influence. In a moonlit scene, the frozen, statue-like quality of the prickly pear cactus with its many arms growing in different directions («llena de manos torturadas») [202] is compared to the statue of Laocoon and his sons in their tortured battle against the snakes. This poem has been criticized for being a purely decorative composition with no connection to the world of the *cante jondo* [203] and for being too coldly intellectual.[204] Yet it continues the mirthful, non-serious tone established by «Crótalo.» By means

---

[199] *Op. cit.*, p. 123.
[200] *Op. cit.*, p. 117.
[201] *Federico García Lorca* (New York: Twayne Publications, 1967), p. 89.
[202] MANUEL FERNÁNDEZ GALIANO, «Los dioses de Federico,» *Cuadernos Hispanoamericanos*, núm. 217 (1968), p. 35.
[203] MORA GUARNIDO, *op. cit.*, p. 193.

of gay, fanciful comparisons, the plant is next converted into a «múltiple pelotari,» whose arms seem to be threatening the wind, and finally into a remembrance of Daphne and Atis: «Dafne y Ais / saben de tu dolor. / Inexplicable.» In spite of its lighthearted tone, however, J. M. Aguirre believes that it has ominous implications, primarily because of its association with the moon which is almost always a malevolent object in Lorca's imagery.[205] Finally, Jean-Louis Schonberg interprets the poem as a subconscious reflection of a psychosexual problem: «Comment comprendre autrement la pièce allégorique intitulée 'Chumbera', le figuier de Barbarie, sorte de Laocoon aux bras tendus contre la lune, aussi châtre qu'Atis, aussi lignifié que Daphne? Qui ce Laocoon tentaculaire, sinon l'incarnation du chancre que stérilise?»[206]

The following poem, «Pita,» has been described correctly as having no theme and as being based solely on one image.[207] Like «Crótalo» it is a humorous composition of popular inspiration, and like «Chumbera» it uses a desert plant common to the Andalusian landscape. The poem compares the maguey plant with its long tapered arms to a petrified octopus. This same metaphor had been used once before by Lorca in an earlier work, *Impresiones y paisajes,* written in 1918. In the section in which he described the Albaicín in Granada, Lorca spoke of the «covachas abandonadas, declives de tierra roja en donde viven los pulpos petrificados de las pitas.»[208] After the initial image, the poet addresses the humanized maguey plant directly and states:

> Pones cinchas cenicientas
> al vientre de los montes
> y muelas formidables
> a los desfiladeros.

The poem then closes with a restatement of the original metaphor.

The final composition, «Cruz,» is remarkable for its concision and intensity of feeling:

> La cruz.
> (Punto final
> del camino.)
>
> Se mira en la acequia.
> (Puntos suspensivos.)

It could serve as an example of the Juan Ramonian ideal of *poesía pura* in which all superfluous words are eliminated so that the composition

---

[204] PEDRO ROCAMORA, «Imagen lírica y teatro pasional en García Lorca,» *Arbor,* LXVIII, 264 (1967), p. 296.
[205] «El sonambulismo de Federico García Lorca,» *Bulletin of Hispanic Studies,* XLIV, 4 (1967), p. 280.
[206] *A la Recherche de Lorca,* p. 189.
[207] FLYS, *op. cit.,* p. 123.
[208] *Obras Completas,* p. 1566.

is reduced to the essential minimum necessary to convey an exact poetic sensation. But this ability to express a maximum of feeling with a minimum number of words is also part of folk tradition. Lorca described this tendency in his lecture on the *cante jondo*: «Causa extrañeza y maravilla cómo el anónimo poeta del pueblo extracta en tres o cuatro versos toda la rara complejidad de los más altos momentos sentimentales en la vida del hombre.» [209]

The five short verses of this poem convey a double image: a solitary cross stands at the end of the road and then becomes a series of suspended points of light reflected in the water of an irrigation ditch. The two images are parallel, for they depict the same scene, the first directly and the second by reflection. Furthermore, the *camino* and *acequia* are co-ordinate symbols: each is a man-made object representing the course of human life. [210] The cross in the first image represents a finite, concrete reality. Standing at the end of the road, it suggests a symbol for the cemetery and death. [211] In the second image, however, this same cross loses its material form to become a series of disjointed, reflected dots of light. This series of dots implies continuation or the infinite, and as such it is in opposition to the concept of a terminal point. Thus, the specific, concrete reality of the first image leads into irreality of the second, which may represent that which is beyond the cross or death. This interpretation seems to be supported by the fact that the *acequia* contains moving water whose purpose is to sustain life. Although the cross, or death, is reflected in the water and is therefore a part of it, nevertheless, the water continues to flow. Thus, this final poem, like so many in the *Poema del Cante Jondo*, is based on the eternal conflict between life and death, and the book seems to close on a positive, perhaps religious note which emphasizes life's indefinite continuation beyond death.

[209] «El cante jondo,» p. 45.
[210] CORREA, «El simbolismo religioso,» p. 45; *La poesía mítica,* p. 10.
[211] FLYS, *op. cit.,* p. 206.

Chapter IV

LANGUAGE AND POETIC TECHNIQUES—ANALY

Before beginning the analysis of the specific poetic techniques encountered in the *Poema del Cante Jondo,* some attention should be given to the vocabulary used in this work. Even the most superficial examination of the individual words reveals that Lorca's poetic language encompasses a world of objects, people, music and dance that is extraordinarily rich and varied when one considers the limited scope and brevity of this book. The poetic vocabulary may best be analyzed by dividing it into categories that relate to inanimate nature, animate nature, the human realm (which includes man-made objects as well as human figures and activities), and the supernatural, a general term we have used to designate all extraordinary beings and forces not considered to be entirely within the realm of normal reality. A careful examination of all images used in this work reveals that objects or phenomena pertaining to the human realm appear with the greatest frequency, followed by the realms of inanimate nature, animate nature, and the supernatural.

SPECIFIC CATEGORIES

Inanimate nature.

That portion of the vocabulary pertaining to this category contains the many terms used to depict the richly varied Andalusian landscape. There are the contrasting rivers, Guadalquivir, Darro and Genil; the trees and their related objects: *naranjos, naranjas, olivos, alamedas, ciprés, limonero, limón, rama, madera, bosque,* and *huertos.* There are the flowers: *azahar, camelias, adelfa, tulipán, lirio, clavel, jazmín, nardo, rosa* and the general word *flor,* as well as other plants or parts of plants: *trigo, junco, tallo, parra, albahaca, hierbabuena, algodón, biznagas, espinas, chumbera,* and *pita.* There is a rich variety of terms referring to celestial phenomena such as: *cielo, luceros, aire, arco iris, luna, rayo, sol, constelación, estrella, culebrinas, atmósferas sin viento,* and *nubes.* Another group of landscape terms includes the aquatic words: *agua, lluvia, estanque, mar, orilla, marea, río, alberca, rocío, flotar, aljibe, sal marina,* and *marina.* There is also a group that refers to time: *madrugada, mañana, tarde, noche, tiempo, aurora, alba,* and *amanecer.* The largest group, however, includes the miscellaneous landscape words: *horizonte, viento, nieve, nevada, fuego fatuo, arena, monte, cueva, silencio ondulado, valles, ecos, suelo, humo, niebla, tierra, luz, oro, plata, azogue, cal, montañas, desierto, sierra, yermo, hondonadas, mundo, veredilla, piedra, llano, polvo, miel, llama, palo, desfiladeros,* and *laberintos.* Other terms also used as part of the landscape are the colors: *blanco, plata, negro, oscuro, moreno, amarillo, rojo, granate, cárdeno, encarnado, verde, oro, gris, ceniciento, morado, violeta, cobre,* and *azul,* as well as the numbers *uno, dos, tres, cinco, seis, siete,* and *ciento* which frequently have a symbolic value.

Animate nature.

Among the words referring to this realm of nature are the following, designating animals and animal phenomena: *serpiente, caballos, jacas, caracolear, unicornios, topo,* and *vientre.* There are also terms relating to birds: *pájaros cautivos/muertos, colas, gritos, gorrión, canario, trino, ruiseñores, cigüeña, nido,* and some referring to various insects such as: *moscardón, tarántula, luciérnaga, mariposas negras/indecisas, escarabajo, araña,* as well as one word designating a fish, the *pulpo.*

Human realm.

The many words related to this category can be subdivided into several groups. The first consists of historical personages and characters from literature; the second contains general human figures; the third is composed of terms referring to parts of the human body; the fourth to man-made objects; the fifth to human activities; the sixth group includes all words describing human emotions; the seventh contains the names of cities, countries, and nationalities; the eighth, and perhaps the most important group, consists of those terms conveying an impression of music and dance.

The historical and literary personages mentioned in this work are: Homer, Amparo Medina, the performers of the *cante jondo* Silverio Franconetti, Juan Breva, and Dolores Parrala, and the fictional characters Laocoon, Merlin, Durandarte, Orlando, Don Juan, and Carmen. The additional human figures include the following: the *gentes de las cuevas,* the *muchacha morena, muchachas ciegas, hijo mío, Lola,* the personified *siguiriya, soleá,* and *petenera,* various *niños, niñas buenas, niña muerta, hombres embozados, gitano, siguiriyero, hombres misteriosos, tú, yo,* the *arqueros oscuros, astrónomos, toreritos* and *torerillos, barberillo, jinetes enlutados, seis gitanas, gente siniestra, cien enamorados, gigante, hembra, galanes, doncellas, faquir indio, gitanillo muerto, jardinero, creador,* and the collective noun *pueblo.*

The third group of words, that relating to parts of the human body, includes: *barba, corazón, diestra, cabeza, pecho, ojos, pupilas, pie menudo, frentes, guedejas, pómulos, mano, boca, dientes de nácar, muelas, muslos, cabellos, cuerpo, cabellera,* and *sangre.*

The fourth and largest group of terms contains all words relating to man-made objects: *barcos de vela, camino, torres* and *torrecillas, abanico, guitarra, copas, flecha, blanco, espadas, arco de viola, arco, cuerdas, velones, puñal, candiles, hondas cisternas, veletas, callejas, calles, reja del arado, reja, farol* and *farolito, mantos, balcón, clavos, campanas, falda* and

118

faldas de moaré, luces, encrucijadas, sombreros, capas, cristal, cirio, saeta, ventanitas, cruces, ciudad, vino, miriñaque, barco de luces, cauces, puerta, quilla, aljabas, proras, rosas de papel, casa, bordón, mantillas, pañales, ace-quia, jabón, surtidor, patio, letras, cañamazo, espejos, glorietas, lámparas, tablado, seda, as de bastos, tijeras en cruz, incienso, taberna, cortinas, vi-huela, and *cinchas.*

The next group includes those words describing human activities: *remar, encadenar, clavar, hogueras, saeta* (meaning «song»), *herir, morir, sueños, coronar, escribir, afilar, entierro, ferias,* and *bordar.*

The sixth word group is comprised of all terms relating to human emotions. These include: *amor, llanto, llorar, suspiros, gritos, dolor, de-seo, ilusión, pena, calvario* (representing suffering), *sollozos, voz entrecor-tada, temblar,* and *temblor, ayes,* and *sonrisa.*

The seventh contains all words relevant to cities, countries, and nationalities: *Sevilla, Granada, Córdoba, Málaga, países remotos, Judea, España, Italia, italiano,* and *flamenco.*

The most important category of terms are those that convey a sensation of music or dance, either directly or by association. We have already seen that the entire first division of this work and many individual poems in the second are a poetic transcription of various aspects of the *cante jondo* and flamenco. Thus, the first way in which music is expressed is through the poem titles themselves. For example: «Poema de la si-guiriya gitana,» «La soleá,» «Las seis cuerdas,» «Falseta,» or «Café can-tante.» Often individual words, such as *vibrar, tono, trino, ritmo, cantar, glitarra, cuerda en tensión* or *melodía,* convey suggestions of musical sound. Frequently, the exclamations that a singer interjects into the verses of a song appear as part of a poem. For example: «¡Ay, petenera gitana! / ¡Yayayay, petenera!» («Falseta»), «¡Señor del mayor dolor!» («Lamenta-ción de la muerte»), or the refrain frequently used in many *saetas* «¡Mi-radlo por donde viene!» «¡Miradlo por donde va!» («Saeta»). A third and extremely important source of music is the poet's use of rhyme and meter. Occasionally, a musical effect is implied in a particular succession of vowels. For example: «Entre la albahaca / y la hierba-buena, / la Lola canta / saetas.» («Balcón»). The succession of the open and relaxed vowel «a» suggests the joyful mood of the girl's song. Another example occurs in the verse «un silencio ondulado» («El silencio») in which the vowels «o» and «u» convey a definite, rolling tonal effect. In another poem the «no's» of the *estribillo,* «No. / No me lo claves. / No.» («Puñal»), create a staccato effect suggestive simultaneously of dagger thrusts and syncopated rhythm. In some poems the meter and cadence of the verses are like the reitereated strumming of a guitar:

> Empieza el llanto
> de la guitarra.
> Es inútil callarla.
> Es imposible

callarla.
Llora monótona
como llora el viento
como llora el agua,
sobre la nevada.
                    («La guitarra»)

Another poem achieves the same reiterative effect without mentioning the guitar directly.

La muerte
entra y sale,
y sale y entra
la muerte
de la taberna.
                    («Malagueña»)

Other images convey a sense of music by their poetic content. Examples:

Campanas de Córdoba
en la madrugada.
Campanas de amanecer
en Granada.
                    («Alba»)

«Pasaba por los tonos / sin romperlos» («Retrato de Silverio Franconetti»), or this image describing Juan Breva's singing style:

Su voz tenía
algo de mar sin luz
y naranja exprimida.
                    («Juan Breva»)

Music is also expressed by natural phenomena, especially the sound of birds: «El débil trino amarillo / del canario» («Amparo») or «Seis ruiseñores la lloran / en la reja.» («Barrio de Córdoba«). Finally, some verses convey a musical impression through the use of onomatopoeic words, such as the following image describing the sound of a flamenco dancer's castanet:

Crótalo.
Crótalo.
Crótalo.
Escarabajo sonoro.
                    («Crótalo»)

The sources of dance impressions are less numerous than those suggesting music. Only two poem titles, «Danza» and «Baile,» and a very limited number of individual words like *caracolear, bailar, girar, temblar, alargar, ondulado,* and *paso* are suggestive of dance movements. Occasionally, dance is depicted directly. For example:

> En la noche del huerto,
> seis gitanas
> vestidas de blanco
> bailan.
>
> («Danzas»)

The rhythm of these verses together with the visual image they create convey an impression of ordered, dance steps. Likewise in this image:

> En la redonda
> encrucijada
> seis doncellas
> bailan.
>
> («Adivinanza de la guitarra»)

More frequently, however, the sensations of dance are implied rather than directly stated. For example: «Las niñas de España / de pie menudo / y temblorosas faldas» («Alba») conveys an impression of delicate, light, dance movements while not actually mentioning dance. Another image:

> Sobre el humo blanco
> del incienso, tiene
> algo de topo y
> mariposa indecisa
>
> («Conjuro»)

describes the movements of a hand which could be that of a flamenco dancer. Occasionally, the movements of animals also suggest dance rhythms: «Cien jacas caracolean. / Sus jinetes están muertos.» («Muerte de la petenera»).

Supernatural realm.

The final category of terms, those we have designated by the general word «supernatural,» consists of all extraordinary beings and forces and includes the Christian deities *Dios, Cristo,* the quasi supernatural beings *la Virgen, San Cayetano,* the pagan god *Dionisio,* the pagan semi-divinities *Dafne* and *Atis,* the mythological-legendary figures *Medusa, Polifemo,* and, finally, the words *almas* and *la muerte,* for the latter is not only a part of the natural realm, but it also appears in this book as a personified being.[1] In addition, there are various human figures that give the impression of sinister, supernatural beings, like the *Cien jinetes enlutados* who travel «por el cielo yacente / del naranjal» («Camino»), or the *arqueros oscuros* who come from «los remotos países de la pena» («Arqueros»).

In the creation of his poetic imagery, Lorca uses all of the words from these four categories in different combinations. Our analysis of

---

[1] Although it may be argued that since death is a normal and indeed expected aspect of nature, it should not be regarded as an extraordinary, much less supernatural force. However, we have placed it in this category precisely because it usually appears in human form in the *Poema del Cante Jondo.*

the individual poetic techniques in the *Poema del Cante Jondo* will be based, in fact, on a careful examination of the image which we believe is the principle poetic unit in all the poems of this book. Each poem is, in reality, an assemblage of closely or loosely interrelated images ranging from one to six lines in length. We are defining «poetic image» as any group of words or verses that in conjunction presents a single, *unified* poetic intuition, a definition that is extremely broad, but which has been suggested by Rafael Bosch in his study of García Lorca's poetry.[2]

In practice, a single image usually, though not necessarily, corresponds to one strophe, since each stanza normally conveys a separate poetic intuition. We believe that all images in this work are carefully constructed around one fundamental poetic element: a symbol, a simile, or a metaphor. Although all three may be present at any one time, only one of then constitutes the basic element. However, other symbols, similes, or metaphors are often added in order to increase the total poetic effect. For example:

> La mano crispada
> como una Medusa
> ciega el ojo doliente
> del candil.
>
> («Conjuro»)

The fundamental poetic element in these verses is the simile which states that a human hand with its moving fingers is like the legendary Medusa whose head was covered with snakes. In addition to this basic element, the image contains three subordinate metaphors and two symbols. The metaphors are: the hand «blinds» the lamp (it hides or extinguishes its flame), the «grieving» eye, and the «eye» of the lamp (its flame). The symbols are *ojo,* which in Yorca's poetry stands for communication and life,[3] and *candil,* a death symbol.[4] It is important to recognize that these additional, subordinate poetic elements have a significant function in that they develop the inherently sinister overtones implicit in the initial comparison and thereby increase the poetic effectiveness of the image.

SYMBOLS

The symbol is one of the most widely used poetic devices in this work, and there is a remarkable variety in the types of words conveying symbolic meanings. Almost any object of inanimate nature, the animal world, the human, and supernatural realms can be used symbolically, a fact we have

---

[2] «Los poemas paralelísticos de García Lorca,» *Revista Hispánica Moderna,* XXVIII, núm. 1 (1962), p. 41.
[3] GUSTAVO CORREA, *La poesía mítica de Federico García Lorca* (Eugene: Univ. of Oregon Publications, 1957), pp. 12-13.
[4] *Ibid.,* pp. 14-15.

already observed in Chapter III, and which will be even more apparent in Chapter V. Many words are symbols for destiny, tragedy, death, or specific emotions like love, joy, happiness, sorrow, or despair. Others symbolize nations, such as Spain or Judea, geographical areas, like Andalusia, or cities, such as Granada, Cordova, or Seville. Other symbols represent various aspects of the world of the *cante jondo,* with its different styles of music and dance, its singers, and *cafés cantantes.* Even certain nonmaterial phenomena, like the *grito* of a *cantaor,* can be a symbol for a different affective reality. A complete examination of all symbols utilized reveals that there is no limitation on what a particular term can represent, and, as we shall see in the poems explicated in the next chapter, a particular symbol may have several levels of meaning simultaneously.

Symbols are not confined solely to nouns. The chromatic adjectives white, silver, dark, yellow, red, garnet, livid, green, gold, gray, purple, violet, orange, blue, the achromatic black, and certain specific combinations of these colors, like white-red or black-red, as well as the descriptive adjectives *hondo, lejano, ondulado, quieto, seco,* and the numbers one, two five, six, seven, and one hundred have symbolic meanings. In addition, certain verbs such as *llegar, no llegar, clavar, amanecer,* and *temblar* are symbolic of certain existential or affective states. All of the symbols in the *Poema del Cante Jondo* may be divided into emblems and symbols proper. The latter are further classified in two functional categories: independent and complex.

Emblems. The emblem is defined by Jaroslaw F. Flys as: «un antiguo símbolo, prácticamente fosilizado, que existe en la mente del pueblo y en el uso del lenguaje diario. Consiste en una permanente asociación de ciertos objetos o colores con los sentimientos humanos. Especialmente los colores tienen frecuentemente este valor simbólico.» Flys goes on to state, quite erroneously we believe, that: «el 'Poema del cante jondo' reduce el empleo de los emblemas a las sensaciones de color.» [5] A closer analysis shows that García Lorca uses many other kinds of emblems as well, especially trees, flowers, stars, and numbers. Examples of Lorca's use of emblems in images where the emblem forms the basic poetic element are the following:

> ¡Ay, amor,
> bajo el naranjo en flor!
>
> («La Lola»)

The *naranjo* is frequently used in literature as an emblem for love or, more specifically, the flowering of love.[6]

> Agua clara
> y olivos centenarios.

[5] *El lenguaje poético de Federico García Lorca* (Madrid: Gredos, 1955), pp. 150, 162.

[6] CORREA, «El simbolismo del sol en la poesía de Federico García Lorca,» *Nueva Revista de Filología Hispánica,* XIV, núms. 1-2 (1960), p. 112.

This image, taken from the poem «Pueblo,» presents a vision of the Andalusian people. It utilizes three emblematic symbols: *agua, olivos,* and *centenarios. Agua* is a common emblem for fertility and life [7] and is used here to represent the continuing life of the people. The *olivos* can symbolize strength, labor, forcefulness,[8] even sadness or tragedy, all of which are characteristics of the *pueblo* after whom the poem is named. *Ciento* is a common emblem signifying not just one hundred, but any indefinite number or an indefinite period of time.[9] Hence, the «olivos centenarios» are best understood as «timeless olive trees» rather than «century-old olive trees,» and in these verses the number is used to signify the eternal or timeless characteristics of the Andalusians themselves.

García Lorca also uses what J. M. Flys calls «emblemas recreados» which keep the essential meaning of the traditional emblem, but which also have an additional, personal significance added by the poet.[10] For example:

> En la noche del huerto,
> coronadas
> con rosas de papel
> y biznagas.
>
> («Danza»)

The *rosa* is a common emblem for love,[11] but in this image the *rosas* are not real; they are false, imitation roses made of paper, symbolizing false or deceptive love.[12]

Independent symbols. Most of the symbols found in Lorca's imagery are structurally independent of each other. For example:

> Muerto se quedó en la calle
> con un puñal en el pecho.
>
> («Sorpresa»)

Calle, like *camino,* stands for the trajectory of human life.[13] *Puñal* is, of course, a death symbol, and *pecho,* the site of the heart, represents life itself. The meaning of the image is obvious. It is a pessimistic statement about the human condition: Death suddenly and unexpectedly destroys life in the middle of its normal course. Although all three symbols function together, their individual meanings are independent of one other.

A variation of this process occurs whenever the independent symbols re-

[7] CELIA S. LICHTMAN, «Federico García Lorca: A Study in Three Mythologies,» Diss. New York Univ., 1965, p. 203.

[8] JAROSLAW M. FLYS, *Op. cit.,* p. 155.

[9] CORREA, «El simbolismo de la luna en la poesía de Federico García Lorca,» *PMLA,* LXXII, 5 (1957), p. 1081.

[10] *Op. cit.,* p. 161.

[11] *Ibid.,* p. 154.

[12] LICHTMAN, p. 138.

[13] CORREA, *La poesía mítica,* p. 9.

present the same rather than different things. In a poem whose major themes are death and burial, the poet states:

> Cuando yo me muera,
> enterradme con mi guitarra
> bajo la arena.
>
> Cuando yo me muera,
> entre los naranjos
> y la hierbabuena.
>
> Cuando yo me muera,
> enterradme si queréis
> en una veleta.

(«Memento»)

In the second strophe he expresses the desire to be buried among orange trees and mint, to join with nature and become a part of it. The *naranjos* and the *hierbabuena,* two plants common to the Andalusian countryside, are used jointly to symbolize the same thing, nature or Andalusia itself.[14]

Complex symbols. The complex symbol is formed by the interaction of two or more independent symbols which together acquire a new meaning that neither had separately. For example:

> Los dos ríos de Granada
> bajan de la nieve al trigo.
> («Baladilla de los tres ríos»)

In this image *nieve* and *trigo* represent respectively the mountain ranges and the plains through which the two rivers flow. However, these mountain ranges and plains are also the most prominent features of the Andalusian landscape; together they may be considered a joint symbol for the whole of Andalusia. This new meaning is suggested only when the two symbols function together to indicate the vast geographical expanse of the region. Singly, neither would be adequate to represent the entire province. Thus the new symbol alters slightly the meaning of the image which now states that the rivers not only flow from the mountains to the plains, but through the entire region of Andalusia. A second example of a complex symbol occurs in «De profundis»:

> Córdoba, olivos verdes
> donde poner cien cruces
> que los recuerden.

Cordova has been described as a melancholy city whose atmosphere is both stoic and tragic.[15] It is a city of: «calles profundas, largas, de un

---

[14] The reader will note that in this poem the *naranjo* is not used as an emblem signifying love as in a previously cited example, but as a generalized symbol for Andalusia.

[15] GUILLERMO DÍAZ-PLAJA, *Federico García Lorca* (Madrid: Espasa-Calpe, 1961), pp. 43, 44, 47.

azul, un verde y un rosa . . . Da la sensación de verticalidad y desnudez
—de misterio.» [16] In the above image, the *olivos* (symbolically associated
with shadows and tragedy),[17] *verde* (which in Lorca's poetry usually has
connotations of mystery, fatality, death, and frequently replaces blue
or red in his imagery),[18] and *cruces* (a vertical death symbol) [19] are equated
with Cordova. Hence, these three independent symbols functioning together
acquire a new meaning within the context of the image that they did not
have separately.

SIMILES

The second major poetic element in Lorca's imagery is the simile.
Although it appears only fifteen times in the *Poema del Cante Jondo,* many
of these similes display a level of intricacy seldom attained by other
poets using this relatively simple, poetic device.

Direct similes. All of the similes used in this work compare two
objects, A and B, and explain directly in what way they are alike. For
example:

> Como Homero cantó
> ciego . . .
>> («Juan Breva»)

This simile compares the singer Juan Breva to Homer and gives the justification for the comparison: They both sang blind, meaning that Juan
Breva habitually sang with his eyes closed. A variation of the direct simile
occurs in two poems in which there is a multiple comparison:

> Llora monótona,
> como llora el agua,
> como llora el viento
> sobre la nevada.
>> («La guitarra»)

Here the forlorn, repetitious strumming of the guitar is said to be like the
«weeping» of water and wind over new-fallen snow. The explanation is
that they share the common trait of an unvaried, monotonous sound.

Complex similes. In the complex simile, used four times in this work,
two objects, A and B, are compared, but in the explanation of how A and B

---

[16] MODESTO RIVERA, «Federico García Lorca, motivos naturales—Sevilla, Córdoba,
Granada,» *Brújula,* II, 3-4 (1936), p. 32.

[17] LICHTMAN, pp. 158-159.

[18] CONCHA ZARDOYA, «La técnica metafórica de Federico García Lorca,» in *Poesía
española contemporánea* (Madrid: Ediciones Guadarrama, 1961), p. 387.

[19] CORREA, *La poesía mítica,* p. 10.

are alike, two other objects or phenomena, A^1 and B^1, are also compared.
Thus, the first comparison originates a second. For example:

> El puñal
> entra en el corazón
> como la reja del arado
> en el yermo.
>
> («Puñal»)

Object A *(puñal)* is compared to object B *(reja del arado)*. In order to
explain how they are alike, we are told that A acts in its realm («entra
en el corazón»), which we shall call A^1, just as B acts in its own realm
(«entra en el yermo»), designated B^1. Consequently, not only are A and
B directly compared, but the two realms within which they function are
also implicitly compared, thereby establishing an implied metaphor that
equates *corazón* with *yermo*. This type of complex simile can be diagramed
as follows:

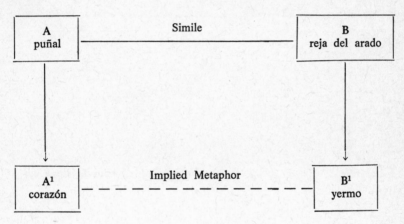

There are, however, two important variations of this pattern in
the *Poema del Cante Jondo*. The first occurs in those images in which the
relationship between elements A and A^1 and B and B^1 is distorted by the
fact that A^1 is missing. As a result, B^1 is forced to replace A^1, and in so
doing, it assumes the same relationship to A that it has to B. The following
image, taken from the same poem as the preceding example, illustrates this
technique:

> El puñal,
> como un rayo de sol,
> incendia las terribles
> hondonadas.
>
> («Puñal»)

In these verses object A *(puñal)* is compared to object B *(rayo de sol)*.
The basis for this comparison is that just as B acts in its realm, B^1 *(las*

127

terribles hondonadas), so too does A act in its own region, A^1 *(el corazón).* However, A^1 has been omitted, although its presence is implied because of the preceding image. Therefore, instead of stating that the dagger, A, acts upon the human heart, A^1, like a sun's ray, B, reacts with the depths of the earth, B^1, the image actually states that the dagger enters and sets fire to the terrible depths, that A acts upon B^1. Thus, the elimination of A^1 *(el corazón)* means that not only is a metaphoric relationship established between A and B^1, but the new metaphor resulting from this rearrangement is a direct rather than an implied metaphor as in the preceding example. This new metaphor, «el puñal incendia las terribles hondonadas,» becomes the actual basis for the image and the simile is reduced to a secondary poetic element. The relationship of these terms may be diagramed as follows:

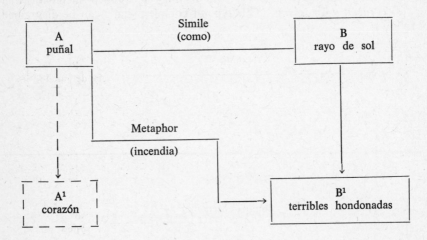

The second kind of variation is found in an image in which objects A and B are introduced in reverse order, and the two additional elements, A^1 and B^1, are not separate entities, but are already fused in a metaphor:

Como un arco de viola
el grito ha hecho vibrar
largas cuerdas del viento.

The image, taken from «El grito,» states that a human cry, A, is like a viola bow, B, and that just as the viola bow makes the strings of the viola (B^1) vibrate, the cry likewise acts upon the wind (A^1) and causes it to vibrate. However, the two concepts, viola strings and wind, are already joined in a metaphor, «largas cuerdas del viento,» so that there is no implied comparison produced as in the first example, nor is there a rearranging of the functional relationship between A and A^1 and

B and B¹ as in the second example studied. A diagram of this image would be as follows:

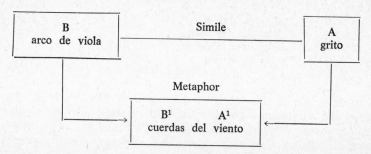

Similes combined with symbols and metaphors. When functioning in combination with symbols and metaphors, the simile can either contain the symbol or metaphor as part of the terms compared, or they can be utilized as additional elements that are not a structural part of the simile.

Symbol within the simile. An example of the procedure in which one of the terms in the comparison is also a symbol occurs in the following image:

> Una ciudad que acecha
> largos ritmos
> y los enrosca
> como laberintos.
>
> («Sevilla»)

In this simile that compares rhythms with labyrinths, the second term of the comparison is a symbol variously interpreted as representing the insoluble perplexities of life, death, a cemetery,[20] or the fate that awaits man at the end of his life.[21]

Symbol apart from the simile. In such images the symbols are not one of the terms compared. For example:

> El puñal
> como un rayo de sol
> incendia las terribles
> hondonadas.
>
> («Puñal»)

Hondonadas is a symbol for death and the sinister forces that influence man's destiny.[22] In this case, however, the symbol is not one of the two terms compared in the simile that equates the dagger with the rays of the sun.

[20] *Ibid.,* pp. 9-10.
[21] LICHTMAN, p. 216.
[22] CORREA, *La poesía mítica,* p. 14.

9

Metaphors within the simile. In images of this type, at least one of the terms compared is also a metaphor.[23] For example:

> Llora monótona
> como llora el agua,
> como llora el viento
> sobre la nevada.
>
> («La guitarra»)

The double simile in this image is composed of three separate metaphors linked by the conjunction *como*. The first of these metaphors (the guitar «weeps» monotonously) is actually the first term of the comparison. The next two metaphors, «weeping water» and «weeping wind,» constitute the other two parts of the double simile.

Metaphors apart from the simile. In such images the metaphors are structurally separate from the similes and are used to augment the poetic effect created by the direct comparison. For example:

> La mano crispada
> como una Medusa
> ciega el ojo doliente
> del candil.
>
> («Conjuro»)

This image actually contains three metaphors, two of which («ojo doliente» and «ojo del candil») are structurally apart from the simile that compares the clenched hand of a dancer to the Medusa.

METAPHORS

For the purpose of this study, we are using the term «metaphor» in a wider sense than its traditional meaning of an identification (either complete or partial) between two objects or ideas. In our opinion a metaphor may be said to consist of any group of words that, functioning together, conveys a single impression or makes a single statement that is contradictory to literal reality as we normally perceive it. It does not have to involve a form of identification. In the traditional concept of metaphor, the necessary identification of one phenomenon with another usually involves a change in the basic nature of at least one of the terms. In modern poetry, however, this change, while it may be present, does not seem to be strictly necessary. Indeed, modern poets seem to put more emphasis on other means to bring about a figurative, non-literal association or relationship.

In García Lorca's poetry, there is an abundant use of traditional as well as modern metaphors. In the case of the former type, Lorca's metaphor formation centers around the principle of intervalence-plurivalence, a poetic

[23] See the following section on metaphors for a definition of the term as it applies to this study.

process by means of which the phenomena of inanimate and animate nature, the human, and supernatural realms are often made equivalent to or substituted for one another. Through intervalence-plurivalence objects lose their own form and become other objects. Edwin Honig believes that intervalence-plurivalence expresses a dynamic conflict between abstract and concrete forces that runs throughout this poet's works: A second way in which Lorca dramatizes the conflict between abstract and concrete forces is by revealing the compulsion of one element or quality of nature to become another and throw off its own inevitable form to live vicariously in one of its own choosing.» [24] Andrew P. Debicki regards the process as part of Lorca's attempt to overcome death. Any perishable object (especially one pertaining to the human realm) can escape its inevitable fate by changing its essential nature and becoming an integral part of some other object or sphere of existence; hence the frequency with which human phenomena show a desire to become objects of nature.[25] Unquestionably, the most detailed study of intervalence-plurivalence is that of Concha Zardoya who states that the basis for this poetic process is found in Lorca's poem «Sur»:

> La clave de esta intervalencia y plurivalencia del mundo acaso está presente en su poema «Sur» *(Poemas varios)*, en el que F. G. L. dice: «da lo mismo decir estrella que naranja, cauce que cielo.» Esto significa que astros, flora, fauna, hombres y cosas participan de una esencia común que los hace identificarse entre sí y equivalerse . . . Las imágenes intervalentes y plurivalentes constituyen el fenómeno metafórico más continuo y constante de toda la obra lorquiana, pues no falta en ninguno de sus libros y ni aun en su teatro. Cada elemento de lo creado se trasfunde a otro, aunque pertenezca al plano más alejado.[26]

García Lorca viewed the universe as a unified creation whose component elements interacted upon each other to create a continuous pattern of change. The various planes of existence, whether inanimate objects, animals, humans, or supernatural beings, did not merely exist side by side in a tangential relationship, but were closely interlocked in a basic existential unity of being. Therefore, to be one thing was to be all things or to be capable of becoming any other thing.

A careful examination of the imagery in the *Poema del Cante Jondo* reveals that there are twenty-four kinds of intervalence-plurivalence and that they can be divided into four categories: inanimate nature, animate nature, the human world, and the supernatural realm. The first category (inanimate nature) contains six kinds of changes. Frequently, one inanimate object replaces another (intervalence). For example:

---

[24] *García Lorca* (Norfolk: New Directions 1963), p. 206.

[25] «Federico García Lorca: estilización y visión de la poesía,» in *Estudios sobre poesía española contemporánea* (Madrid: Gredos, 1968), pp. 218-220.

[26] *Op. cit.,* pp. 367-368.

> Bajo las estremecidas
> estrellas de los velones.
>> («Muerte de la petenera»)

The lamps' flames are replaced by stars. In other images an object of inanimate nature becomes a creature of the animal kingdom (plurivalence). Thus, the century plant cactus becomes a «pulpo petrificado» («Pita»).

In one poem an inanimate, natural object takes on the form of a human figure. The prickly pear cactus is a «Laoconte salvaje» and a «múltiple pelotari» («Chumbera»). Occasionally, an inanimate object is replaced by a part of the human body. Example: «El río Guadalquivir / tiene las barbas granates» («Baladilla de los tres ríos»). The river's granite-red, clay banks become a beard. In some images an inanimate object performs human activities or shows human emotions:

> Llora monótona
> como llora el agua,
> como llora el viento
> sobre la nevada.
>> («La guitarra»)

The water and wind react with human feelings and weep. The most frequent kind of plurivalence takes place when an object of inanimate nature is equated with a man-made object. For example:

> Bajo el arco del cielo
> sobre su llano limpio
> dispara la constante
> saeta de su río.
>> («Sevilla»)

The sky becomes a bow and the river an arrow.

The next type of plurivalence, of which there are two varieties, involves creatures of the animal kingdom. The first concerns the equating of animals with human beings. An example is found in a poem in which six nightngales are personified as mourners who weep for a dead child:

> Dentro hay una niña muerta
> con una rosa encarnada
> oculta en la cabellera.
> Seis ruiseñores la lloran
> en la reja.
>> («Barrio de Córdoba»)

The second type involves the changing of a legendary animal into a supernatural, divine figure. The single example of this phenomenon occurs in a poem in which «strange unicorns» are seen to take on many forms including that of Christ:

> Por la calleja vienen
> extraños unicornios.
> ... ...
> Más cerca
> ya parecen astrónomos.
> Fantásticos Merlines
> y el Ecce Homo,
> Durandarte encantado,
> Orlando furioso.
>
> («Procesión»)

The third and largest category of intervalence-plurivalence pertains to elements of the human realm. There are fourteen types of changes within this group. The first occurs in the poem just quoted and involves the equating of human figures with legendary animals. In the religious processions of Holy Week, the hooded penitents are described as unicorns: «Por la calleja vienen / extraños unicornios» («Procesión»).

Occasionally, a part of the human body is converted into an element of inanimate nature: «su falda de moaré tiembla / entre sus muslos de cobre» («Muerte de la petenera»). The Gypsy girl's thighs are equated with a metal. At other times a part of the human body becomes an animal: «En la araña / de la mano» («Crótalo»). In one image a part of the human body is equivalent to a human being:

> Las calles están desiertas
> y en los fondos se adivinan
> corazones andaluces
> buscando viejas espinas.
>
> («Baile»)

The «corazones andaluces» designate the human figures searching in the background. Sometimes a part of the human body becomes a man-made object:

> ¡Oh guitarra!
> Corazón malherido
> por cinco espadas.
>
> («La guitarra»)

The five fingers of the guitarist are like five swords.

Frequently, a human phenomenon is transformed into an object of nature, as in these verses in which the cry of the singer becomes a black rainbow:

> Desde los olivos
> será un arco iris negro
> sobre la noche azul.
>
> («El grito»)

At times a human phenomenon, like the singer's voice, is identified with a human emotion such as grief:

> Nada como su trino.
> Era la misma

> pena cantando
> detrás de una sonrisa.
>
> («Juan Breva»)

In many images a man-made object becomes an object of nature, as in the following example in which the street is transformed into a river carrying a statue of the Virgin to the sea:

> Virgen con miriñaque,
> tú vas
> por el río de la calle
> ¡hasta el mar!
>
> («Paso»)

Frequently, a man-made object is equated with a member of the animal kingdom. In the following verses a flamenco dancer's castanet becomes a beetle:

> Crótalo.
> Crótalo.
> Crótalo.
> Escarabajo sonoro.
>
> («Crótalo»)

In several images a man-made object is changed into a human being. Example:

> En la redonda
> encrucijada,
> seis doncellas
> bailan.
>
> («Adivinanza de la guitarra»)

These six *doncellas* are the six strings of a guitar that dance as the instrument is played. Occasionally, a man-made object is equivalent to a part of the human body, as in the following in which the guitar becomes a human heart.

> ¡Oh guitarra!
> Corazón malherido
> por cinco espadas.
>
> («La guitarra»)

Often a man-made object acquires human qualities and performs human actions, as in this image announcing the «weeping» of the guitar: «Empieza el llanto / de la guitarra» («La guitarra»). Very frequently, one man-made object is equated with and substituted for another man-made object. For example:

> Pasan caballos negros
> y gente siniestra
> por los hondos caminos
> de la guitarra.
>
> («Malagueña»)

The strings of a guitar become roads along which various figures move. Sometimes a man-made phenomenon is changed into a supernatural being, as in the following verses in which the music of the guitar is compared to the sobbing of lost souls, suggesting an unworldly, infernal atmosphere:

> El sollozo de las almas
> perdidas
> se escapa por su boca
> redonda.
>
> («Las seis cuerdas»)

The final kind of plurivalence, of which there are two types in this book, pertains to the trancformation of supernatural forms of beings. The first involves a deity who becomes two flowers:

> Cristo moreno
> pasa
> de lirio de Judea
> a clavel de España.
>
> («Saeta»)

The second type is found in images in which supernatural beings become personified figures, as in the following lines in which death is transformed into a bride crowned with a wreath of withered orange blossoms:

> Por un camino va
> la muerte, coronada
> de azahares marchitos.
>
> («Clamor»)

Types of metaphors.

Like the symbols and similes, the metaphors in this work are employed either as the basic poetic unit around which an image is formed or as secondary elements within the image. Almost all metaphors in the *Poema del Cante Jondo* can be classified as substantival, adjectival, or verbal metaphors, depending on whether their principal element is a noun, an adjective, or a verb.

Substantival metaphors. Such metaphors result from a non-literal, figurative use of a noun. For example:

> Empieza el llanto
> de la guitarra.
>
> («La guitarra»)

The use of *llanto* instead of the more logical *música* creates the metaphor. Another example appears in the verses: «Sevilla es una torre / llena de arqueros finos» from «Sevilla.» The statement that the city is a tower is a metaphor based on the equation of two nouns.

Adjectival metaphors. Such metaphors are produced by modifying a noun with an adjective that is illogical and which contradicts literal reality. For example: «Es un silencio ondulado» («El silencio»). The use of *ondulado* with *silencio* gives an auditory phenomenon a visual dimension not normally expected. Another example occurs in the following verses:

> Largas sombras afiladas
> vienen del turbio horizonte
> y el bordón de una guitarra
> se rompe.
>
> («Muerte de la petenera»)

The basis for the image is the metaphor in the first line in which *sombras* is modified by *afiladas.* The justaposition of these two words attributes a solid, material form to a non-material phenomenon through the implication that the shadows are converted into knives.

Verbal metaphors. In some cases it is the verb that creates the metaphor, often by attributing actions to inanimate objects. For example:

> Las montañas miran
> un punto lejano.
>
> («Después de pasar»)

Miran imputes a conscious act to an inanimate object, thereby creating a metaphor. Another example is found in «Barrio de Córdoba»: «La noche se derrumba.» Here the verb does not necessarily imply that the night has become animate, but it does perform an action that would be possible only for objects having a physical mass.

Implied metaphors. These metaphors are never actually stated, but their presence is strongly implied by the interrelationship of other elements within the image. One of the sources of the implied metaphor is, as we saw in our discussion of similes, the complex simile. For example:

> Un puñal
> entra en el corazón
> como la reja del arado
> en el yermo.
>
> («La guitarra»)

The direct comparison of a dagger with a plowshare also implies an equivalence between their two realms, the heart and barren land. Hence there is the unstated but implied metaphor: «El corazón=el yermo.» The following lines provide another illustration:

> ¡Oh guitarra!
> Corazón malherido
> por cinco espadas.
>
> («La guitarra»)

This image is based on a metaphor that equates a guitar with a heart which has been badly wounded by five swords. However, if the guitar is a heart and the heart is badly wounded, then, by implication, the guitar is also badly wounded. The expression «guitarra malherida» is an unstated metaphor. But there is also a second implied metaphor in this image. The five swords that wound the guitar are, undoubtedly, the five fingers of the guitarist. But this metaphorical transformation of fingers into swords is only inferred.

Symbolic metaphors. In some images a metaphor may also be a symbol. For example:

> Vienen de los remotos
> países de la pena.
>
> («Arqueros»)

This image refers to the dark archers who are approaching Seville. The metaphor «países de la pena» is possibly a symbol for the realm of the dead. Another example of a symbolic metaphor occurs in «Baladilla de los tres ríos»:

> ¡Quién dirá que el agua lleva
> un fuego fatuo de gritos!

According to Concha Zardoya, «un fuego fatuo de gritos» very likely refers to Granada, and it may represent symbolically the past and therefore now dead inhabitants of the city, since the *fuego fatuo* is often associated with cemeteries. Hence, it may symbolize the city's historic past: «. . . *fuego fatuo* es, primero, reflejo, luz reflejada, pero la propiedad que posee de aparecer generalmente en los cementrios, se irradia sobre *gritos,* significando que éstos pertenecen a muertos, los cuales, a su vez, evocan el pasado histórico de Granada; el agua, en síntesis, llévase luces y gritos trágicos o de muerte.» [27]

Metaphors by literary analogy. At times a metaphor is based on an allusion to literary figures from classical mythology, the Bible, or Spain's national literature. For example:

> Los sueños de ayer las buscan,
> pero las tiene abrazadas
> un Polifemo de oro.
> ¡La guitarra!
>
> («Adivinanza de la guitarra»)

The quitar is like the mythological creature Polyphemus because its round opening is reminiscent of the cyclop's one eye in the center of his forehead. An example of a metaphor by Biblical analogy appears in «Encuentro»:

> En las manos
> tengo los agujeros

---

[27] *Ibid.,* pp. 391-392.

de los clavos.
¿No ves cómo me estoy
desangrando?

The martyrdom of the poet is metaphorically compared to that of Christ on the cross. The following verses allude to characters from Spanish literature:

Y loca de horizonte,
mezcla en su vino
lo amargo de Don Juan
y lo perfecto de Dionisio.

(«Sevilla»)

La Carmen está bailando
por las calles de Sevilla.

(«Baile»)

Visionary metaphors. In his work on the principles of modern poetry, Carlos Bousoño describes the visionary image or metaphor as a poetic device fundamentally different from the traditional image.[28] According to him, traditional images and metaphors are based on rational similarities between two or more phenomena. These rational comparisons fall into three main categories: physical resemblance (which includes function, purpose, and behavior), moral similitude, and value equivalency. Furthermore, these similarities are the result of an objective, intelectual recognition that exists prior to our esthetic response to them. In modern poetry, however, the image or metaphor is often irrational and highly subjective as it is based on subconscious comparisons:

Pues el poeta contemporáneo llamará iguales a los términos A y B «en principio» no porque objetivamente se parezcan, en su figura material, en su configuración moral o en su valor . . . sino porque despiertan en nosotros, sus contempladores, un sentimiento parejo . . . Nuestra emoción es independiente y «previa» al reconocimiento intelectual del parecido objetivo, que sólo alcanzamos a vislumbrar después . . . En la metáfora tradicional ocurre justamente al revés: en ella el reconocimiento intelectual de la semejanza objetiva es «anterior» a toda posible emoción poética, pues precisamente ésta depende de aquél.[29]

Bousoño repeatedly stresses the point that the visionary image and metaphor frequently are not derived from sensory perception, for no physical similarity necessarily unites the plane of reality with the imaginary plane. The only real connection between the two is the subjective, emotional response that they elicit from the poet, and not only is «emotional» recognition prior to «intellectual» recognition, but the latter is not even necessary.

---

[28] BOUSOÑO does not distinguish between image, metaphor, and symbol, terms which he regards as essentially synonymous since they all involve the principle of comparison. See his *Teoría de la expresión poética* (Madrid: Gredos, 1970), p. 139.
[29] *Ibid.*, pp. 143-145.

However, it is frequently possible to perceive the intellectual basis for the comparison, but only after a subtle analysis, whereas in the traditional metaphor this rational basis is more readily apparent. In «Encrucijada,» for example, the poet describes the east wind as being like a lantern and a dagger in the heart.

> Viento del Este:
> un farol
> y el puñal
> en el corazón.

Obviously, the comparison between the wind and these two objects cannot be based on any of the three traditional categories; the reason for the comparison must lie in the common emotion that all three evoke. The lantern and the dagger are common death symbols that suggest a foreboding of violence, doom, anihilation—all of which are repeated or included symbolically in the East wind which apparently elicites the same series of feelings from the poet. This similarity of emotional response, however, is not immediately apparent; it becomes so only after analysis.

A more complicated example occurs in «Madrugada.»

> Sobre la noche verde,
> las saetas
> dejan rastros de lirio
> caliente.

In these verses the songs or *saetas* leave trails of a warm lily. This poem, the last one in the «Poema de la saeta,» depicts a generally positive affective atmosphere. The *saeteros* who first appeared as dark archers coming from «the remote lands of grief,» are now associated with love, and their songs, also sharing in this new association, are compared to the warmth and softness of a lily, the Easter flower symbolizing the resurrection and triumph of Christ. It is precisely these pleasing, positive associations that form the emotional connection between the flower and the *saetas* which at this point are no longer treated as embodyments of pure suffering, but as symbols of triumph over suffering and death.

A second «visionary» phenomenon described by Bousoño is the *visión*, a type of metaphor or image in which unreal qualities or functions are attributed to real objects or phenomena. The justification for the metaphor lies in the like emotional response produced in the poet by the real object and by the unreal quality or function attributed to it. Hence, just as in the visionary image, the key to understanding the *visión* lies in the analysis of the poet's and, by extension, of our own emotional reaction to each of these two elements.[30]

[30] *Ibid.,* pp. 177-182. 196-197. The main difference between the *imagen visionaria* and the *visión* is purely formal rather than essential. The former is based on the like sentiment occasioned by two objects; the latter, on the similar emotions produced by the association of an object with an unreal quality or function.

The *visión* occurs very few times in this work. In speaking of the girl Lola, for example, Lorca states:

> Tiene verdes los ojos
> y violeta la voz.
>
> («La Lola»)

The girl's violet voice, an example of synesthesia, is also a *visión* whose justification can be found through an analysis of the emotions traditionally suggested by this color. Violet is often associated with sensuality, passion, or voluptuousness, and it is precisely these qualities that are attributed to the girl as she washes diapers beneath a flowering orange tree.

A second example of this poetic device occurs in «Candil»:

> ¡Oh, qué grave medita
> la llama del candil!

Obviously, the attribution of an unreal function (meditating) to a real object (lamp) is based upon the feelings of quiet, peaceful serenity conveyed by both the verb and the noun.[31]

Functioning of the metaphor.

Independent metaphors. These metaphors form the basis of an image which does not have other symbols or similes as additional elements. Example: «Por la calleja vienen / extraños unicornios.» («Procesión») As we saw in Chapter III, these «unicorns» are the robed, hooded figures of the marchers in a religious procession. Another example:

> Pones cinchas cenicientas
> al vientre de los montes.
>
> («Pita»)

This image is composed exclusively of three independent metaphors: (1) The desert cactus, the *pita,* the subject of this poem, is said to «place itself» on the landscape; (2) these plants are compared to ash-colored girths; (3) the side of the mountain becomes the mountain's «belly».

Symbols within the metaphor. In these images a symbol is one of the elements of the metaphor. For example:

---

[31] The reader will note that this example of a *visión* is also a verbal metaphor, and the preceding example—Lola's «violet voice»—is both an adjectival metaphor and a *visión* simultaneously.

> Cuando yo me muera,
> enterradme, si queréis,
> en una veleta.
>
> («Memento»)

The metaphor «enterradme en una veleta» contains a symbol, *veleta,* which represents the everchanging vicissitudes of a man's life.[32] Hence the image may express the poet's desire to be a part of or to have his life identified with the eternal history of his race, or, possible, with mankind in general. Another example of this use of symbols occurs in a poem describing the music of the *siguiriya gitana.*

> ¿Qué luna recogerá
> tu dolor de cal y adelfa?
>
> («El paso de la siguiriya»)

These verses have two metaphors: «moon which gathers in» and «grief of quicklime and rosebay.» In the first, *luna,* a death symbol, may represent the final destiny of the personified *siguiriya.*[33] The second metaphor containts two symbols: *cal* and *adelfa,* which together represent, in the view of Jean-Louis Schonberg: «une impuissance totale et douloureuse qui cherche soulagement»[34] and, in the opinion of Gustavo Correa, they signify a foreshadowing of death.[35]

Symbols apart from the metaphor. In such images the symbols are not a structural part of the metaphor. For example:

> Oyes los maravillosos
> surtidores de tu patio
> y el débil trino amarillo
> del canario.
>
> («Amparo»)

In this poem describing the confined, sheltered life of a young girl, the verses quoted contain one metaphor, «el débil trino amarillo del canario,» and three symbols, two of which are not structurally a part of it: the upward reaching *surtidores,* which may represent the freedom the girl lacks, and the *patio,* symbolizing her enclosed, restricted existence. Another example is the following:

> Sobre el tablado oscuro,
> la Parrala sostiene
> una conversación
> con la muerte.
>
> («Café cantante»)

---

[32] LICHTMAN, pp. 213-214.
[33] CORREA, *La poesía mítica,* pp. 159, 7.
[34] *A la Recherche de Lorca* (Neuchâtel, Swisse: Éditions de la Baconnière, 1966), p. 190.
[35] *La poesía mítica,* p. 7.

The metaphor describing the singer's song as «una conversación con la muerte» provides the basis for the image. In addition to this metaphor, there is one symbol, *oscuro,* which complements the notion of death.

Metaphors within metaphors. An example of a metaphor within a metaphor occurs in the following verses:

> Tierra
> de la muerte sin ojos
> y las flechas.
>
> («Poema de la soleá»)

This image is based on the phrase «land of death and arrows» meaning Andalusia. Within this metaphor, however, «death without eyes» constitutes a second metaphor that is structurally within the first and is included to increase its poetic effectiveness. Another example is the following:

> En la noche del huerto
> sus dientes de nácar
> escriben la sombra
> quemada.
>
> («Danza»)

The metaphor «sus dientes escriben» contains another, «dientes de nácar,» that is structurally a part of it.

Interlinking metaphors. Interlinking metaphors are structurally connected to one another by sharing one of their terms. In this way the two are joined as though in a chain. For example:

> Sobre el olivar
> hay un cielo hundido
> y una lluvia oscura
> de luceros fríos.
>
> («Paisaje»)

Here «lluvia de luceros» is linked to a subsequent metaphor «luceros fríos» through a mutual sharing of *luceros.* It is important to note that «cielo hundido» that precedes «lluvia de luceros» is an independent metaphor, for it has no such structural connection to the two that follow. Another example is found in «El paso de la siguiriya»:

> Va encadenada al temblor
> de un ritmo que nunca llega;
> tiene el corazón de plata
> y un puñal en la diestra.

The first two lines contain three interlinking metaphors: «va encadenada al temblor,» «temblor de un ritmo» (within the context of the image «temblor» seems to imply fear as well as a wavering of the sound's pitch), and «ritmo que nunca llega.» The first and second metaphors are linked by their common use of *temblor,* and the second is joined to the third by the word *ritmo.* This technique of interlinking successive metaphors is, of course, one of the means by which García Lorca achieves a high degree of concision and poetic concentration.

TECHNIQUES OF SENSE PERCEPTION

Every image in the *Poema del Cante Jondo* contains specific, material objects or phenomena that are perceived not only in terms of their metaphorical relationship to each other, but also by the definite sense experience that each conveys to the reader. The importance of sense perceptions in imagery was fully understood by García Lorca who, in his lecture «La imagen poética de don Luis de Góngora» in 1926, stated: «Un poeta tiene que ser profesor en los cinco sentidos corporales. Los cinco sentidos corporales, en este orden: vista, tacto, oído, olfato y gusto. Para poder ser dueño de las más bellas imágenes tiene que abrir puertas de comunicación en todos ellos, y con mucha frecuencia ha de superponer sus sensaciones y aun de disfrazar sus naturalezas.» Lorca then remarked that the sense of sight was basic to all imagery and that the last three senses were subordinate to sight and touch: «Todas las imágenes se abren, pues, en el campo visual. El tacto enseña la calidad de sus materias líricas. Su . . . calidad casi pictórica. Y las imágenes que construyen los demás sentidos están supeditadas a los dos primeros.» [36]

An analysis of all images in the *Poema del Cante Jondo* reveals that Lorca generally followed these statements about sense perception. A tabulation of the actual frequency of occurance differs only slightly from his theoretical order in that sight and touch are used with almost equal frequency, followed by hearing, taste, and smell in descending order. In fact, touch is utilized in one more image that sight, and the last two senses, taste and smell, are reversed from the sequence given by Lorca. These two senses appear, however, in almost the same number of images, so that the percentage difference between them (less than 1%) is insignificant. Lorca often combined several different sense perceptions within each image, associating two or more with a single object simultaneously.

Of the 278 poetic images in this book, tactile sensations are present in 273 of them. A visual impression is found in 272 images, an auditory sensation is conveyed in 154, and impressions of taste and smell are utilized in 38 and 36 images respectively. Thus it is apparent that the last three senses are numerically subordinate to sight and touch, either of which is used in more images than the last three combined. Translated into percentages, touch is used in 98.2% of all images, sight in 97.8%, hearing in 55.3%, taste in 13.6%, and smell in 12.9%. The reader will note that

---

[36] *Obras completas* (Madrid: Aguilar, 1963), pp. 67, 68-69.

the sense of hearing occurs with more than twice the frequency of taste and smell together. Hearing seems to occupy an intermediate frequency level, distinctly below the first two senses, but clearly above the last two.

Single sense perception. This group contains those few images in which the poet attempts to convey an impression that utilizes only one of the five senses—sight. Example:

> (Lo negro
> sobre lo rojo.)
> («Cueva»)

This image mentions no tangible objects and is composed almost exclusively of words denoting color. Thus it is perceived only through the sense of sight. Another example occurs in a poem in which the abstract, non-tangible labyrinths created by time slowly vanish:

> Los laberintos
> que crea el tiempo
> se desvanecen.
> («Y después»)

Since the labyrinths are not concrete objects, they may be said to have only visual rather than visual and tactile qualities.

Double sense perception. There are three kinds of images whose component objects or phenomena are perceived simultaneously by two of the senses: those utilizing sight and touch, those of touch and hearing, and one image experienced through sight and hearing. The following presents an example of sight and touch sense perceptions:

> Nadie
> pudo asomarse a sus ojos
> abiertos al aire duro.
> («Sorpresa»)

Both *nadie,* suggesting a human figure, and *ojos abiertos* are perceived in the visual terms of size, shape, and position. The *aire duro* conveys a definitive tactile sensation. Another example:

> Lámparas de cristal
> y espejos verdes.
> («Café cantante»)

The lamps and green mirrors convey visual impressions to the reader and the hardness and texture of the glass suggest a strong tactile sensation.

The two best examples of an image experienced by touch and hearing occur in the same poem, «Retrato de Silverio Franconetti.» In speaking of the singer's cry, the poet says:

> Pasaba por los tonos
> sin romperlos.

Pasaba suggests freely flowing movement and therefore provides a tactile or kinesthetic sensation of relaxation. The subject of this verb, *el grito,* is in direct contrast with it, for in addition to its auditory dimension, it implies kinesthetic tension, as does *romper. Tonos* supplies an additonal auditory element. The other image involving touch and hearing appears in the final verses of the poem:

> Ahora su melodía
> duerme con los ecos.
> Definitiva y pura.
> ¡Con los últimos ecos!

Melodía and *ecos* present auditory sensations and *duerme* creates an impression of kinesthetic relaxation.

The one example of an image perceived by both sight and hearing is: «Es un silencio ondulado» («El silencio»). Silence, the absence of sound, is as much an auditory phenomenon as sound itself. In this verse silence is given a visual aspect by *ondulado,* which suggests a rolling, up and down movement. The classification of this verse as a double sense perception image is open to question, however, since to many readers *ondulado* may also suggest a pulsating, throbbing sensation conveying a tactile impression. In that event the image would be perceived by three of the senses: sight, touch, and nearing.

Triple sense perception. These images occur in three combinations: sight-touch-hearing, which is by far the largest group, sight-touch-smell, and sight-touch-taste. The following is an example of the first combination, sight-touch-hearing:

> Sobre el viento
> amarillo
> se abren las campanadas.
> («Campana»)

The yellow wind is experienced by the combined senses of sight (its color and movement), touch (the feeling of the wind), and hearing. The *campanadas* are perceived audibly and their presence in the image implies the existence of bells that also convey visual and tactile impressions. Another example of the same three senses occurs in «Encrucijada»:

> La calle
> tiene un temblor
> de cuerda
> en tensión,
> un temblor
> de enorme moscardón.

The metaphor «la calle tiene un temblor» conveys sensations that are perceived visually (the street's movement and relative size and shape), and tactually (its hardness and the kinesthetic tension implicit in *temblor*). The «temblor de cuerda en tensión» is experienced visually (size, shape,

145

movement), tactually (the material of which it is made and its kinesthetic tension), and audibly (the vibrating cord's sound). The sound of these vibrations is then compared to: «un temblor de enorme moscardón,» which is visual (size, shape, movement), tactile (vibrations), and audible (the bat-fly's buzzing sound).

The next type of triple sense perception, sight-touch-smell, is exemplified by the following image:

> Cristo moreno,
> con las guedejas quemadas,
> los pómulos salientes
> y las pupilas blancas.
>
> («Saeta»)

The figure of a dark Christ with jutting cheek bones and gleaming white eyes conveys a strong visual impression. The statue's scorched locks of hair also add sensations of touch (the texture of the burned hair) and smell to the image. Another example:

> Sobre el humo blanco
> del incienso, tiene
> algo de topo y
> mariposa indecisa.
>
> («Conjuro»)

The «humo blanco del incienso» has a visual dimension (color, relative shape, and movement), a tactile aspect (the texture of the incense), and it provides a definite olfactory sensation. The *topo* and the *mariposa* are experienced visually and tactually.

The final kind of triple sense perception combines sight-touch-taste. Example:

> El campo
> de olivos
> se abre y se cierra
> como un abanico.
>
> («Paisaje»)

The swaying field or olive trees is experienced visually (size, shape, characteristic color, movement), tactually (the texture of bark and leaves), and gustatively (the characteristic taste of the tree's fruit). Another example of this combination occurs in «De profundis»:

> Córdoba, olivos verdes
> donde poner cien cruces
> que los recuerden.

Cordova, green olive trees, and one hundred crosses suggest visual and tactile sensations conveyed by the texture and feel of stone, bark, leaves, and wood. Again the olive trees impart a sensation of taste because of their fruit.

Quadruple sense perception. There are three combinations of four senses used in this book. The first in order of frequency combines sight-touch-hearing-taste and is exemplified by the following image:

> Os sienten todas las muchachas
> que lloran a la tierna
> soleá enlutada.
>
> («Alba»)

The «muchachas que lloran» are perceived visually, audibly, and tactually (kinesthetic tension caused by weeping), but there is also an implied sense of taste in the tears. The «soleá enlutada» is a visual as well as an auditory phenomenon since she is a personified song. Another example:

> (Dejadme en este campo
> llorando.)
>
> («¡Ay!»)

In these verses the *campo* conveys visual and even tactile sensations. *Llorando* adds an auditory dimension, suggests kinesthetic tension, and implies the taste of tears.

The second type of quadruple sense perception combines sight-touch-hearing-smell. Example:

> Como tallos de parra
> encendidos.
>
> («Sevilla»)

This image describes the way Seville twists the rythms of the *saeta*. The vines have a visual dimension, and the fact that they are burning suggests sensations of touch, hearing (the crackling sound that dried vine stocks make), and the smell of smoke. The following provides an additional example of these same sense perceptions:

> Dentro hay una niña muerta
> con una rosa encarnada
> oculta en la cabellera.
>
> («Barrio de Córdoba»)

The «caballera» of the «niña muerta» and the «rosa encarnada» offer visual and tactile sensations. A profound silence seems to pervade the entire scene and adds an auditory dimension to the image. Finally, a rose implies an olfactory sensation.

The third type of quadruple sense perception combines sight-touch-taste-smell. For example:

> Cuando yo me muera
> entre los naranjos
> y la hierbabuena.
>
> («Memento»)

Both the orange trees and the mint convey sensations that are visual (size, shape, color), tactile (the texture of the plants and, in the case of the orange trees, of their fruit), olfactory (the characteristic aroma of oranges and mint), and gustatory. Another example:

> Y loca de horizonte,
> mezcla en su vino
> lo amargo de Don Juan
> y lo perfecto de Dionisio.
> («Sevilla»)

Horizonte and *vino* have visual qualities. The former is perceived in terms of position and brightness and the latter by color and matter. In addition, *vino* implies a tactile sensation of wetness as well as impressions of smell and taste.

Quintuple sense perception. The following is an example of an image combining all five of the senses:

> Entre la albahaca
> y la hierbabuena
> la Lola canta
> saetas.
> («Balcón»)

The two plants and the girl convey visual impressions. The fact that she is singing *saetas* adds an auditory quality. Touch and smell are inferred by the texture of the leaves and the characteristic aroma of these plants. In addition, the *hierbabuena* suggests a strong sensation of taste. Another example of quintuple sense perception occurs in the poem dedicated to Silverio Franconetti:

> La densa miel de Italia
> con el limón nuestro
> iba en el hondo llanto
> del siguiriyero.
> («Retrato de Silveiro Franconetti»)

Miel, limón, and *siguiriyero* communicate impressions of color, size, and shape. Thick honey and lemons also suggest distinct tactile, olfactory, and gustative sensations. *Llanto* not only provides an auditory dimension, but it also reinforces the tactile aspect by adding kinesthetic tension.

A statistical analysis of the various combinations of sense perceptions within the *Poema del Cante Jondo* reveals that images with three sense perceptions are the most frequent and those with one, the least. Double sense perception ranks second in frequency with quadruple and quintuple sense perceptions third and fourth respectively. The actual number of images in each category can be listed in order of descending frequency as follows:

Triple sense perception	(Total: 121 images)
Sight-Touch-Hearing	112 »
Sight-Touch-Smell	5 »
Sight-Touch-Taste	4 »

Double sense perception	(Total: 111 images)
Sight-Touch	104 »
Touch-Hearing	6 »
Sight-Hearing	1 »

Quadruple sense perception	(Total: 26 images)
Sight-Touch-Hearing-Taste	11 »
Sight-Touch-Hearing-Smell	8 »
Sight-Touch-Taste-Smell	7 »

Quintuple sense perception	(Total: 16 images)

Single sense perception	(Total: 4 images)
Sight	4 »

OTHER IMAGE TECHNIQUES

We are including in this section, in alphabetical order, those poetic techniques used in the creation of imagery which we did not discuss previously.

Alliteration. The repetition of the same sound or group of sounds (whether consonants or vowels) within a verse is used sparingly in this work. In the following verses, for example, there is a succession of «a» vowels:

> Entre la albahaca
> y la hierbabuena
> la Lola canta
> saetas.
>
> («Balcón»)

«La guitarra» makes use of alliteration in the repetition of «o»'s and «a»'s:

> Llora monótona
> como llora el agua,
> como llora el viento
> sobre la nevada.

Anaphora. The repetition of a word or group of words at the beginning of each verse, stanza, etc. is infrequent in the *Poema del Cante Jondo.* Two examples of this technique, however, are the following:

> Que muerto se quedó en la calla
> que con un puñal en el pecho
> y que no lo conocía nadie.
>
> («Sorpresa»)

Tierra
vieja
del candil
y la pena.
Tierra
de las hondas cisternas.
Tierra
de la muerte sin ojos
y las flechas.

(«Poema de la soleá»)

Antonomasia. This technique, closely related to the synechdoque, refers to the designation of an object by one of its qualities, an epthet, or
by a proper name. Several examples appear in this book:

Y la cueva encalada
tiembla en el oro.

(«Cueva»)

The sunlight is referred to by a word describing one of its qualities, its
golden color. Another example:

Evoca los limonares
de Málaga, la dormida.

(«Juan Breva»)

Here a city is characterized by an epithet, «la dormida,» the sleeping one.
Asyndeton. This poetic technique—the omission of conjunctions, especially the word «and»—occurs only twice in this work.

Piensa que el suspiro tierno,
el grito, desaparecen
en la corriente del viento.

(«La soleá») [37]

Anchos sombreros grises,
largas capas lentas.

(«Poema de la Saeta»)

The *y* is omitted before the second verse in both examples.
Animation. Animation normally is defined as a process whereby inanimate objects acquire life and movement, but this restricted meaning is not
adequate to describe all the types of life transference found in the *Poema
del Cante Jondo.* There are, in fact, five different forms of animation.
It will be apparent in the course of our analysis that this wider definition
is closely related to intervalence-plurivalence, discussed earlier in this
chapter.

---

[37] This example, appearing in the Aguilar edition of García Lorca's *Obras completas,* may be the result of a publisher's error in that the two major previous
editions of the *Poema del Cante Jondo,* the Ulises and the Losada, both include the
word *y* at the beginning of the second verse.

The first type of animation refers to the dynamization of static forms, by means of which inanimate objects seem to acquire life and perform actions. In «Sevilla» for example, the city appears to act with a life force of its own:

> Una ciudad que acecha
> largos ritmos,
> y los enrosca
> como laberintos.

In another composition a street light seems to tremble in fear:

> ¡Cómo temblaba el farol!
> Madre.
> ¡Cómo temblaba el farolito
> de la calle!
>
> («Sorpresa»)

At times inanimate objects are transformed into animals. Thus, a castanet becomes an «escarabajo sonoro» («Crótalo») and the century plant, a «pulpo petrificado» («Pita»).

The second type of animation, personification, is closely related to dynamization, but in this case inanimate or non-human, animate objects acquire human physical-psychological traits or perform human actions. For example:

> El río Guadalquivir
> tiene las barbas granates.
>
> («Baladilla de los tres ríos»)

The red banks of the river become a red beard.

> Seis ruiseñores la lloran
> en la reja.
>
> («Barrio de Córdoba»)

The nightingales perform a specifically human action and weep like mourners for a dead child inside a house.

The third kind of animation, dehumanization, imputes non-human qualities to human figures, usually by comparing them to plants or animals. Examples of both kinds of dehumanization occur in poems in which the singing voice of Juan Breva is said to resemble both a lightless ocean and a squeezed-out orange:

> . . . Su voz tenía
> algo de mar sin luz
> y naranja exprimida.
>
> («Juan Breva»)

151

and the hooded marchers in a religious procession become «strange unicorns»:

> Por la calleja vienen
> extraños unicornios.
>> («Procesión»)

The fourth type of animation is divinization, usually defined as a metaphoric process whereby objects from inanimate and animate nature are identified with or take on the attributes of divinities. When the word is defined in these terms, there appear to be no examples of divinization in the *Poema del Cante Jondo*. However, if we extend the meaning of divinization to include an identification with any extramundane or supernatural being or force, we find two images in which human phenomena are transformed into beings of this type. Example:

> Los sueños de ayer las buscan,
> pero las tiene abrazadas
> un Polifemo de oro.
> ¡La guitarra!
>> («Adivinanza de la guitarra»)

A man-made object, a guitar, is identified with the cyclops, Polyphemus. In the second example, a guitar's music becomes the sobbing of lost souls that presumably come from an infernal, supernatural realm:

> La guitarra
> hace llorar a los sueños.
> El sollozo de las almas
> perdidas
> se escapa por su boca
> redonda.
>> («Las seis cuerdas»)

The final category of animation, disdivinization, is a process by which divine beings are equated with animate or inanimate natural objects. The only genuine example of disdivinization that we have found [38] occurs in the «Poema de la saeta» where Christ is converted into two flowers.

> Cristo moreno
> pasa

[38] Although CONCHA ZARDOYA states that the image:

> Virgen con miriñaque,
> virgen de la soledad,
> abierta como un inmenso
> tulipán
>> («Paso»)

also presents an example of disdivinization, we feel that such an assertion is incorrect, since it is the Virgin's crinoline dress that is compared to a tulip rather than the Virgin herself. Secondly, she is not «transformed» into any other thing; hence her status as a semi-divine figure has not been changed. See CONCHA ZARDOYA, *op. cit.*, p. 366.

de lirio de Judea
a clavel de España.
(«Saeta»)

Apposition. Apposition is occasionally used in this work to create a metaphor or to point out a special relationship between two phenomena. The ten examples appearing in the book can be subdivided into the four categories established by Concha Zardoya in her study of García Lorca's metaphors.[39] The first type, of which there is only one example, occurs when an appositive follows the subject of a sentence:

El corazón,
fuente del deseo,
se desvanece.
(«Y después»)

The second group, of which there are four examples, is created by the ellipsis of a verb:

Córdoba, olivos verdes
donde poner cien cruces
que los recuerden.
(«De profundis»)

In this image, *tiene* has been omitted after Córdoba. The third type consists of apposition by means of a vocative. The single example is:

¡Oh guitarra!
Corazón malherido
por cinco espadas.
(«La guitarra»)

Finally, there are four appositives created by simple juxtaposition. Example:

Los sueños de ayer las buscan,
pero las tiene abrazadas
un Polifemo de oro.
¡La guitarra!
(«Adivinanza de la guitarra»)

It has been suggested that most of Lorca's appositives form metaphors which are not strictly necessary for understanding the poetic content of the image and are included only as secondary elements whose purpose is to increase the total poetic effect.[40]

---

[39] *Op. cit.,* pp. 393-395.
[40] BRUNO TURCATO, «Struttura ed evoluzione delle prime metafore lorchiane,» *Quaderni Ibero-Americani,* 4 (1960-62), p. 133.

Chiasmus. This technique, involving the inversion of the word order in one member of a parallel expression, appears in three poems. Example:

> Campanas de Córdoba
> en la madrugada.
> Campanas de amanecer
> en Granada.
>
> («Alba»)

The pattern established in the first two verses: bells + city + time of day is altered in the following two lines: bells + time of day + city.

> La muerte
> entra y sale,
> y sale y entra
> la muerte
> de la taberna.
>
> («Malagueña»)

In these verses the reversal of both the subject *(la muerte)* and the verbs *(entra-sale* vs *sale-entra)* crates a chiasmus.

Contrast. The technique of contrast, also called antithesis or union of opposites, is, in terms of both frequency and variety, one of the most widely used poetic devices in this work. There are, in fact, close to forty different types employed.

In Lorca's hands this traditional poetic technique becomes a highly sophisticated principle that underlies the dynamics of his poetic creation. According to Rafael Bosch, contrast in this poet goes beyond the usual meaning of antithesis. He views it as a dynamic clash of images resulting from a struggle between contending opposites:

> En los numerosos estudios que se han realizado hasta ahora de García Lorca no se encuentra ninguna referencia a la cuestión fundamental del contraste como principio de creación. Esto ha de aplicarse al contraste como principio general, más amplio que otros vocablos, como «antítesis», que también servirán para describir la actitud de García Lorca ante la imagen poética. Y hay que acentuar que ese contraste se realiza en la forma de choques de imágenes. . . . La expresión «contraste» o «choque» se usa aquí en un sentido muy particular por lo intenso, con la significación de lucha de contrarios.[41]

The most frequent type of contrast encountered in the *Poema del Cante Jondo* is between life and death. This struggle, which, as we saw in Chapter III, provides one of the book's major themes, is expressed by an almost endless variety of symbols, usually occurring in pairs rather than singly. For example:

> Vine a este mundo con ojos
> y me voy sin ellos.
>
> («Lamentación de la muerte»)

[41] «El choque de imágenes como principio creador de García Lorca,» *Revista Hispánica Moderna*, XXX, Núm. 1 (enero 1964), p. 35.

To be «with eyes» symbolizes life and to be «without eyes,» death.[42] Another example:

> Cien jinete enlutados,
> ¿dónde irán,
> por el cielo yacente
> del naranjal?
>
> («Camino»)

In this image the riders in mourning, symbolizing death, form a contrast to the orange grove, a common symbol for both life and love. Further examples:

> Dentro hay una niña muerta
> con una rosa encarnada
> oculta en la cabellera.
>
> («Barrio de Córdoba»)

The flesh-colored rose, symbolic of life, is in ironic contrast to the fact of death.

> As de bastos.
> Tijeras en cruz.
>
> («Conjuro»)

The Ace of Wands of the Tarot cards is associated with life [43] and the crossed scissors are an ominous sign in Andalusian folklore. In another stanza in the same poem, the death versus life motif seems to be exemplified by contrasting animals:

> Sobre el humo blanco
> del incienso, tiene
> algo de topo y
> mariposa indecisa.

The light, graceful butterfly is equated with life whereas the earth-bound mole, living in the ground, may symbolize death. Occasionally, the contast between life and death is represented by a symbolic opposition between a noun and its adjective. For example:

> Entre mariposas negras
> va una muchacha morena
> junto a una blanca serpiente
> de niebla.
>
> («El paso de la siguiriya»)

Again the butterfly is a life symbol, but these butterflies are black, a color associated with death. Likewise, there is an inherent conflict between

---

[42] CORREA, *La poesía mítica*, pp. 12-13.

[43] EDEN GRAY, *A Complete Guide to the Tarot* (New York: Crown Publishers, 1970), p. 48.

«serpent,» an animal symbolizing beatrayal and death, and «white» which can represent purity and life. At other times the life-death theme is expressed by symbols representing communication versus non communication or stagnancy. Such is the case with two consecutive poem titles in the «Poema de la siguiriya gitana»: «El grito» and «El silencio.» The former implies the desire to affirm life through communication, and the latter, antithetically, expresses death through silence.[44] Sometimes the life-death theme is stated by verbs conveying an idea of tranquility or peace versus those symbolizing fear. For example:

> Por la tarde ves temblar
> los cipreses con los pájaros,
> mientras bordas lentamente
> letras sobre el cañamazo.
>
> («Amparo»)

Here *bordas,* with its implied feeling of serenity and creative activity, is in direct contrast to *temblar* which, within the context of the poem, implies fear or dread since it is associated with the cypresses, traditional cemetery trees.[45]

At times contast takes the form of opposition between conflicting emotions like sorrow and happiness, implicit in such words as *pena* and *sonrisa*:

> Era la misma
> pena cantando
> detrás de una sonrisa.
>
> («Juan Breva»)

In other poems symbols of freedom are contrasted with those representing restriction or limitation. For example:

> Para los barcos de vela
> Sevilla tiene un camino;
> por el agua de Granada
> sólo reman los suspiros.
>
> («Baladilla de los tres ríos»)

The *barcos de vela,* which can sail on the open sea and hence represent freedom of movement, form a contrast to the more limited row boats whose presence is implied in the last verse.

At times the contrast is between the abstract and the concrete, between an illusion and a reality. Example:

> La ilusión de la aurora
> y los besos
> se desvanecen.
>
> («Y después»)

---

[44] HOWARD T. YOUNG, «The Magic of Reality,» in *The Victorious Expression* (Madison: Univ. of Wisconsin Press, 1966), p. 155.
[45] LICHTMAN, p. 156; CORREA, «El simbolismo del sol,» p. 112.

The ephemeral *ilusión de la aurora* is contrasted with the more nearly concrete *besos* though they both share a similar fate.

On other occasions two Andalusian cities are used as antithetical elements:

> Para los barcos de vela
> Sevilla tiene un camino;
> por el agua de Granada
> sólo reman los suspiros.
>
> («Baladilla de los tres ríos»)

This image, already quoted in another context, states an essential difference between Seville and Granada.

At times the opposing aspects of a single city form the basis for a contrast:

> Y loca de horizonte,
> mezcla en su vino
> lo amargo de Don Juan
> y lo perfecto de Dionisio.
>
> («Sevilla»)

Seville's «perfection» is contrasted with its «bitterness.»

Some images utilize antithetical human figures. For example:

> ¡Ay, petenera gitana!
> ... ...
> Tu entierro no tuvo niñas
> buenas.
> ... ...
> Tu entierro fue de gente
> siniestra.
>
> («Falseta»)

And in the section «Dos muchachas,» the personalities and social circumstances of two Andalusian girls, Lola and Amparo, provide the basis for two contrasting poems, as we shall see later in this discussion.

Often the contrast between two objects or phenomena is based on size:

> Juan Breva tenía
> cuerpo de gigante
> y voz de niña.
>
> («Juan Breva»)

On other occasions the size of an object forms a contrast to its transcendental importance. Example:

> Cigüeña incandescente
> pica desde su nido
> a las sombras macizas,
> y se asoma temblando
> a los ojos redondos
> del gitanillo muerto.
>
> («Candil»)

In these verses the small size of the Gypsy boy seems to imply a contrast to the enormity of death.

Occasionally, symbolic colors are used antithetically. We have already seen one such example in an image discussed in a different context:

> Entre mariposas negras
> va una muchacha morena
> junto a una blanca serpiente
> de niebla.
>
> («El paso de la siguiriya»)

Here black is contrasted with white. But in addition to any symbolic significance they may have, partially opposing colors also create a striking chromatic effect. For example:

> Sobre el cielo negro
> culebrinas amarillas.
>
> («Lamentación de la muerte»)

Part of the esthetic appeal of this image comes from the contrast between darkness and light, between black and yellow.

In many poems contrast is achieved through the opposing sensations of kinesthetic tension and relaxation. In describing Silverio Franconetti's singing, Lorca states:

> Su grito fue terrible.
> ... ...
> Pasaba por los tonos
> sin romperlos.
>
> («Retrato de Silverio Franconetti»)

The *grito* produces psychologically a sense of kinesthetic tension, and yet the fact that it gently «passes» through Franconetti's «tones» without damaging them implies the opposite, kinesthetic relaxation.

At times opposing auditory sensations are utilized, as in the following example in which a tender sigh forms a contrast to a cry carried by the wind:

> Piensa que el suspiro tierno
> y el grito desaparecen
> en la corriente del viento.
>
> («La soleá»)

In one poem a special auditory phenomenon, the singing of Silverio Franconetti, is analyzed as being both melodious and strident, two opposite qualities symbolized by *italiano* and *flamenco*:

> Entre italiano y flamenco,
> ¿cómo cantaría
> aquel Silverio?
>
> («Retrato de Silverio Franconetti»)

This same idea is then expressed with another type of contrast, this time involving opposite taste sensations:

> La densa miel de Italia
> con el limón nuestro,
> iba en el hondo llanto
> del siguiriyero.
>
> («Retrato de Silverio Franconetti»)

In the process of making this gustative contrast, two nations, Italy and Spain, are also compared.

In other images the physical materials of which an object is made become the basis for a contrast:

> En la redonda
> encrucijada,
> seis doncellas
> bailan.
> Tres de carne
> y tres de plata.
>
> («Adivinanza de la guitarra»)

The distinction is drawn between a guitar's three gut and three wire strings.

At times birds or animals are used as contrasting symbolic elements. In «La Lola» and «Amparo,» to be discussed at the conclusion of this section, the *gorrión* and *canario* are symbolic opposites, and in «Conjuro» the *topo* and *mariposa* become contrasting symbols for death and life.

Occasionally, the poet contrasts two different realms of existence, such as inanimate and animate nature. For example:

> Los olivos
> están cargados
> de gritos.
> Una bandada
> de pájaros cautivos
> que mueven sus larguísimas
> colas en lo sombrío.
>
> («Paisaje»)

In these verses a state of emotional tension exists betmeen the olive trees and the band of birds whose cries weigh them down.

In other poems two geographical regions are contrasted:

> Los dos ríos de Granada
> bajan de la nieve el trigo.
>
> («Baladilla de los tres ríos»)

The *nieve,* representing the rugged mountains, is in contrast with the *trigo,* symbolizing the flat plains.

Another image in the same poem uses rivers for contrast:

> Guadalquivir, alta torre
> y viento en los naranjales.
> Darro y Genil, torrecillas
> muertas sobre los estanques.
> («Baladilla de los tres ríos»)

The gayer Guadalquivir, associated with life, forms a contrast to the somber, tragic Darro and Genil, allied with death.

Trees can also be used for purposes of contrast:

> El río Guadalquivir
> va entre naranjos y olivos.
> («Baladilla de los tres ríos»)

Although the image may be simply an expression of a totality, it is possible that the two types of trees may represent opposite emotions. We have already noted that the *naranjos* are symbolic of love and joyousness, whereas the *olivos* are often associated with shadows, human destiny, and sadness.[46]

Occasionally, two flowers are used as symbolic opposites. For example:

> Cristo moreno
> pasa
> de lirio de Judea
> a clavel de España.
> («Saeta»)

The lily, a symbol of purity, spirituality, serenity, or the ascetic, is in contrast to the carnation, symbolic of passion, carnal love, or the earthly and mundane.

In some poems contrast takes the form of opposite directions of movement on the same plane. For example:

> El campo
> de olivos
> se abre y se cierra
> como un abanico.
> («Paisaje»)

The visual effectiveness of this image depends on motion in two contrary directions indicated by the opening and closing of a fan.

Sometimes there is contrast between movement on two different planes. Example:

---

[46] Luis Felipe Vivanco, «Federico García Lorca, poeta dramático de copla y estribillo,» in *Introducción a la poesía española contemporánea* (Madrid: Ediciones Guadarrama, 1957), pp. 414-415.

> Los niños miran
> un punto lejano.
> ... ...
> y por el aire ascienden
> espirales de llanto.
>
> («Después de pasar»)

The *punto lejano* presumable lies on a horizontal plane, whereas the *espirales de llanto* are ascending vertically.

At other times contrast exists between the foreground and background of an image. Example:

> Las calles están desiertas
> y en los fondos se adivinan
> corazones andaluces
> buscando viejas espinas.
>
> («Baile»)

The emptiness of the streets in the forground is in contrast to the activity taking place in the background.

As we saw in the introductory comments to this section, Lorca often employs contrast as a basic principal of structure. The following analysis of a single stanza from the «Baladilla de los tres ríos» illustrates this use:

> El río Guadalquivir
> va entre naranjos y olivos.
> Los dos ríos de Granada
> bajan de la nieve al trigo.

There is contrast within the verses because the *naranjos* and *olivos* may simbolize the positive-negative emotions of joy and sadness, and the *nieve* and *trigo* can represent opposing geographical areas—mountains and plains. Furthermore, the snow and wheat may have the additional symbolic meanings of sterility-lifelessness and fertility-life respectively. There is also the implied tactile-thermal contrast between the coldness of the snow and the warmth of wheat (a warmth supplied by the sun's rays). In addition, there are several types of contrast between the two pairs of verses. The Guadalquivir is contrasted with the two rivers of Granada, the Darro and Genil. Their directions of movement are opposite, for the Guadalquivir flows in a horizontal direction, while the other two rivers descend on a more nearly verticle plane. Furthermore, the implied orange and ashen-white colors in the first two verses find their counterpart in the following two lines, but in *reverse order*. Finally, the positive-negative sequence established by the emotional values of the symbols *naranjos-olivos* in verses one and two, is reversed in lines three and four by the tactile-thermal impressions conveyed by *nieve-trigo*, for these impressions suggest a negative-positive ordering of physical sensations. Thus, it is quite apparent that this quatrain is based on a principal of multiple contrasts. In these four verses the poet has included a maximum of thirteen kinds: (1) contrast within each pair of verses; (2) between two varieties of trees; (3) the positive-negative emotions these trees represent; (4) between snow and wheat; (5) the opposing geographical areas they symbolize; (6) sterility-lifelessness versus fertility-life; (7) the opposing tactile-thermal sensations of coldness and warmth; (8) contrast between the *pairs* of verses; (9) opposing rivers; (10) their opposite directions of movement; (11) the color sequences in each pair of lines; (12) between the positive-negative sequential pattern of verses one and two and the negative-positive sequence in lines three and four; (13) the implied contrast between words symbolizing emotional responses on the one hand, and those conveying physical sensations on the other.

The final type of contrast in this book is between entire poems and their respective component elements. Such is the case with «La Lola» and «Amparo» that together make up the section «Dos muchachas.» The personalities and social circumstances of the two girls are compared by a series of antithetical image symbols:

«La Lola»	«Amparo»
naranjo (life, love)	ciprés (death)
nardo (robust freedom in growth)	jazmín (delicate cultivation)
lavar (common-place work)	bordar (refined pastime)
acequia (a more freely flowing water)	surtidor (a more carefully controlled jet)
gorrión (common bird, freedom)	canario (caged house pet)
venir de los torerillos (social accessibility)	dificultad en hablarle (social inaccessibility) [47]

Diminutives. The twelve examples of diminutives in the *Poema del Cante Jondo* exhibit a variety of poetic functions, but rarely are they used solely to express small size. In Andalusia diminutives are a common feature of every-day speech, and, as Oreste Macrì has pointed out: «il diminutivo andaluso . . . non tanto diminuisce le dimenzione, quanto accresce la grazia dell'oggetto naturale.» [48] So it is not surprising to find that the diminutive is often used by García Lorca to impart a typically Andalusian, colloquial grace and charm to his verses. In «La Lola,» for example, he states:

> El agua de la acequia
> iba llena de sol,
> en el olivarito
> cantaba un gorrión.

The *olivarito* may be in diminutive form in order to create a popular atmosphere suggestive of Andalusian speech.

---

[47] See Chapter III for a more complete discussion of these two poems.
[48] *Canti Gitani e Andalusi* (Guanda: Collezione Fenice, 1961), p. 9.

At other times the diminutive communicates an infantile vision of certain phenomena. Example:

> Limoncito amarillo,
> limonero.
> Echad los limoncitos
> al viento.
>> («Lamentación de la muerte»)

These verses are reminiscent of children's nursery rhymes.

As we saw in the preceding section, the diminutive is occasionally employed to express a contrast in which an object's small size is antithetical to its significance. For example:

> Cigüeña incandescente
> pica desde su nido
> a las sombras macizas
> y se asoma temblando
> a los ojos redondos
> del gitanillo muerto.
>> («Candil»)

Gitanillo suggests the contrast between the small size of the child and the importance of his death.

At times the poet uses a diminutive in order to intensify the emotional force of an image. For example:

> ¡Cómo temblaba el farol!
> Madre.
> ¡Cómo temblaba el farolito
> de la calle!
>> («Sorpresa»)

The use of *farolito* instead of *farol* reduces the physical dimensions of the scene and creates an intensifying contrast that enhances the image's affective impact.

In his prose work *Impresiones y paisajes,* García Lorca declared: «Granada ama lo diminutivo . . . Por eso la estética genuinamente granadina es la estética del diminutivo, la estética de las cosas diminutas.»[49] This association between Granada and the diminutive is reflected in the first composition of the *Poema del Cante Jondo*: the Guadalquivir is said to be an «alta torre» whereas the two rivers of Granada, the Darro and the Genil, are «torrecillas / muertas sobre los estanques,» («Baladilla de los tres ríos»). But in these verses, the diminutive also has another function, that of reducing the affective impact of *muertas*. In other words, it becomes a device to diminish the reader's psychological reaction to certain emotionally negative words.

[49] *Op. cit.,* pp. 5-6.

At times Lorca uses the diminutive to categorize the members of a particular profession. For example:

> Los toreritos
> la rodean
> y el barberillo
> desde su puerta
> sigue los ritmos
> con la cabeza.
>
> («Balcón»)

In this poem the *toreritos* and the *barberillo* should not be understood to mean small, but rather young or novice members of their trades.[50]

Upon occasion a diminutive is used for emphasis. For example:

> Vestida con mantos negros,
> piensa que el mundo es chiquito
> y el corazón es inmenso.
>
> («La Soleá»)

A widow dressed in black robes is comparing the immensity of her grief to the relative insignificance of the world in general. *Mundo* is then modified by *chiquito,* which causes the noun to stand out precisely because the diminutive is an unexpected modifier.

Finally, the diminutive is utilized to put into relief and to focus attention on a small detail that might otherwise pass unnoticed. Example:

> Ventanitas de oro
> tiemblan,
> y en la aurora se mecen
> cruces superpuestas.
>
> («Noche»)

In these verses describing a religious procession during Holy Week, the reader's attention is focused more sharply on the windows by making them *ventanitas*. Without the use of a diminutive, these golden windows would be obscured by the larger, swaying crosses, since these command greater attention due to their symbolic importance.

Ellipsis. This poetic device appears five times in this work. In every instance the omitted word is a verb. Examples:

> Andalucía tiene
> largos caminos rojos.
> Córdoba, olivos verdes
> donde poner cien cruces
> que los recuerden.
>
> («De Profundis»)

---

[50] MANUEL MUÑOZ CORTÉS and JOAQUÍN GIMENO CASALDUERO, «Notas sobre el diminutivo en García Lorca,» *Archivos de Oviedo,* IV (1954), p. 284.

Cuando yo me muera,
enterradme con mi guitarra
bajo la arena.

Cuando yo me muera,
entre los naranjos
y la hierbabuena.

(«Memento»)

Enjambement. Because of the poet's frequent use of free verse, the run-on line is one of the most widely employed techniques in this book. There is scarcely a single poem in which it does not occur. The most common forms of enjambement are:
1) between subject and predicate

El río Guadalquivir
va entre naranjos y olivos.

(«Baladilla de los tres ríos»)

2) between the noun and a modifying prepositional phrase

El campo
de olivos
se abre y se cierra
como un abanico.

(«Paisaje»)

3) between two parallel prepositional phrases

La elipse de un grito
va de monte
a monte.

(«El grito»)

4) between a noun and its modifying adjective

(Torres altas y hombres
misteriosos.)

(«Cueva»)

5) between the verb and its direct object.

Las montañas miran
un punto lejano.

(«Después de pasar»)

Extension of the basic image. Another poetic technique frequently found in the *Poema del Cante Jondo* is the continued or extended image or metaphor in which physical objects, sense perceptions, an emotional-dramatic situation, or an idea appearing in a particular image (usually the initial one) become the basis for subsequent images. Normally, it is altered with

165

each successive repetition in order to increase its poetic effectiveness. In this way an entire poem can be created from one central image whose poetic elements or theme are incorporated in the succeeding verses. Hence, the extension of the basic image becomes a method of developing a theme with variations. For example:

> Empieza el llanto
> de la guitarra.
> ... ...
> Llora monótona
> como llora el agua,
> como llora el viento
> sobre la nevada.
> ... ...
> Llora por cosas
> lejanas.
> Arena del Sur caliente
> que pide camelias blancas.
> Llora flecha sin blanco,
> la tarde sin mañana,
> y el primer pájaro muerto
> sobre la rama.
>
> («La guitarra»)

The image-metaphor of the weeping guitar in the opening lines becomes the focal point of the poem, for it is re-expressed and given further elaboration in many subsequent verses. The guitar's weeping is said to be like the crying of water and wind, the sand of the warm south, an arrow, an afternoon, or the first dead bird upon a branch. Each of these images marks a further step in the poem's affective development, and each gives new meaning to the two initial lines.

Another example of the extended image occurs in «El grito,» quoted here in its entirety:

> La elipse de un grito
> va de monte
> a monte.
>
> Desde los olivos
> será un arco iris negro
> sobre la noche azul.
>
> ¡Ay!
>
> Como un arco de viola
> el grito ha hecho vibrar
> largas cuerdas del viento.
>
> ¡Ay!
>
> (Las gentes de las cuevas
> asoman sus velones.)
> ¡Ay!

The first three verses present an image (the ellipse of a cry that goes from mountain to mountain) which becomes the basis for all subsequent images. Each suceeding stanza utilizes either the visual shape of the ellipse or the actual sound of the cry as part of its component elements. In the second strophe this elliptical cry is transformed into a curved rainbow that spans the night sky. The third stanza compares or changes this cry into the bow of a viola that makes the wind vibrate. The closing lines show the effect of this cry, now carried by the wind, on the human beings who hear it. Each new use of these same elements expands their poetic effectiveness, and an entire poem is created from the variations on an initial, basic image.

Integration and disintegration of elements. Another technique used in image formation is the integration of separate elements into a whole and the disintegration of a complete unit into its separate parts. For example:

> Cirio, candil,
> farol y luciérnaga.
>
> La constelación
> de la saeta.
>> («Noche»)

These verses describe a religious procession moving through the early dawn. The candles carried by the marchers join with the street lamps and the glow worms shining in the surrounding countryside to form a constellation of lights called the constellation of the *saeta*. First the poet names the separate light-producing objects, and then he integrates them into a complete unit.

Another example occurs in «Retrato de Silverio Franconetti»:

> La densa miel de Italia
> con el limón nuestro,
> iba en el hondo llanto
> del siguiriyero.

In these verses, the separate elements Italian honey and Spanish lemon are integrated in the deep cry of the singer.

The opposite procedure, the analysis of a phenomenon into its constituent parts, is exemplified by the following image:

> Y van a un laberinto.
> Amor, cristal y piedra.
>> («Arqueros»)

A metaphorical labyrinth is broken down into its three component elements: love, crystal, and stone. A second example appears in an image attempting to define Spain geographically by analyzing the features of its landscape:

De España.
Cielo limpio y oscuro,
tierra tostada,
y cauces donde corre
muy lenta el agua.
                    («Saeta»)

Materialization and dematerialization. The former occurs whenever non-material phenomena or non-solid objects acquire material form or solidity. Dematerialization refers to the opposite procedure by which material objects become non-material and frequently lose their form and mass. The following illustrates materialization:

¿Qué luna recogerá
tu dolor de cal y adelfa?
                    («El paso de la siguiriya»)

In this image non-material grief is composed of two material objects and is gathered in by the moon.

The next image, taken from the same poem, illustrates both materialization and dematerialization:

Tierra de luz,
cielo de tierra.

The second verse, «sky of earth,» is an example of materialization in that a non-solid phenomenon, the sky, acquires solid mass and is said to be made of earth. The first line, «earth of light,» illustrates dematerialization, for a solid object is transformed into a non-solid phenomenon. Another example of dematerialization appears in an image which also illustrates the principle of integration of elements:

La densa miel de Italia
con el limón nuestro,
iba en el hondo llanto
del siguiriyero.
                    («Retrato de Silverio Franconetti»)

The solid objects honey and lemon become non-material, for they are transformed into pure sound upon entering the singer's deep wail.

Metonymy. This poetic technique is related to the synechdoche, and it refers to the substitution of an object by something associated with it. For example:

Anchos sombreros grises,
largas capas lentas.
                    («Arqueros»)

The two articles of clothing are used to designate their wearers, the *ar-*

queros oscuros who are approaching Seville. A second example ocurs in
«Paisaje.»

> Los olivos
> están cargados
> de gritos.

Here the cries, associated with the ominous birds roosting on the branches,
are a substitute for the birds themselves.

Mystery. In many poems of the *Poema del Cante Jondo,* there is a
deliberate use of the mysterious. Frequently, a feeling of mystery is brought
about by the presence of sinister elements whose purpose is not directly
indicated. Example:

> Por las callejas
> hombres embozados
> y en las torres
> veletas girando.
> Eternamente
> girando.
> ¡Oh, pueblo perdido
> en la Andalucía del llanto!
> («Pueblo»)

The poet never states who these men are or why they are here; their very
presence seems to be an ominous sign. At other times he portrays or
suggests a sinister situation without stating its cause:

> En la casa se defienden
> de las estrellas.
> («Barrio de Córdoba»)

Unquestionably, the most frequent method of creating a sense of mystery
is through the use of the unasked-unanswered question. For example:

> Unas muchachas ciegas
> preguntan a la luna
> y por el aire ascienden
> espirales de llanto.
> («Después de pasar»)

Our immediate reaction to this image is to inquire, what did the
girls ask the moon? Since we never learn the moon's answer, a mystery
results that is further enhanced as spirals of weeping ascend through
the air. What has caused this weeping? Does it precede the question or
is it a direct consequence of the moon's reply, or has a new event taken
place? No indication is given in the text, and the reader is left to con-
jecture for himself.

Onomatopoeia. There is only one example of onomatopoeia in the
Poema del Cante Jondo. As we saw earlier in our discussion of García

Lorca's poetic vocabulary, the initial and closing verses of «Crótalo» use this onomatopoeic word to convey the sound of a Gypsy dancer's castenettes.

> Crótalo.
> Crótalo.
> Crótalo.
> Escarabajo sonoro.

Oxymoron. This poetic device, which joins two inherently contradictory terms in a single metaphoric concept, appears but once in this collection:

> Tierra de luz,
> cielo de tierra.
>
> («El paso de la siguiriya»)

Parentheses. In his article on the function of the parenthesis in Lorca's poetry, Roberto Yahni discusses five different uses, all of which apply to the *Poema del Cante Jondo.*[51] Perhaps the most important is to diminish the emotional tone of an image or to instill a note of gravity in order to enhance it. Citing Tomás Navarro Tomás' *Manual de Entonación Española,* Yahni quotes: «'La entonación del paréntesis se caracteriza por su nivel grave respecto al de las unidades inmediatas. . . . La línea melódica del paréntesis se desenvuelve de ordinario a unos seis o siete semitonos por debajo de la altura media de la frase en que se halla intercalado.'»[52] The following verses provide an example of this usage:

> El corazón,
> fuente del deseo,
> se desvanece.
>
> (Sólo queda
> el desierto.)
>
> La ilusión de la aurora
> y los besos
> se desvanecen.
>
> («Y después»)

The parentheses create a subtone and increase the sense of stillness already inherent in the image of a lonely desert.

On other occasions the parentheses fulfill the function of a theatrical stage direction. In Yahni's words: «Interesa destacar la que llamamos acotación dramática, que tiene el mismo valor que la acotación en el teatro.

---

[51] «Algunos rasgos formales en la lírica de García Lorca: función del paréntesis,» *Bulletin Hispanique,* LXVI, 3-4 (1964), pp. 106-124.

[52] *Ibid.,* p. 107.

El poeta sugiere con ella un ambiente, un clima, un traje, un sonido, en suma: una escenografía.»[53] The following example illustrates this type:

> La cruz.
> (Punto final
> del camino.)
>   («Cruz»)

The words in parentheses clearly are used both as a «stage direction,» indicating the location of the cross, and as a symbolic statement about man's fate, for the cross stands at the end of a road (a frequent Lorquian symbol for the trajectory of human life) like a grave marker indicating that death is the final reality.

A third use is to create an interior dialogue or monologue in which the poet conveys his personal feelings directly. At times he seems to be conversing with the reader and at other times with himself. In fact, these interior dialogues establish a commentary in two voices, each of which has its own special tone and feeling. As Yahni has observed: «La intercalación de paréntesis en sus obras líricas configura una verdadera poesía de dos veces, en las que aparecen quizá los 'dos yo' del poeta, creando a veces una composición de estructura verdaderamente coral. Pero dos voces son fundamentalmente tensión, conflicto, desdoblamiento del poeta que dialoga a veces consigo mismo o a quien la vida se le muestra siempre en doble faz.»[54] The poem «¡Ay!» provides an example of this technique:

> El grito deja en el viento
> una sombra de ciprés.
>
> (Dejadme en este campo
> llorando.)
>
> Todo se ha roto en el mundo.
> No queda más que el silencio.
>
> (Dejadme en este campo
> llorando.)
>
> El horizonte sin luz
> está mordido de hogueras.
>
> (Ya os he dicho que me dejéis
> en este campo
> llorando.)

The verses in parentheses represent the poet's personal, subjective commentary to the reader.

[53] *Ibid.*, p. 108.
[54] *Ibid.*

Another example of an interior dialogue, this time between two conflicting sets of symbols that may represent two opposing affective realities,
occurs in the first section of the «Poema de la soleá»:

> Tierra seca,
> tierra quieta
> de noches
> inmensas.
>
> (Viento en el olivar,
> viento en la sierra.)

Seca, quieta, and *noches inmensas* are death symbols that create an
impression of emptiness, aridity, and lifelessness. This reality is then
contrasted to the words in parentheses that contain the life symbol *viento,*
associated with *olivar* and *sierra* representing destiny. Hence, the verses
in parentheses act as a second voice in a symbolic dialogue between the
forces of life and death.

A fourth use discussed by Yahni is the «paréntesis explicativo» whose
purpose is to complete or complement a previously expressed idea, metaphor, image, or simply to give an explanation. Example:

> Como un arco de viola
> el grito ha hecho vibrar
> largas cuerdas del viento.
>
> ¡Ay!
>
> (Las gentes de las cuevas
> asoman sus velones.)
>
> («El grito»)

The last verses complete and complement the previous image by showing
what effect the cry has on the human inhabitants of the region. In another
poem the *paréntesis explicativo* is used to explain a prevoius statement:

> El gitano evoca
> países remotos.
>
> (Torres altas y hombres
> misteriosos.)
>
> («Cueva»)

The verses in parentheses explain that these remote lands are characterized
by high towers and mysterious men.

The final usage occurs in those compositions in which it organizes
the formal structure of the poem and therefore is of primary rather
than secondary importance. Probably the best example is found in

«Cueva,» two of whose verses were used previously:

> De la cueva salen
> largos sollozos.
>
> (Lo cárdeno
> sobre lo rojo.)
>
> El gitano evoca
> países remotos.
>
> (Torres altas y hombres
> misteriosos.)
>
> En la voz entrecortada
> van sus ojos.
>
> (Lo negro
> sobre lo rojo.)
>
> Y la cueva encalada
> tiembla en el oro.
>
> (Lo blanco
> sobre el rojo.)

We saw in our discussion of this poem in Chapter III that each pair of verses is followed by another pair in parentheses which restates symbolically or elaborates further the theme of the first of the two pairs. Thus, the narrative content of verses one and two (sobbing coming from the cave) is reiterated in the form of two chromatic symbols: *cárdeno* (flesh color) which may represent either the human being, a Gypsy, who is weeping in the cave, or the fatal wound (torn flesh) which will be the cause of his death later in the poem. The second symbol, *rojo,* may stand for the tragedy or misfortune causing his anguish, or it may represent his blood issuing from the wound. As we have just seen, the next two lines in parenthesis, «(Torres altas y hombres / misteriosos),» complete by further explanation the concept of *países remotos.* These remote lands seem to suggest the dying man's mental state in that they could symbolize the after-life or «other world» towards which his thoughts are now directed, or they may indicate delirium, in the sense that he can no longer perceive people or places clearly, and so everything seems far off. The next verses: «En la voz entrecortada / van sus ojos» develop both the idea of a knife wound, since his voice is «entre*cortada*,» and the idea that the Gypsy, now growing weaker, is near death. His voice seems to be faltering, for it is no longer producing the drawn-out *largos sollozos* of the first image. Because the poet states that the man's eyes join with his voice, it appears that his vision is also failing. The following set of lines in parentheses, («Lo negro / sobre lo rojo),» seems to restate in chromatic form the content of the preceding verses. The dark eyes, represented by *negro,* are «within» i.e., they join with the man's faltering voice in lamenting the tragedy, again indicated by *rojo.* It is also possible, however, that these two verses in parentheses represent the Gypsy's death, an event prepared for by all the preceding lines. Thus, *negro* may refer to the fact that the man's eyes can no longer see light, that he is dead. *Rojo,* the color of his blood, acts as a reminder of the violent nature of his death. In the final strophe, the *cueva encalada,* shimmering in the intense sunlight, is re-expressed in the form of *lo blanco* (white-washed cave) upon *lo rojo* (the human tragedy or blood of the dead Gypsy). In summation, the poem utilizes an essentially bipartite structure in which the words in parentheses express on a symbolic level the drama presented by direct statement.

Refrains. Refrains appear in twenty-five of the fifty-one poems in the *Poema del Cante Jondo.* Undoubtedly the most common use of the refrain is to create a musical atmosphere by the reiteration of a fixed, rhythmic sound pattern. For example:

> Cien jacas caracolean.
> Sus jinetes están muertos.
> («Muerte de la petenera»)

The impression of prancing horses in reinforced by the sharp, staccato sound of the «c» in the first verse and the «e» in the second.

Lorca's musical refrains occasionally include *estribillos* from actual folk songs, either intact or in a slightly altered form. The double refrain: «¡Miradlo por donde viene!» and «¡Miradlo por donde va!» in the poem «Saeta» comes directly from Spanish popular songs, possibly from a *saeta.*[55]

The exclamation *¡Ay!,* found in many folk songs and frequently heard in the *cante jondo,* appears in several Lorca poems. For example: «¡Ay, yayayayay / que vestida con mantos negros!» («La soleá») or «¡Ay, petenera gitana! / ¡Yayay, petenera» («Falseta»). In this book the refrain *¡Ay!* has a double function: it acts as an intruding element that interrupts the normal flow of the verses, and it often serves as a focal point for the emotions conveyed in the preceding lines.[56] In

---

[55] DANIEL DEVOTO, «Notas sobre el elemento tradicional en la obra de García Lorca,» *Filología,* año II, núm. 3 (1950), p. 318.

[56] This particular function of the refrain is not limited solely to the exclamation *¡Ay!,* however, as the following example, in which a different refrain acts as an interrupting element, clearly shows:

> La Carmen está bailando
> por las calles de Sevilla.
> Tiene blancos los cabellos
> y brillantes las pupilas.
>
> ¡Niñas,
> corred las cortinas!
> («Baile»)

such cases the *¡Ay!* becomes a cathartic cry of angush. «El grito,» to be analyzed in detail in our Chapter V, will serve as an illustration of both uses:

> La elipse de un grito
> va de monte
> a monte.
> ... ...
>
> ¡Ay!
>
> Como un arco de viola
> el grito ha hecho vibrar
> largas cuerdas del viento.
>
> ¡Ay!
>
> (Las gentes de las cuevas
> asoman sus velones.)
>
> ¡Ay!

Constant reiteration of the refrain often serves to accentuate and individualize the particular idea or emotions expressed in the poem. In «Lamentación de la muerte,» for example, the continuous repetition of «luego / un velón y una manta / en el suelo» increases the emotions of fear, dread, and stoic resignation inherent in the death symbols *velón* and *manta*. Their effect is cumulative, so that by the end of the poem, the refrain has actually become the most important emotional element. Through an intense concentration of feeling, these verses establish and maintain the affective mood of the entire composition.

In some poems, however, the refrain not only sets the emotional tone, but it prepares for subsequent events. The opening verse of each strophe in «Memento»: «Cuando yo me muera,» prepares for three subsequent variations on the theme of burial, a logical consequence of the death motif:

> Cuando yo me muera,
> enterradme con mi guitarra
> bajo la arena.
>
> Cuando yo me muera,
> entre los naranjos
> y la hierbabuena.
>
> Cuando yo me muera,
> enterradme si queréis
> en una veleta.
>
> ¡Cuando yo me muera!

In «Conjuro» the dramatic power of the refrain results from tension and conflict between two opposing symbols. As we saw in Chapter III, the theme of the poem is the struggle between the forces of life and death, a struggle that is reflected in the symbolism of every stanza. The refrain, «As de bastos. / Tijeras en cruz,» reiterates and emphasizes this conflict by its two opposing elements: the Ace of Wands representing life and the crossed scissors signifying death.

At times the refrain becomes the poet's direct commentary to the reader. For example:

> El puñal
> entra en el corazón
> como la reja del arado
> en el yermo.
>
> No.
> No me lo claves.
> No.

> («Puñal»)

There are two poems in the *Poema del Cante Jondo* that utilize alternating refrains. In the first, «Baladilla de los tres ríos,» the two refrains function together harmoniously. The second is merely a variation of the first: « ¡Ay, amor / que se fue y no vino! » and « ¡Ay, amor / que se fue por el aire! » In «Arqueros,» however, the alternating refrains form a constrast that produces emotional tension: «Guadalquivir abierto» and « ¡Ay, Guadalquivir! » The first has positive connotations in that *abierto* often is a symbol for communication, freedom, and the possibility of fulfillment.[57] The second refrain, on the other hand, is associated with anguish and pain.

Ruptura del sistema. This poetic technique, described in detail by Carlos Bousoño in *Teoría de la Expresión Poética,* consists of the introduction of the unexpected into a particular theme or into any logically anticipated sequence of elements. In Bousoño's own words:

«Sistema» significa aquí norma de relación entre dos términos, establecido por nuestro instinto de conservación o por nuestra razón, o por nuestro sentido de la equidad o por nuestra experiencia: hasta por nuestras convenciones. Lo importante es que esa relación de que hablamos *se nos imponga por sí misma,* al hallarse profundamente arraigada en la conciencia humana. Dicho de un modo ligeramente distinto: el análisis descubre en tal sistema un par de elementos, A y *a,* tan íntimamente vinculados, que cuando se produce el término A, o radical, aparece en el sistema, normalmente, el término asociado *a.* Ahora bien: ocurre que el poeta puede destrozar súbitamente esa esperada relación A-*a* si cambia *a* por *b,* de suerte que en vez del usual

[57] CORREA, *La poesía mítica,* pp. 11-12.

emparejamiento A-*a* surja un emparejamiento diverso A-*b*. Cuando tal acaece, decimos que el sistema A-*a* se ha *roto,* que hay una *ruptura* en ese sistema.[58]

García Lorca occasionally uses this technique in the *Poema del Cante Jondo.* Example:

> Ni tú ni yo estamos
> en disposición
> de encontrarnos.
> Tú . . . por lo que ya sabes.
> ¡Yo la he querido tanto!
> Sigue esa veredita.

> («Encuentro»)

The poem begins as a conversation between the poet and a loved one in which the former announces that they cannot be reconciled. In line four he tells her that she already knows why. But in the next verse, instead of explaining what that reason is, he interjects: « ¡Yo la he querido tanto! » which not only is an unanticipated element quite different from the expected explanation, but it even changes the nature of the dialogue from a conversation *with* the woman to a statement *about* her in the form of an aside remark. The expected pronoun *te* (you) is replaced by the unexpected *la* (her). The next line, «Sigue esa veredita,» continues the *ruptura,* for it merely affirms the poet's determination to separate from the woman, and it does not help us understand why they cannot be reconciled. The anticipated explanation is never given.

Another example of the *ruptura del sistema* occurs in «Baile» whose principal figure is the legendary Carmen:

> La Carmen está bailando
> por las calles de Sevilla.
> Tiene blancos los cabellos
> y brillantes las pupilas.

The very mention of Carmen inmediately evokes an image of the heroine of Bizet's opera, a beautiful, exotic, dark-haired, young woman. This psychologically anticipated image is suddenly destroyed, however, when we learn that this Carmen is an old woman with white hair. This impression is confirmed again in the following strophe in which we are told:

> En su cabeza se enrosca
> una serpiente amarilla,
> y va soñando en el baile
> con galanes de otros días.

[58] *Op. cit.,* p. 388.

12

Thus, Carmen (A) evokes a certain anticipated image (a), which is replaced by (b), a portrait of her as a sinister and repulsive hag.

Signos de sugestión. This technique, also described by Carlos Bousoño,[59] refers to a process by which the poet uses a series of words as *indicios* of a particular idea or feeling not enunciated directly. These «suggestive signs» insinuate certain qualities that are not made manifest until the end of the poem, at which point they are seen to form a consistent chain of indicators, all leading up to a final poetic image. Although this device is not frequently encountered in the present work, it does appear in some poems. For example:

> Los arqueros oscuros
> a Sevilla se acercan.
>
> Guadalquivir abierto.
>
> Anchos sombreros grises,
> largas capas lentas.
>
> ¡Ay, Guadalquivir!
>
> Vienen de los remotos
> países de la pena.
>
> Guadalquivir abierto.
>
> Y van a un laberinto.
> Amor, cristal y piedra.
>
> ¡Ay, Guadalquivir!
>
> («Arqueros»)

The «dark archers» convey a sinister impression implying violence and death. The fact that they are wearing «wide gray hats» and «long capes» adds to their generally menacing appearance. The *Ay* of the second refrain conveys a feeling of surprise or pain, though the cause is unknown. This over-all impression of approaching disaster is reinforced by the fact that these mysterious figures come from «remote lands of grief» and, in the final, culminating image, they are seen to go towards a labyrinth of love, crystal, and stone. We saw in Chapter III that this labyrinth may represent a fatal enigma, and it may suggest that man's final destiny is death. The last image is the climax of the poem because it communicates a basic attitude about the human condition. The other elements—the sinister dark archers, their wide, gray hats and long, slow capes, the exclamation *¡Ay!*, and the remote lands of grief—are all *signos de sugestión* that prepare for the final image.

Another example of this technique appears in «Muerte de la petenera»:

---

[59] *Ibid.,* pp. 122-124.

En la casa blanca muere
la perdición de los hombres.

Cien jacas caracolean.
Sus jinetes están muertos.

Bajo las estremecidas
estrellas de los velones,
su falda de moaré tiembla
entre sus muslos de cobre.

Cien jacas caracolean.
Sus jinetes están muertos.

Largas sombras afiladas
vienen del turbio horizonte
y el bordón de una guitarra
se rompe.

Cien jacas caracolean.
Sus jinetes están muertos.

This poem presents a succession of stanzas whose common theme is the arrival of death. The death of the *petenera* finally occurs in the last image when the «long sharpened shadows» cut the guitar's bass string symbolizing her life. Prior to this event, there is a series of indicators or *signos de sugestión* that, as a group, lead up to that final, culminating image. The expectation of death is established in the first verses which state that the *petenera* lies dying in a house whose very color can be symbolic of grief or sorrow. Next appear the one hundred prancing horses whose riders are dead. There is the implication that these figures are emmisaries of death who are waiting to carry her off. Both the number one hundred [61] and the horse [62] can be death symbols, with the latter often representing a mysterious journey that invariably ends in death.[63] In the next strophe the lamp's flames and the *petenera's* mohair skirt are trembling, suggesting fear. Her thighs are of copper; they have the rigidity of death. The shadows are *afiladas,* knife-like, and the horizon from where they come is «turbid,» a word also associated with extinction.[64] This series of signs, all implying death's imminent arrival, culminate in the last two verses with the symbolic cutting of the thread of life.

Space-Time-Movement. Many images use space, time, or movement to produce poetic effects. Space, in the form of great distance or depth,

[60] FLYS, p. 152.
[61] MACRÌ, p. 24.
[62] JOSÉ FRANCISCO CIRRE, «El caballo y el toro en la poesía de García Lorca,» *Cuadernos Americanos*, XI, 6 (1952), pp. 240-241.
[63] MARÍA TERESA BABÍN, *García Lorca, vida y obra* (New York: Las Américas Pblg. Co., 1955), p. 73.
[64] CORREA, *La poesía mítica,* p. 14.

frequently is employed to create a three dimensional effect, to focus attention on specific objects, or to give a special emotional tone to an image. For example:

> Las calles están desiertas
> y en los fondos se adivinan
> corazones andaluces
> buscando viejas espinas.
>
> («Baile»)

The fact that the main action is taking place in *los fondos,* meaning background or depths, creates a three dimensional effect that would be lacking were the activity occurring in the foreground. This sensation of distance also comes from the use of *adivinan,* which makes the human figures searching for old thorns scarcely discernible, thus emphasizing the spatial distance between them and the reader. Psychologically, the reader is compelled to focus his attention more sharply than if they were nearer and more readily perceptible.

Another example occurs in «Después de pasar»:

> Los niños miran
> un punto lejano.
> ... ...
> Las montañas miran
> un punto lejano.

Because the object at which the children and the mountains are gazing lies at a «far-away point,» there is an increased sense of mystery. Furthermore, vast distance is an important factor in establishing the mood of spiritual desolation and emptiness conveyed by this composition.

Time is used in the *Poema del Cante Jondo* in two ways: it either gives an impression of infinity by stressing the eternal vastness of time, or it points out the specific time, usually at night or just at daybreak, at which an event takes place. For example:

> Los laberintos
> que crea el tiempo
> se desvanecen.
>
> («Y después»)

In this image time's infinite duration creates an impression of temporal vastness. Another example:

> Tierra seca,
> tierra quieta,
> de noches
> inmensas.
>
> («Poema de la soleá»)

Time, in the form of an immense, unending night, is used to create an impression of temporal and perhaps even spatial infinity.

In other poems time is specified in describing a particular event:

> Empieza el llanto
> de la guitarra.
> Se rompen las copas
> de la madrugada.
>
> («La guitarra»)

The specific time of day is early dawn. Since one often associates serenity, calm, and a peaceful stillness with the early morning hours, the sudden, violent shattering of the glass goblets is a completely unexpected development for which the reader is psychologically unprepared. On other occasions, a night setting, the most widely used time reference in this book, is essential for conveying the desired poetic effect. Example:

> En la casa se defienden
> de las estrellas.
> La noche se derrumba.
> Dentro hay una niña muerta
> con una rosa encarnada
> oculta en la cabellera.
>
> («Barrio de Córdoba»)

In many images movement or a lack of movement is an important factor. Frequently, motion forms the metaphorical basis for an image. Example:

> Oye, hijo mío, el silencio.
> Es un silencio ondulado.
>
> («El silencio»)

The poetic effectiveness of these lines lies precisely in ascribing motion to silence. Another example of movement occurs in «Paisaje,» where it creates an unusual visual effect:

> El campo
> de olivos
> se abre y se cierra
> como un abanico.

At other times a lack of motion is used to intensify a dramatic situation. For example:

> ¡Oh, qué grave medita
> la llama del candil!
>
> Como un faquir indio
> mira su entraña de oro
> y se eclipsa soñando
> atmósferas sin viento.
>
> («Candil»)

181

The implied stillness of the scene creates a mood of intense concentration and helps build a feeling of suspenseful tension. Another example occurs in the book's final poem, «Cruz»:

> La cruz.
> (Punto final
> del camino.)
>
> Se mira en la acequia.
> (Puntos suspensivos.)

Again the emotional intensity evoked is due in part to a lack of movement, which allows the reader to focus his attention on a specific object, the cross, whose motionless reflection seems suspended in a timeless state.

Special visual phenomena. Two of the most frequently used visual phenomena not previously discussed are light and its absence, darkness. In many images a background of either light or darkness plays an important role in creating the desired emotional tone. For example:

> Y la cueva encalada
> tiembla en el oro.
>
> («Cueva»)

The *oro* is, of course, the intense sunlight whose shimmering brightness gives the impression that the dazzling, white-washed cave is trembling. This painful sensation of brightness contributes much to the emotional intensity of these verses.

A strophe from «Paisaje» offers an example of the poetic use of darkness:

> Sobre el olivar
> hay un cielo hundido
> y una lluvia oscura
> de luceros fríos.

The dark rain and a sunken or somber sky add immeasurably to the emotional tone, the sense of mystery and suspense that predominate in this picture of a menacing landscape.

A second type of special visual phenomenon is reflection, though it is not widely used in the *Poema del Cante Jondo*.

Usually, reflection not only portrays a physical reality, but it suggests an emotional atmosphere as well. In the following verses, for example, the train of a singer's silk dress, or possibly those of the women in the audience, are reflected in the cafe's mirrors:

> Las gentes
> aspiran los sollozos.
> Y en los espejos verdes,
> largas colas de seda
> se mueven.
>
> («Café cantante»)

182

These long green silken tails have a serpentine quality that gives an ominous tone to the image.

At times reflection metaphorically fuses one object with another. For example:

> El agua de la acequia
> iba llena de sol.
>
> («La Lola»)

The water in the irrigation ditch reflects the sun whose rays appear to be fused with it.

In some images reflection creates a dazzling optical effect:

> Ventanitas de oro
> tiemblan,
> y en la aurora se mecen
> cruces superpuestas.
>
> («Noche»)

The sun's reflection on the windows seems to make them shimmer or tremble with light.

Synecdoche. This term is usually defined as the designation of the whole by one of its parts or, less frequently, the part by the whole. Examples:

> Sevilla es una torre
> llena de arqueros finos.
>
> («Sevilla»)

The tower referred to is the Giralda, Seville's famous landmark, and this building (a part of the city) represents the whole city. In another poem a part of the human body, the heart, represents an entire human figure:

> Las calles están desiertas
> y en los fondos se adivinan
> corazones andaluces
> buscando viejas espinas.
>
> («Baile»)

Synesthesia. This word may be defined as a process by which we experience certain phenomena through senses other than those normally used. In the *Poema del Cante Jondo*, García Lorca utilizes six kinds of synesthesia. The most frequent is the perception of purely auditory phenomena by visual means. For example:

> Tiene verdes los ojos
> y violeta la voz.
>
> («La Lola»)

183

The second type, experiencing a visual phenomenon by auditory means, occurs but once:

> ¡Quién dirá que el agua lleva
> un fuego fatuo de gritos!
> («Baladilla de los tres ríos»)

Very often a visual phenomenon is perceived by touch, as in the following verses:

> y una lluvia
> de luceros fríos.
> («Paisaje»)

The fourth kind, sound experienced primarily by taste, is found in a single image:

> y hay en su llanto dejos
> de sal marina.
> («Juan Breva»)

In the fifth kind of synesthesia, an auditory sensation is perceived simultaneously by two other senses, sight and touch:

> y te ahogas en tu trino
> de palo.
> («Crótalo»)

The final type of synesthesia, also appearing in only one image, involves the perception of an auditory sensation by sight, touch, smell, and taste:

> Su voz tenía
> algo de mar sin luz
> y naranja exprimida.
> («Juan Breva»)

Verb tenses. The three major tenses appearing in this work, the present indicative, imperfect indicative, and preterite, all have special poetic functions in addition to their normal grammatical uses. The most frequently occurring tense, the present indicative, vivifies and intensifies by transporting the reader to the moment at which an action is taking place. In an article on García Lorca's use of verb tenses, Juan Cano Ballesta has stated:

> García Lorca, que por vocación es un dramaturgo y por andaluz vigorosamente sensorial, reproduce sus escenas míticas apelando a los sentidos todos, más que a la memoria, y actualizando los objetos de la narración como en un escenario ante nuestros ojos. . . . *El principio básico de la actualización es, pues, el empleo continuo del presente.* El narrador, en lugar de instalarse en su presente, como el historiador, para ver el desarrollo de los hechos como pasados lejanos o próximos, desaparece tras la palabra, poniendo el «devenir» de la acción en el centro de nuestra atención.[65]

Examples of this usage are found in «Café cantante»:

> Lámparas de cristal
> y espejos verdes.
>
> Sobre el tablado oscuro,
> la Parrala sostiene
> una conversación
> con la muerte.
> La llama,
> no viene,
> y la vuelve a llamar.
> Las gentes
> aspiran los sollozos.
> Y en los espejos verdes,
> largas colas de seda
> se mueven.

The continuous use of the present indicative, especially in the middle section of the poem, vivifies Dolores Parrala's song and intensifies the poetic drama, for this tense reduces to a minimum the psychological distance between the reader and the action described; the present puts us at the very center of these events.

The present tense frequently has the least temporal significance precisely because its vividness removes it from the flow of time and fixes the moment it portrays. It is, therefore, an extensive rather than a momentary present. As González Muela has pointed out: «. . . el interés del poeta no está en 'localizar' muy concretamente la acción o proceso dentro de una porción del tiempo real, sino en dejar a esa acción o proceso eternizada, en un mundo en el que el tiempo no se mide en extensión, sino en profundidad.» [66] An example of this occurs in the poem dedicated to Silverio Franconetti:

> Ahora su melodía
> duerme con los ecos.
> Definitiva y pura.
> ¡Con los últimos ecos!
> («Retrato de Silverio Franconetti»)

The poet uses the present tense to create an illusion of eternity rather than just to describe the present, passing moment.

The normal grammatical-stylistic uses of the imperfect indicative as the tense that describes the setting for an action, or which carries the reader into the past and narrates events while slowing down the flow of time

---

[65] «Una veta reveladora en la poesía de García Lorca,» *Romanische Forschungen,* LXXVII, 1-2 (1965), p. 81.
[66] «El aspecto verbal en la poesía moderna española,» *Revista de Filología Española,* XXXV, (1951), p. 78.

to allow him to focus on the details or attendant circumstances, are well known and do not need to be elaborated further in this study. Perhaps the most frequent additional use for the imperfect in the *Poema del Cante Jondo* is to designate an event of secondary importance taking place on the periphery of the central action, usually narrated in the present. In such cases, the imperfect brings about a momentary change of scene or a change in the order of importance of events, as the focus of attention shifts to record a minor action or detail occurring simultaneously with a central episode.[67] In «La Lola,» for example, the central episode, narrating the girl's actions, is entirely in the present tense:

> Bajo el naranjo lava
> pañales de algodón.
> Tiene verdes los ojos
> y violeta la voz.

But the next strophe and the peripheral events it relates are of only secondary importance, and this is indicated by the use of the imperfect:

> El agua de la acequia
> iba llena de sol;
> en el olivarito
> cantaba un gorrión.

The second additional use for the imperfect is to indicate a permanent change of theme. Example:

> La Lola
> canta saetas.
> Los toreritos
> la rodean
> y el barberillo,
> desde su puerta,
> sigue los ritmos
> con la cabeza.
> Entre la albahaca
> y la hierbabuena
> la Lola canta
> saetas.
> La Lola aquella,
> que se miraba
> tanto en la alberca.
>
> («Balcón»)

Verses one through twelve describe Lola singing while surrounded by a group of admirers. So far the poem deals only with the girl's outward acts, not with her personality or motives. The last three lines (verses thirteen to fifteen), however, present a new theme: either they suggest a

---

[67] CANO BALLESTA, pp. 92-94.

possible interest in suicide, as indicated in Chapter III, or they form an ironic commentary by implying that she is apparently a vain woman who habitually admires her own image in the pond. In order to indicate this thematic change from a superficial observation of actions to a more psychologically perceptive analysis of personality, the poet has chosen a different verb tense, the imperfect.

The final use of the imperfect is in combination with the preterite to depict both a finite action and its results. For example:

> Su grito fue terrible.
> Los viejos
> dicen que se erizaban
> los cabellos,
> y se abría el azogue
> de los espejos.
> («Retrato de Silverio Franconetti»)

Silverio's cry (related in the preterite tense) produced two immediate results described in the imperfect: his listeners' hair stood on end and the mirrors shattered.

The preterite is employed frequently to portray a sudden, unexpected interruption in the flow of events, an interruption that is usually sinister. In «Retrato de Silverio Franconetti,» for example, the preterite suddenly intrudes into the smooth narration in the imperfect to introduce a fearful element implying pain or death:

> La densa miel de Italia
> con el limón nuestro,
> iba en el hondo llanto
> del siguiriyero.
> Su grito fue terrible.

This tense thus divides the poem into two opposing perspectives: those events that have emotionally positive associations and those that are emotionally negative.

The appearance of the preterite often signals a change in a poem's emotional tone, thereby creating a new poetic atmosphere, as in the following example:

> Tu entierro fue de gente
> siniestra.
> Gente con el corazón
> en la cabeza,
> que te siguió llorando
> por las callejas.
>
> («Falseta»)

Finally, as Cano Ballesta has observed, the preterite is consistently used

187

to capture the most tragic and terrible moments, and it is therefore the tense most frequently employed to portray sudden death:[68]

> Muerto se quedó en la calle
> con un puñal en el pecho.
> No lo conocía nadie.
>
> («Sorpresa»)

Zeugma. The zeugma is usually defined as a figure of speech in which a single modifier, usually a verb or an adjective, is applied to two or more words simultaneously, although it is logically appropriate for only one of them. This poetic device appears infrequently in the *Poema del Cante Jondo*. The following verses, however, provide examples:

> El puñal
> como un rayo de sol
> incendia las terribles
> hondonadas.
>
> («Puñal»)

«Incendia» is logical with «sol,» but not with «puñal.»

> Largas sombras afiladas
> vienen del turbio horizonte
>
> («Muerte de la petenera»)

«Largas» is appropriate for «sombras,» but «afiladas» is not.[69]

---

[68] *Ibid.*, p. 106.
[69] The reader will note that in this last example it is not an adjective which modifies two nouns, but rather a noun that is modified by two adjectives.

CHAPTER V

INTERACTION OF POETIC TECHNIQUES—SYNTHESIS

In this final chapter we shall show how the poetic techniques studied individually in Chapter IV function together in the creation of a poem. We have chosen as examples six poems from what we consider to be the most representative sections of the book. As we saw in Chapters I and III, the cry or *grito* of the *cantaor* is an essential element in singing the *siguiriya gitana*, for this cry is frequently used either to create or cathartically release the dramatic tension generated by the song. García Lorca declared: «la 'siguirilla' gitana comienza por un grito terible. Un grito que divide el paisaje en dos hemisferios iguales; después la voz se detiene para dejar paso a un silencio impresionante y medido.»[1] It is not surprising, therefore, to find that «El grito» from the «Poema de la siguiriya gitana» is devoted to a poetic interpretation of this cry and that it is logically placed between the guitar introduction and the composition «El silencio.» Lorca also stated: «La figura del 'cantaor' está dentro de dos grandes líneas: el arco del cielo en lo exterior, y el zig-zag que asciende dentro de su alma.»[2] This «arco del cielo» will be a key element in every image of «El grito,» and the ascending zig-zag movement will take the form of a vibrating chord. The poem begins with the verses:

> La elipse de un grito
> va de monte
> a monte

which present, through synesthesia, a perfect fusion of sight and sound as the audible cry is given a visual dimension. The first image is, in reality, an «extended image» in that it will provide the basis for the rest of the poem, because each succeding stanza, except the final one, will utilize a variation of this cry's elliptical shape as its principal element.

The image is based on a substantival metaphor, «la elipse de un grito,» which contains one symbol, *grito,* whose meaning is ambiguous. Traditionally, the cry often suggests pain, tragedy, fear, terror, or death, and indeed, it has many of these associations here. In Lorca's poetry, however, this word frequently has a positive significance in that it expresses a desire to communicate, to affirm life, and so to ward off the forces of death.[3] The *grito* is, in fact, the symbolic opposite of the

---

[1] «Arquitectura del cante jondo,» in *Obras completas* (Madrid: Aguilar, 1963), p. 57.
[2] *Ibid.,* p. 60.
[3] GUSTAVO CORREA, «El simbolismo religioso en la poesía de Federico García Lorca,» *Hispania*, XXIX, núm. 1 (1956), p. 44.

silencio that follows, for silence represents the absence of communication and a denial of the life forces.[4] It is likely that both sets of meanings are utilized in this image—the traditionally negative, folk meaning, as well as the more positive, special meaning given it by Lorca. Hence, the *grito* is actually an *emblema recreado*. Within the context of this poem, the cry creates a dramatic tension by unleashing a sensation of cosmic terror that has all the negative connotations stated above, but, at the same time, it acts as a life-asserting, cathartic release of tension [5] and a symbolic protest against these very forces. The cry represents the singer's attempt to ward off silence, to fight against death. Among the other poetic techniques employed are materialization—an essentially non-material phenomenon, the cry, acquires visual shape—and animation, since the cry seems to acquire a life-force of its own and to travel from mountain to mountain. There is also a feeling of mystery based on the unasked-unanswered question: «What has caused this cry?» This sense of mystery is further enhanced by both distance, in terms of a vast geographical area traversed by the *grito,* and a night setting. An enambement between the second and third verses speeds up the pace of these lines and contributes to the impression of swift movement. Much of the vividness of this image is due to the present tense that reduces to a minimum the psychological distance between the reader and the event described. The scene seems to be removed from the flow of time and to continue indefinitely as an extensive rather than a passing, momentary present. Finally, three sense perceptions are utilized: hearing, sight, and touch in that order of importance. The tactile sensations include the material hardness of the mountains and the kinesthetic tension produced by the piercing *grito.*

The next verses:

> Desde los olivos
> será un arco iris negro
> sobre la noche azul

present the first of the two transformations that the singer's cry will undergo, and they remind us of the reference to «la noche azul» appearing in the poet's original lecture on the *cante jondo* where he states: «. . . sus textos como sus melodías antiquísimas tienen su mejor escenario en la noche . . . en la noche azul de nuestro campo.» [6] Furthermore, the *arco iris negro* suggests the *arco del cielo* which Lorca called the first of the «grandes líneas» of the *cantaor.* Likewise, this image, with its imposing black rainbow, is equivalent to the first of the «dos hemisferios iguales» into

---

[4] CORREA, *La poesía mítica de Federico García Lorca* (Eugene: Univ. of Oregon Publications, 1957), p. 18.

[5] HOWARD T. YOUNG, «The Magic of Reality,» in *The Victorious Expression* (Madison: Univ. of Wisconsin Press, 1966), p. 157.

[6] «El cante jondo, cante primitivo andaluz,» in *Obras completas,* p. 47.

which he claimed the singer's terrible cry divided the landscape. This first «hemisphere» is of striking visual magnitude and the second will be of grandiose sound. The image conveyed here is partially an extension of the previous one in both its affective atmosphere and in its use of the cry's geometric shape. The ellipse now becomes a cosmic rainbow spanning the night sky instead of the mountains. The use of the same element creates a sense of continuity, but at the same time, it is offset by contrast. The previous verses relied primarily on auditory and secondly on visual sense perceptions, but in this image the visual, including the chromatic, is predominant. It has no auditory dimension; the scene depicted is almost completely static. The other two senses, touch (the bark and leaves of the olive trees) and taste (suggested by the olives), are of only secondary importance.

The image contains two metaphors and six symbols. The first is a substantival metaphor (*el grito* «será un arco iris») which involves synesthesia, for it gives a visual, chromatic dimension to a phenomenon of sound. But within this metaphor there is a second, an adjectival metaphor, «arco iris negro». A rainbow cannot be black, since black implies an absence of light and therefore of color. The two are interlinking in that they share a common element, the *arco iris*. This unexpected depiction of a rainbow as «black» also produces a *ruptura del sistema*. The affective significance of these verses, however, is fully understood only through an analysis of its symbols. The olive trees, an emblem, are symbolic of tragedy, and they stand as witnesses to the fullfillment of man's fate.[7] The cry, as we know, represents fear, but also a desperate wish to overcome death or the tragic fate implicit in both the *olivos* and the *siguiriya* itself. The rainbow is an emblem for hope or life, while black and night are emblems for death. Blue is an emblematic symbol for truth, innocence, hope, and illusion.[8] Thus, we may now understand the meaning of the image as follows: Above the olive trees, that stand as witnesses to the unfolding of a tragic destiny, the cry of the *cantaor* is both a cry of fear and a protest against man's preordained fate. The cry attempts to become a rainbow (hope and life), but this attempt is doomed to fail, for this rainbow will be black: it too will be overcome by death. It is therefore apparent that although the metaphors create a striking visual impression, the emotional power of the image resides in its symbols. These symbols are, in fact, the major poetic element and the metaphors are subordinate to them.

It is significant that the dynamic power of the image is a direct result of contrast between opposing symbolic elements. The rainbow and blue are symbolically opposite to night and black. The principle of

[7] LILIA V. BOSCÁN, «La muerte en la poesía de Lorca,» *AFZ*, IV, núm. 4 (1965), p. 290; CELIA S. LICHTMAN, «Federico García Lorca: A Study in Three Mythologies,» doctoral dissertation, New York University, 1965, pp. 158-159.

[8] JAROSLAW M. FLYS, *El lenguaje poético de Federico García Lorca* (Madrid: Gredos, 1955), p. 152.

dynamic contrast is complicated even further by the fact that these conflicting symbols are not grouped together in like pairs, but in contrasting pairs. Thus, we do not find the positive life symbols «rainbow» and «blue» together, nor the negative death symbol «night» joined with «black.» Instead, the rainbow is black (positive-negative sequence) and the night is blue (negative-positive order). This arrangement increases the number of points of conflict within the image and thereby adds to the emotional tension it conveys.

Of particular interest is the poet's use of the future tense which effects both the image's literal meaning and its affective qualities. The future conveys the idea that the cry will become a rainbow at some distant, unspecified time. We are suddenly transferred from the world of present realities (the present tense was the only one used until now), and we are unexpectedly told that what we are witnessing is not an actual event, but a potential one; something anticipated rather than something that is. This second stanza, like the first, involves vast spacial distance, but it also employs two additional poetic techniques: dehumanization (the human cry is compared to a rainbow) and plurivalence (a phenomenon from the human realm is converted into a phenomenon of inanimate nature).

The «¡Ay!» which follows is the poem's refrain. As a cathartic cry, it is the singer's or the poet's personal response to the foregoing scenes. It intrudes into the sequence of consecutive images and shifts the composition back to a purely auditory and kinesthetic plane. The reader now experiences the cry directly in its full auditory form, rather than through a visual medium, and this directness serves to draw him psychologically deeper into the dramatic atmosphere of the poem. The brevity and extreme condensation of this refrain intensify its dramatic qualities and prepare the way for the following verses.

In the next stanza:

> Como un arco de viola
> el grito ha hecho vibrar
> largas cuerdas del viento

the concept of the *arco* is again the basis for the image, but this time the «arco iris» has been replaced by an «arco de viola,» the cry's second transformation. The total image, however, contrasts with the previous one in two ways: its auditory aspect is of greater importance than its visual dimension, and because of its use of movement, it is dynamic rather than static. Like the first verses in the poem, it combines three sense perceptions in the following order of importance: hearing, sight, and touch (the cords under tension, the verb *vibrar,* the kinesthetic reaction to the *grito,* the feel of the wind, and the hardness of the viola bow's wood.) This strophe presents the second of the two hemispheres into which Lorca claimed the *paisaje* is divided by the singer. It is a «hemisphere» of sound in which «el zig-zag que asciende dentro del alma» of the *cantaor* is portrayed by the vibrations that move the «cuerdas del viento.»

As we saw in the preceeding chapter, the image is based on a «complex simile» comparing the cry to a viola bow. It also contains two direct metaphors, one implied metaphor, and three symbols within the metaphors. The two direct metaphors are: «the cry has made the wind vibrate,» a verbal metaphor, and «cords or strings of the wind,» a noun metaphor. The second or shorter metaphor is, of course, contained within the first. In stating that just as a viola bow makes the strings of a viola move, so the cry causes the strings of the wind to vibrate, there is the implied metaphorical comparison of the wind to a viola, since each becomes the instrument acted upon. The symbols are *arco,* which may stand for communication and the forces that assert life,[9] *grito,* whose contradictory meanings have already been discussed, and *viento,* a traditionally ambiguous emblem. *Viento* usually represents the creative life forces: fertility, virility, and communication,[10] but it can also be a symbol for the very opposite: destructive violence and death.[11] When the two symbols react together (the wind is animated by the cry), they both represent positive and negative forces simultaneously, thereby maintaining the dramatic conflict between life and death implicit in all the preceding verses.

The present perfect tense places the action in the recent past and forms an effective temporal contrast to the future used in the preceding strophe. This sudden change of verb tense has the effect of disorienting the reader, thereby increasing the level of affective tension and the mood of mystery. The realms of man and nature interact, and in the process several other poetic techniques are used: dehumanization, for a human sound *(grito)* is likened to an object *(arco de viola)*; animation, since the cry moves the cords of the wind; intervalence-plurivalence and materialization, because the cry is equated to a viola bow (both belong to the realm of man and man-made objects) and the wind becomes the strings of an instrument (something from the realm of nature crosses over into that of man-made objects). There is an enjambement between the second and third verses (between the verb and its direct object), and finally, we find a pervasive feeling of mystery resulting from an unasked-unanswerer question regarding the cry's origin and meaning.

The final image:

(Las gentes de las cuevas
asoman sus velones)

acts as a concluding epilogue to the preceding drama in that the inhabitants of the surrounding countryside hold up their lanterns to see what has happened. The image is unusual because it is composed exclusive-

---

[9] YOUNG, *op. cit.*, p. 157.

[10] CORREA, *La poesía mítica*, p. 12; LICHTMAN, *op. cit.*, pp. 49, 181.

[11] JUAN EDUARDO CIRLOT, *Diccionario de símbolos* (Barcelona: Editorial Labor, 1969), p. 476; LICHTMAN, *op. cit.*, p. 201; MARÍA TERESA BABIN, *García Lorca, vida y obra* (New York: Las Américas Pblg. Co., 1955), p. 69.

13

ly of symbols, three of which are present and the fourth implied. The *gentes* are Gypsies who, in Lorca's poetry, often represent mankind in general or tragic fate.[12] *Cuevas* is a death symbol, an *ataúd en vida*.[13] The *velón* suggests death since it is frequently placed at the head of a corpse during a wake.[14] Finally, there is an implied silence in these verses which are enclosed in parentheses precisely to indicate a diminished tone or semi-stillness. Since silence is also a death symbol, it becomes the antithesis of the *grito,* when the latter represents communication and life. But because silence is not actually mentioned, it is an implied element, although paradoxically, it may be the most important symbol used. In this concluding stanza the *grito* is no longer heard; only death associated words are present. Silence has won and the next phase of the «Poema de la siguiriya gitana» will be called «El silencio» precisely because the struggle between the forces of life and death seems to be resolved at last in favor of the latter. The poem then closes with a final *¡Ay!* of defeat and despair.

Contrast has an important function in this part of the poem. The entire image is in contrast to the preceding verses in that it relies primarily on visual preception rather than on auditory sensations. Secondly, there is the visual contrast within the image between the darkness of the landscape and the brightness of the glowing lanterns. Finally, there is a symbolic contrast between the implied silence and the *grito* that dominates the rest of the poem.

The parentheses serve not only to create a diminished tone and an impression of stillness, but they also perform the same function as a stage direction in a play. Roberto Yahni claims, in fact: «'El Grito' es un microdrama presentado 'in medias res.' . . . El paréntesis que encierra la acotación nos sugiere este drama trunco, por una parte, y por otra realza la nota de misterio con lo que podría interpretarse como una referencia a los movimientos de supuestos actores, testigos mudos de la tragedia.»[15] The poet again evokes a sense of mystery by means of a new unasked-unanswered question: «What do these people see?» Although we never learn the answer, we suspect that what the lanterns reveal confirms the triumph of death.

In conclusion, the poem has a definite, well marked structure consisting of an introduction, a first phase, a second phase, and an ending, with the refrain «¡Ay!» serving as an affective commentary on the scenes described. The two principal images describe two «hemispheres» (one visual, the other primarily auditory) into which the poet claims the landscape of the *siguiriya gitana* is divided. There is also a fluctuation in the use of verb tenses. The poem opens with the present indicative, follows with the future, moves back to the present perfect, and finally returns to the present to complete a kind

---

[12] Arturo Barea, *Lorca, the Poet and his People* (London: Faber and Faber, 1941), p. 122.

[13] Correa, *La poesía mítica,* p. 17.

[14] Young, *op. cit.,* p. 158.

[15] «Algunos rasgos formales en la lírica de García Lorca: función del paréntesis,» *Bulletin Hispanique,* LXVI, núm. 1-2 (1964), p. 110.

of temporal cycle. A technique of alternating sense perceptions is also apparent. The first strophe is primarily auditory, the second visual, the third auditory, and the fourth visual. Finally, the poem shows a clear dramatic development: Its opening image establishes a dynamic tension and balance between the forces of life and death through the use of an ambiguous symbol, the cry, that connotes both simultaneously. This conflict grows more intense in the two subsequent images as the life-asserting symbols struggle for dominance over those denying life, but it concludes with the eventual victory of death.

The next poem chosen for analysis is from the «Poema de la soleá.» *Soleá* is actually an Andalusian, regional pronunciation of *soledad,* meaning loneliness, a highly appropriate title for this poem. «La soleá» is one of the few compositions in which the poet utilizes the actual metrical form of the *cante* in addition to evoking its mood of contemplative melancholy and stoic resignation. The musical *soleá* is normally written in octosyllabic tercets with the first and third verses rhyming in assonance. The first line of the initial tercet becomes the refrain and is repeated before each succeding stanza. These characteristic are strictly maintained throughout this composition.

The first tercet presents the *soleá* as a woman dressed in black robes who reflects upon the insignificance of the world when compared to the human heart:

> Vestida con mantos negros,
> piensa que el mundo es chiquito
> y el corazón es inmenso.

The image is based on three metaphors: «Vestida con mantos negros» (the song has been transformed into a woman), «el mundo es chiquito,» and «el corazón es inmenso.» Each contains one symbol: *negros,* an emblem representing death, tragedy, or mourning; *mundo,* which stands for human society, or simply, that which is outside the individual; and *corazón,* an emblem symbolizing not only love, but the spiritual-emotional in general. The first is a verbal metaphor, but the second and third are adjectival metaphors formed by interchanging the two adjectives that would logically modify *mundo* and *corazón.* This unexpected exchange not only converts what would be literal statements of fact into metaphoric statements, but it also produces a *ruptura del sistema* in that it introduces an unexpeced element into a logically anticipated sequence of nouns and adjectives.

Contrast is extremely important in this image, for not only is *mundo* contrasted to *corazón,* and *chiquito* to *inmenso,* but each noun is contrasted to its modifying adjective. The verses seem to express, through symbols, the idea that the world, external reality, or the rest of human society is of little importance, or is possibly indifferent to the individual whose emotions are of much greater magnitude. The image utilizes materialization and personification. A non-material element, the song of the *soleá,* is transformed poetically into a woman. This metaphorical change also involves intervalance in that a human creation, a song, becomes a human being. As Andrew Debicki has pointed out, personification adds a dramatic, vital element and creates an illusion of reality that would otherwise be lacking if the ideas expressed by the song had remained only musical abstractions.[16] The image is perceived by sight (black robes, world, heart, relative size conveyed by the adjectives *chiquito* and *inmenso*) and touch (the texture of the robes, the relative hardness and softness implicit in *mundo* and *corazón* respectively).

The diminutive *chiquito* has a special poetic function. Apart from its obvious use as the antithesis of *inmenso,* the *-ito* ending causes the symbol it modifies to stand out. It intensifies the notion of smallness already inherent in *chico* and therefore makes the contrast between the noun and the adjective much more emphatic. Secondly, the diminutive adds a colloquial, familiar tone to the image, reminiscent of the basic folk origin of the *soleá*. Finally, there is a sense of mystery resulting from the unasked-unanswered question of why this woman is dressed in black robes, and what has caused her pensive, even somber frame of mind.

The refrain «Vestida con mantos negros,»[17] repeated after each tercet, provides a reaffirmation of the emotions associated with the black robes. Since the first two stanzas are more concerned with conveying her stoic, philosophical attitude towards life than in directly depicting her emotions, the refrain acts as an emotional element suggesting an undefined tragedy, and it serves as a balance to the intellectual cast of these strophes. It also intimates repeatedly the presence of death, a force lurking just outside the emotional perimeter of each image.

The second tercet continues the personified *soleá*'s thoughts and gives additional emphasis to their stoic content:

> Piensa que el suspiro tierno
> y el grito desaparecen
> en la corriente del viento.

It contains three emblematic symbols: *suspiro tierno,* which we believe represents love rather than sadness, *grito,* which in this poem stands for pain, grief, or suffering, and *corriente del viento,* suggestive not so much of a life or a death force—its usual meanings—but rather, the inevitable passage of time or eternity. These verses imply that all human emotions from happiness to sorrow are dissipated by time. The first two emblems

---

[16] «Federico García Lorca: Estilización y visión de la poesía,» in *Estudios sobre poesía española contemporánea* (Madrid: Gredos, 1968), p. 206.

[17] According to Daniel Devoto, this particular refrain comes directly from a popular folk song. See his «Notas sobre el elemento tradicional en la obra de García Lorca,» *Filología,* Año II, núm. 3 (1950), p. 318.

utilize metonymy in that the abstract concepts love and grief are represented by two of their manifestations, a tender sigh and a scream. Since an entire range of human emotions is suggested by these two extremes, there is a synecdoche in that the whole is symbolized by two of its parts.

The image employs three sense perceptions, the principal one of which is hearing. Sound is conveyed by the symbols *suspiro, grito,* and *viento.* Sensations of touch are implicit in *viento* and in the kinesthetic relaxation and tension associated with *suspiro* and *grito* respectively. The *corriente del viento* imparts a visual perception of rapid movement that lends a more dynamic quality to the image, and this sensation is enhanced by the enjambement between the second and third verses. Contrast is again an extremely important element. This tercet depends largely on auditory sensations, whereas the first stanza was primarily visual. Furthermore, there is a contrast between the positive symbolic associations of *suspiro* and the negative implications of *grito* and between the opposing kinesthetic sensations they convey. Finally, there exists a marked difference in their respective auditory volumes.

The last tercet:

> Se dejó el balcón abierto,
> y al alba por el balcón
> desembocó todo el cielo

is based on the verbal metaphor «desembocó todo el cielo,» but there are also two symbols which are subject to conflicting interpretations. According to Gustavo Correa, both *balcón* and *abierto* are common Lorca symbols for communication and freedom.[18] Consequently, we are tempted to see similar positive associations in *alba,* the time at which the blackness of night, a death symbol, is replaced by light, and in *cielo,* whose vast expanse also suggests freedom. This analysis would seem to indicate that the poem ends on a positive note, for at dawn the light flows into the room behind the balcony, dispelling the shadows, and replacing the somber, melancholy mood of the *soleá* with a feeling of optimism. But such an interpretation would be in direct contrast to the pessimistic, somber attitude expressed in all the preceding verses. Furthermore, the intensified cry, « ¡Ay yayayayay, / que vestida con mantos negros! » that immediately follows would not make sense, since this cry is clearly one of increased rather than diminished anguish. Evidently, the arrival of dawn in this final tercet, far from being a positive event, is a cause for greater despair.

We suggest that this *soleá* is both a song sung at a Gypsy wake and that, through personification, its mood has been identified from the outset

[18] *La poesía mítica,* pp. 11-12.

with the dead man's widow, dressed in the black robes of mourning.[19] The verses of the *cante,* whose tone has been one of stoic resignation, are her thoughts as she struggles to accept the inevitability of death and to resist succumbing to her grief. When the dawn arrives the song ceases; the wake is over and the widow's realization that the burial must inevitably follow produces her final cry of angush. This interpretation not only accounts for the increased emotion in the refrain's final repetition, but it also explains both the title, meaning loneliness, and the reason for the philosophical mood of the first two tercets. In fact, the widow's thoughts seem to form a progression. In the first stanza she seems preoccupied with a grief that is all encompassing. In the second strophe she has turned to a kind of stoic, philosophical rumination on grief mitigated by time (grief self-spent) or, perhaps, to the *tempus fugit* theme of her marriage having lasted but the time involved in a gust of wind. In the third tercet she directs her attention to her present state and her immediate future. The arrival of dawn might imply a demand that the living return to the living, a thought that prompts her anguished cry. It is apparent that the meaning of the poem is fully clarified only in the last tercet and that many of the symbols appearing in the preceding verses, like the *mantos negros, corazón inmenso, suspiro, grito,* and *corriente del viento,* are, in reality, *signos de sugestión* forming a consistent chain of indicators that culminates in the cry of despair in the concluding lines.

These final verses make use of animation, since an inanimate object (the sky) seems to acquire life and enter the room, and its component objects are experienced by sight and touch. The subsequent refrain, however, provides two additional sensations: hearing and kinesthetic tension, both conveyed by the woman's cry. Three kinds of contrast appear in this stanza: (1) Whereas a probable night setting was intended in each of the preceding tercets, the closing lines describe the arrival of dawn. (2) The preterite tense forms a contrast to the present indicative, used exclusively until the third image. This shift in verb tense produces a sudden, unexpected interruption in the succession of thoughts passing through the woman's mind, and it introduces a new event that changes the poem's affective atmosphere. (3) The woman's apparent surrender to despair is in contrast to the stoic resignation that characterized her feelings before.

«Saeta,» a part of the «Poema de la saeta,» does not attempt, except in the refrain, to imitate either the metrical form or the fervent religious content of a genuine *saeta.* As we noted in Chapters I and III, the lyrics of this traditional song are normally a devotional commentary on the sufferings of Christ or the Virgin or on various events in their lives. García

---

[19] «La soleá» immediatly follows «Sorpresa,» whose theme is expressed in the opening lines: «Muerto se quedó / en la calle / con un puñal en el pecho.» «La soleá,» depicting a widow's mourning, seems to be a sequel to this death scene.

Lorca's poem, however, is a description of the float carrying a statue of Christ rather than a recreation of the song addressed to him.

The first image:

> Cristo moreno
> pasa
> de lirio de Judea
> a clavel de España

is based on a verbal metaphor in which Christ is transformed (passes) from the lily of Judea to the carnation of Spain, and the enjambement between each of its four verses tends to reinforce the idea of rapid change. This poetic transformation, however, may not be original with Lorca who may have borrowed it from Spanish popular tradition. According to Gino Rizzo, many traditional *saetas* utilize this theme, although Lorca has apparently reversed the usual pattern in presenting first the *lirio* and then the *clavel*: «Pero el cambio de 'lirio' a 'clavel' es también popular, aunque interpretado por Lorca exactamente al revés:

> En el portal de Belén
> nació un clavel encarnado
> que, por redimir al mundo,
> se ha vuelto lirio morado.

Es que los atributos de 'lirio' y 'clavel' se dan con frecuencia, sea a Cristo, sea a la Virgen.» [20]

In Lorca's poem this metaphor contains two actual symbols or emblems, *lirio* and *clavel*, and two implied symbolic emblems, the presumed white-red colors of these flowers. We must admit, however, that these colors are merely an assumption, since the poet does not specify the kind of lily and carnation he has in mind. The white lily is a common religious emblem for purity, chastity,[21] serenity,[22] and for the death-resurrection cycle, since most of its species perish after the blooming season and are «resurrected» the following year. Consequently, the lily would seem to be opposite to the red carnation, a religious and folk emblem for passion, virility, and love.[23] Based solely on the symbolic meanings of these flowers, the image appears to represent Christ as a figure in whom the pure, ethereal qualities of the lily are contrasted to the passionate, human attributes of the carnation. However, this apparent contrast may not be entirely valid, for the lily sometimes has meanings that are similar to those of the carnation. For example, Celia Lichtman states:

> The lily is utilized by the poet in a completely traditional manner as a religious symbol and in its dual aspect as flower of desire and death. It is

[20] «Poesía de Federico García Lorca y poesía popular,» *Clavileño*, VI, 36 (1955), p. 50.
[21] GEORGE FERGUSON, *Signs and Symbols in Christian Art* (New York: Oxford Univ. Press, 1954), p. 41.
[22] FLYS, *op. cit.*, p. 155.
[23] *Ibid.*, p. 154; FERGUSON, *op. cit.*, p. 34.

one of the flowers of the Virgin, appearing in pictorial representations of the major events in her life, especially the Annunciation . . . In addition to its traditional religious role, the lily has always been indicated as a flower of desire similar to the spikenard and carnation. The blossoms' shape emphasize this by transforming it into a phallic symbol . . . The sexual power of the lily is always either implicit or stated.[24]

Carlos Ramos-Gil feels that Lorca uses the lily as a negative symbol. For him it signifies suffering or frustration.[25]

The search for the exact meaning of these flowers is complicated further by the fact that their implied colors have a symbolic meaning of their own. White not only symbolizes the soul and purity; it can also represent grief and tragedy.[26] Red frequently suggests not only life and love,[27] but passion, violence, and bloodshed. Combining the symbolic significance of the flowers with their colors, the image now seems to portray an ethereal but suffering Christ of the lily who is not so much contrasted to, as combined with the passionate and agonizing Christ of the carnation. Such an interpretation is, of course, consistent with Christian tradition which considers him to be a harmonious and perfect combination of the godly and the human. The color emblems, therefore, tend to complement and extend the various meanings of these two flowers and to diminish considerably the aparent symbolic opposition between them. When combined with their theoretical colors, the two flowers become «complex symbols» in that they acquire a new symbolic meaning they did not have previously. The reader should be aware, however, of a dissenting viewpoint—that of Edward E. Stanton to whom these flowers and their respective colors may be nothing more than a reference to Christ's blood (carnation) against his pale skin.[28] The final color, *moreno,* is not necessarily a symbol, but since it is dark, it does suggest a foreboding of death,[29] the crucifixion. This kind of association may not have been intended, however, because Christ is normally depicted as *moreno* in the folk art of Andalusia.[30]

It is significant, furthermore, that the flowers are the *lirio de Judea* and the *clavel de España.* This association with specific countries may be taken to mean that those qualities of spirituality and passion attributed respectively to the lily and the carnation are symbolic of the character, national temperament, or religious attributes of the two nations. It is also possible, as Carl Cobb observes, that these flowers suggest the contrast

---

[24] *Op. cit.,* pp. 150, 152.
[25] *Ecos antiguos, estructuras nuevas y mundo primario en la lírica de Lorca* (Bahía Blanca, Argentina: Cuadernos del Sur, 1967), p. 73.
[26] FLYS, *op. cit.,* pp. 159, 28.
[27] *Ibid.,* p. 152.
[28] «Federico García Lorca and *Cante Jondo,*» Diss. Univ. of Calif., Los Angeles, 1972, p. 167.
[29] CORREA regards *morado* as a sign of fatality, death. See his reference to it in *La poesía mítica,* p. 8.
[30] GINO RIZZO, *Op. cit.,* p. 50.

between the asceticism of original Christianity and the sensuousness of Catholicism as practiced in Seville.[31]　When Christ «passes» from Judea, he leaves behind the qualities of the lily and becomes, to the Spaniards, the flesh and blood, living Christ of the carnation.

These verses, which join the realms of the supernatural, man, and nature, utilize disdivination and plurivalence, insomuch as a supernatural and divine figure, Christ, is identified with objects of the natural world, and two objects of nature, the lily and the carnation, are equated with things of the human realm, the nations Judea and Spain.　The image combines sensations of sight, touch, and smell.　It also utilizes contrast in that the lily, as we nave seen, forms in some respects a possible contrast to the carnation, and white and red are partially opposed in their symbolic meanings.　Furthermore, the supposed religious attitudes of Judea and Spain may be contrasted with each other.　This image forms the basis of the entire poem, for the rest of the composition is really an extension or further description of some of the objects mentioned here.　Thus, it may be considered an «extended image.»

The next verse, «¡Miradlo por donde viene!», is a refrain taken from the popular *saetas* in which the expression *míralo* or *miradlo por donde viene* is frequently the introductory line.　Rizzo summerizes Lorca's special use of this refrain as follows:

> En cuanto al verso «¡Miradlo por donde viene!», con que empieza un sinnúmero de saetas, observaremos solamente que Lorca, abandonando la estructura y el metro tradicional de las saetas populares, lo utiliza de una manera libre y original, poniéndolo en el centro de su poesía y aislándolo para que adquiera una mayor carga emocional. La repetición final del verso ligeramente variado, que en otros casos es preciosista y artificiosa, completa aquí, de una manera sencilla y eficaz, la visión del paso que se aleja:

> ¡Miradlo por donde va! [32]

This verse gives a musical character to the composition, and it signifies the approach of Christ's statue which will be described at the conclusion of the poem.　It thus prepares the reader for an event that is to follow.

The next image begins with the same words that ended the preceding strophe:

> De España.
> Cielo limpio y oscuro,
> tierra tostada,
> y cauces donde corre
> muy lenta el agua.

The period after the first verse creates a break in the rhythm, and it appears

---

[31] *Federico García Lorca* (New York:　Twayne Publishers, 1967), p. 49.
[32] *Op. cit.*, p. 50.

to function like a colon since a definition or amplification follows. In fact, the entire image seeks to define Spain through a simultaneously realistic and symbolic depiction of its landscape. In this description, the poet seems to counterbalance those words that have positive, life supporting connotations—*cielo, tierra,* and *agua*—against those conveying negative associations—*tostada, corre muy lenta,* and *oscuro*—which represent aridity, the slowing of the life forces, and death. But these symbols are not without ambiguity, for the *cielo* is not only *limpio,* «clear,» but *oscuro,* «dark» as well. The *tierra,* usually associated with fertility, the life instinct, and the womb, is *tostada*—sterile, without life. Even *agua,* the life force, moves slowly and therefore suggests possible stagnation and death.

Contrast is unquestionably one of the most important poetic techniques in the image. By contrasting the three life symbols with three suggesting death, an effective tension is maintained between these two opposing forces. *Cielo* stands geographically in contrast to *tierra,* and *agua* implies a contrast to the dryness associated with *tierra tostada.* Like the *lirio* and *clavel* of the preceding verses, the *cielo* and *tierra* also represent a symbolic contrast between the spiritual-ethereal and the material-physical.

The image also uses «disintegration of elements» in that a whole —Spain— is analyzed into its most characteristic features, and a synedoche, since a few characteristics of the Spanish landscape represent the whole nation. There are sensations of sight and touch with the latter implied by the hardness of the *tierra tostada,* the burning sensation of its sun-baked surface, and the wetness of the water. The image also contains a possible *ruptura del sistema* in that we would expect the expression *cielo limpio y . . .* to be completed by a word like *claro,* but instead we find *oscuro,* the exact opposite of what was anticipated.

The final image returns to the theme of the first stanza, but now it describes Christ directly in terms that seem more realistic than symbolic:

> Cristo moreno,
> con las guedejas quemadas,
> los pómulos salientes
> y las pupilas blancas.

That Christ is *moreno* is probably due to the fact that the statue is carved from dark wood. The *guedejas quemadas* refer to locks of real hair singed by the candles placed around the head. The *pómulos salientes* describe a characteristic facial expression, and the *pupilas blancas* allude to the white crystals used for the statue's eyes.[33] The figure depicted here is a

---

[33] EVELYN M. V. D. FERRIS, «Federico García Lorca: A Study of the Popular and Traditional Inspiration of his Poetry,» M.A. thesis, Columbia University, 1941, p. 124.

Christ of the people, possibly of the Gypsies, since his features generally re-semble theirs. This final image utilizes a double contrast in that the statue's dark wood is contrasted to its white crystal eyes (wood vs glass, dark vs white). There are three sense perceptions: sight (the statue's features), touch (the tactile sensations of wood, hair, glass), and smell (burned or singed hair).

The poem begins with a description of Christ's statue that is largely symbolic; it then proceeds to a depiction of Spain in both symbolic and realistic terms, and it ends with a return to the initial theme, now portraying the statue in a purely realistic way. Thus, the poem displays an essentially circular structure in its thematic development, but within this circle there is a definite linear progression from symbolism to realism.

«Las seis cuerdas,» the third part of the «Gráfico de la petenera,» is an excellent example of the poet's ability to express an essentially auditory phenomenon, the music of the guitar, in terms of visual imagery that successfully conveys the mood or affective values of the music. Once again Lorca has not followed the musical *petenera*'s characteristic pattern of octosyllabic quatrains rhyming in assonance, with an extra verse inter-polated between the third and fourth lines. There are no clearly defined stanzas in «Las seis cuerdas.» The poem consists of a two verse introduc-tion followed by two, four and five line segments, each of which forms a sin-gle image. Assonance it not used; the meter is irregular, ranging from three to eight syllables per line, and no attempt is made to utilize the *petenera*'s traditional themes. The poem is, instead, a highly original composition that presents a series of random associations evoked solely by the haunting music of the guitar.

The introductory verses:

> La guitarra
> hace llorar a los sueños

constitute an «extended image» insofar as they introduce the guitar, the key element that will form the basis of both succeeding images. These initial lines are a verbal metaphor that contains two contrasting symbols: *guitarra,* a sinister object which, in Lorca's poetry, usually represents grief, pain, or death,[34] and *sueños,* an emblem that stands for hope, illusion, and aspiration. Much of the poetic effect is based on personification. The guitar acts like a human agent and causes sorrow and weeping; even dreams weep like human beings. The reader should note that not only in these two verses, but throughout the entire poem the presence of the guitar player

---

[34] CORREA, *La poesía mítica,* p. 9.

will be deliberately suppressed in order to increase the dramatic-poetic role of the instrument which is forced to act as its own personified agent. The sense perceptions include sight, hearing, and touch (the kinesthetic tension implied in *llorar* as well as the feel of the guitar's wood). Of particular importance are the auditory sensations produced by *llorar* and by the implied guitar music transformed into weeping. This conversion of sound involves a form of intervalence since both auditory phenomena pertain to the human realm. An aura of mystery is created by the unasked-unanswered question of why the music should have this effect.

The first of the two principal segments is a partial extension of the introductory verses:

> El sollozo de las almas
> perdidas
> se escapa por su boca
> redonda.

This image contains two substantival metaphors: music equals the sobbing of lost souls, and the round opening in the guitar equals a mouth. The first may be a symbolic metaphor in that the entire phase «el sollozo de las almas / perdidas» may be a symbol for lost illusions, dashed hopes, despair, etc. suggested by the music. The human realm (guitar) combines with the supernatural-spiritual realm represented by «lost souls,» whose presence increases the emotional-dramatic qualities of the poem and heightens its sense of mystery. Both divinization and personification occur because the guitar music has become the sobbing of souls who dwell in an infernal, supernatural place, and the instrument's opening is now a human mouth. These metaphorical comparisons involve intervalence and pluri-valence: A man-made object and its sound are equated with human and supernatural phenomena. Antonomasia is also present since the music is designated by one of its qualities, its sobbing sound. Enjambements occur between the first and second, and the third and fourth verses. The sense perceptions are conveyed visually (the mouth of the guitar and the movement indicated by «se escapa»), audibly (the sobbing), and tactually (the kinesthetic tension suggested by sobbing.)

The next image, the high point of the poem, is structurally one of the most complex images in the *Poema del Cante Jondo*:

> Y como la tarántula
> teje una gran estrella
> para cazar suspiros,
> que flotan en su negro
> aljibe de madera.

Just as a tarantula weaves a web to ensnare its prey floating on the surface of a cistern, so the guitar creates a musical spell that entraps the listeners' emotions as they respond to the music. In other words, these verses evoke and interrelate two kinds of reality: the literal, physical reality of a tarantula and its web,[35] and poetic reality, represented by the guitar and its music. The point of contact between them is the simile «como una tarántula,» which directly compares the guitar to the spider. Having established this connection between the two series of phenomena, the rest of the image forges a chain of comparisons between the various elements in each series.

A careful analysis reveals that in addition to the «complex simile,» which is the basis of the image, there are five direct metaphors, two implied metaphors, and three symbols incorporated as additional poetic elements. The stated metaphors are: (1) the guitar weaves a star (a verbal metaphor); (2) to hunt with a star (substantival metaphor); (3) to hunt for sighs (substantival metaphor); (4) sighs that float (verbal metaphor); (5) the guitar's circular opening equals a wood cistern (substantival metaphor which, as we shall see, is also a symbolic metaphor.) In all likelihood, the first and second metaphors are *visiones* because in each the guitar is described as performing an unreal, non-logical, or irrational function. It is significant that these metaphors not only follow one another in succession, but four of them are conjoined by means of link words. The metaphor chain produced in this fashion is: «teje una gran estrella» — *estrella* «para cazar» — *cazar* «suspiros» — *suspiros* «que flotan.» This use of interlinking metaphors produces a concise, compact total image that is esthetically quite rich, since it allows for a great metaphorical density within the space of a few lines. In stating that the guitar weaves a star just like a tarantula weaves a web, there is the implied equation between star and web. But since this comparison, based on a possible visual similarity between the two objects, is not made directly, it constitutes an implied metaphor. Similarly, there is an implied equivalency between *suspiros* and a tarantula's prey since both are trapped in the web. The three symbols are: *estrella*, an *emblema recreado* which represents the enchanting spell of the music, as well as the ideal or that which is beautiful,[36] enigmatic, and mysterious;[37] *suspiros*, an emblem symbolizing the sorrow, sadness, or tragedy that characterize the music; and *negro aljibe*, a death symbol. The *aljibe* has this meaning for three reasons: its black color suggests as association with death; since it is located within the earth, it has a connection with the sinister, telluric forces that are so much a part of Lorca's Andalusian poetry;[38] this same object referred to here as an *aljibe* (the circular opening in the guitar) was depicted in the preceding image as an infernal realm to the dead, a repository of sobbing, lost souls. Each of these symbols is structurally within a metaphor. This image is partially an extension of the previous one in that it uses some of the same elements:

[35] The logical objection that tarantulas do not weave webs is hardly relevant since we are dealing with a poetic fantasy.

[36] DEBICKI, *op. cit.*, p. 207.

[37] FLYS, *op. cit.*, p. 169.

[38] J. M. AGUIRRE, «El sonambulismo de Federico García Lorca,» *Bulletin of Hispanic Studies*, XLIV, 4 (1967), p. 283; ENRIQUE MARTÍNEZ LÓPEZ, «Aljibe y surtidor o la Granada de Federico García Lorca,» *La Torre*, X, 40 (1962), p. 35.

the music, which has been converted from *sollozos* to *suspiros,* and the round opening of the guitar, which has become an *aljibe* instead of a *boca.* There is an effective triple contrast in the symbols *estrella* and *aljibe.* The words suggest opposing geographical locations (heaven and the sub-surface of the earth), contrasting colors (white and black), and opposite (positive-negative) emotional associations.

Intervalence is present in that one object of nature (a spider's web) is equated with another natural object (a star), and a man-made object (the round opening in the guitar) is equivalent to another man-made object (a cistern). There is also plurivalence since several objects or phenomena from the human realm are equated with objects of nature: the guitar equals a tarantula; its music becomes a star; and human sighs are compared to a tarantula's prey. Materialization is used in converting the abstract enchantment of the music into a star, in transforming the non-material sighs into material objects that float and can be caught, and in changing sheer darkness into a cylindrical container. The image utilizes animation in that a normally inanimate phenomenon, the guitar or its music, weaves and hunts like a tarantula, and dehumanization, for human sighs are equated with insects caught in a web.

These verses also contain two examples of a *ruptura del sistema. Teje* is not followed by an expected word like *telaraña or encantamiento,* but by *estrella.* Similarly, the *suspiros* following *cazar* are an unexpected direct object. An enjambement exists between the penultimate and the final verses, and there are three sense perceptions: sight, hearing, and touch. The contrasting light and darkness implied by the opposite celestial-terrestrial spheres *(estrella—negro aljibe)* are particularity significant in creating a mood of eeriness and mystery. In fact, the sense of mystery and dramatic tension implicit in all the preceding images attain their maximum development here. The overtones of tragedy or death, inherent before in *llorar, sollozo,* and *almas perdidas,* now become a material as well as an emotional reality that takes the concrete form of a tarantula preparing to hunt is prey in a black cistern.

«Retrato de Silverio Franconetti,» the first poem in the «Viñetas flamencas,» is not so much a portrait of the singer as of his song. Our analysis reveals that the poem develops in three essential stages of eight verses each. The first stage, which is divided into two, four line segments, is a general recollection of his singing style. It begins by asking (verses 1-4) and then answering (lines 5-8) a basic question:

> Entre italiano
> y flamenco,
> ¿cómo cantaría
> aquel Silverio?

> La densa miel de Italia
> con el limón nuestro
> iba en el hondo llanto
> del siguiriyero.

The key symbols, *italiano* and *flamenco,* are expanded or changed to «la densa miel de Italia» and «el limón nuestro.» «Italiano» may refer to the melodious, pleasant, or even operatic qualities of his voice, whereas «flamenco» and «limón nuestro» probably represent the strident, piercing intensity of his cry while singing the *siguiriya gitana* in which he was a specialist. In short, Silverio's personal style fused the melodic qualities of Italian music with the bitter mode of the Spanish *cante jondo. Italiano* and *flamenco* may also refer, however, to his mixed parentage, since his father was Italian and his mother, Spanish.[39] An obvious contrast exists in the symbolic meanings of *italiano—flamenco* and *miel—limón,* and the latter pair of words has contrasting taste sensations as well. These symbols are, of course, part of a metaphor using both integration of elements and dematerialization. Italian honey and Spanish lemon are integrated in the deep cry of the singer, but at the same time, these two solid objects become non-material phenomena because they are transformed into sound. There is also a synecdoche in that the entire range of Silverio's singing is represented by its melodiousness and stridency. All of the physical senses are utilized in these verses. Intervalence and plurivalence are present in that one human phenomenon, the *llanto,* is made equivalent to another, Silverio's song, and two objects of nature, honey and lemon, are converted into a human phenomenon, the singer's *hondo llanto.* Finally, an enjambement occurs between the first and second, the third and fourth, and the seventh and eight verses.

The next group of eight lines—the poem's second phase—is introduced by a statement in the preterite tense: «Su grito fue terrible.» This use of the preterite denotes a sudden, unexpected interruption. It presents a new affective reality that abruptly shatters and contrasts with the generally placid recollection of Silverio's singing developed in the previous eight verses. It introduces a new aspect of his style: its jarring, over-whelming power. This verse acts, in fact, like a dividing line between the previous part, whose emotional atmosphere was positive, and the next section whose affective tone will generally be negative.

This phase of the poem, which describes the effects of Silverio's cry on his audience and on the physical milieu surrounding him, seems to develop on an emotional plane dominated by a mysterious force Lorca called the *duende,* and which he defined in his lecture «Teoría y juego del duende» as a dark, telluric power that provides the true basis for all art: «La llegada del duende presupone siempre un cambio radical en todas las formas sobre planos viejos, da sensaciones de frescura totalmente inéditas . . . el duende no llega si no ve posibilidad de muerte . . . el duende hiere, y en la curación de esta herida, que no se cierra nunca, está lo insólito, lo inventado de la

---

[39] Julián Pemartín, *El cante flamenco: guía alfabética* (Madrid: Afrodisio Aguado, 1966), p. 147.

obra de un hombre.» [40] This second part of the poem does indeed involve a «cambio radical en todas las formas» and, as we shall see, there is in most of its images that implication of death so essential for the *duende's* appearance. We believe it extremely likely that the middle section of this poem represents an attempt to convey, through three startling images, this essential, creative force in Silverio's singing. The *grito* may, in fact, be considered a symbol for the demoniac force of the *duende*.

The next seven verses can be divided into three images:

> Los viejos
> dicen que se erizaban
> los cabellos,
> y se abría el azogue
> de los espejos.
> Pasaba por los tonos
> sin romperlos.

The first image (lines 1-3) is actually a «symbolic metaphor» depicting fear or the presence of the uncanny, possibly the awesome *duende*. In conveying a sensation of horror, it provides a rare example of a metaphor that is also a symbol for an affective state. The second part (verses 4-5) is based on a verbal metaphor that shows the effect of Silverio's cry on the physical environment of a cafe in which he is singing. The cry first appears as a discordant, intrusive element producing a jarring dissonance as it pierces the mirrors. But then in lines 6-7 it becomes a harmonious aspect of the song, as it blends into the music «passing through the tones without breaking them.» The sensations of fear and violence that predominated before give way to calm. These two concluding verses form a transitional image that prepares for the third and final phase of the poem, which will be characterized by a return to an atmosphere of peaceful tranquility. The verb tenses have an unusually important function in these images. The preterite, as we saw, introduced a new affective reality, Silverio's *grito terrible*. The imperfect tense then describes the results of this new phenomenon, and it slows the pace of the description in order to allow the reader to absorb it more completely.

Contrast is present on various levels: between the emotional tone of this phase of the poem and the preceding one; between the implications of violence inherent in the first two images and the impression of tranquility conveyed by the last two verses; between the kinesthetic sensations of tension («. . . se erizaban / los cabellos») and relaxation («Pasaba por los tonos»). Finally, there seems to be an essential contrast between the world of the song within which the cry functions as an integral, harmonious element, and the world of the audience where it is an intruding phenomenon producing a violent, dissonant effect. The

[40] *Obras completas,* pp. 113, 117.

other poetic techniques appearing in this section of the «Retrato» include: triple sense perceptions (sight, hearing, touch), enjambement, animation (the inanimate *cabellos* and *azogue* seems to act on their own), and a feeling of mystery.

The poem's final section is composed of two, four line stanzas:

> Y fue un creador
> y un jardinero.
> Un creador de glorietas
> para el silencio.

> Ahora su melodía
> duerme con los ecos.
> Definitiva y pura.
> ¡Con los últimos ecos!

Once again the preterite tense indicates a transition to another phase characterized by a different affective reality, psychologically removed from the previous scenes of tension and fear. But in these verses the preterite also suggests finality and a quality that was unique. Its eulogistic tone is in marked contrast to most of the second section, although the feeling of subdued tranquility had been prepared by the two preceding lines.

The first quatrain has two distinct parts, with the second (lines 3-4) amplifying the statement made in the first (verses 1-2). The total image expresses the idea that Silverio Franconetti was a creative artist, and he was a «gardener» in that what he «planted,» flourished. In point of fact, his style of singing was renowned in his day, and it produced many followers after he became the most prestigious singer of the *cante jondo* of his generation.[41] And Silverio was a «creator of bowers for silence,» a substantival metaphor which can be interpreted to mean that by means of his art he was able to create something that would contain, in the sense of give permanence to, his song which has now been reduced to silence. The image, therefore, would seem to deal with how the artist, through his art, overcomes the limitations imposed by death. Andrew Debicki believes, in fact, that this and the following image specifically treat the problem of art and the artist vis-à vis death:

> El papel específico del artista en este esfuerzo por superar a la muerte se indica en «Retrato de Silverio Franconetti,» . . . Aunque el cantaor y hasta su melodía ya no están directamente presentes en el mundo, la pureza y la cualidad definitiva del canto de Silverio lo relaciona con la naturaleza (Silverio es «jardinero»), despierta ecos en el mundo, y ahora motiva la crea-

---

[41] RICARDO MOLINA and ANTONIO MAIRENA, *Mundo y formas del cante flamenco* (Madrid: Revista de Occidente, 1963), pp. 58-59.

ción de un poema. El arte pasado del *cantaor* ha suscitado y se ha entablado con el arte presente del poeta; los valores de su canto y de su visión no se han perdido por completo. Este poema indica, por lo tanto, las posibilidades del arte para preservar los valores humanos, y sugiere un tema que aparecerá frecuentemente en la obra posterior de Lorca.[42]

Thus, the *glorietas* appear to be a symbol for the art that preserves his now silenced song. However, since *silencio* is a common Lorcan symbol for death or tragedy,[43] the metaphor may signify that Silverio was a creator of new styles *(glorietas)* for expressing the traditional themes of the *cante,* that he was an innovator of a new style of *cante grande.* This interpretation finds support in historical fact, for he was renowned as a singer who not only had mastered all forms of the *cante,* but who expanded it to include many new types of songs.[44] It is also possible to interpret the verses: «Un creador de glorietas / para el silencio» to indicate that Silverio was a master of the dynamics of silence, that he knew how to use it effectively to enhance the sound of his voice or the lyrics of his songs. The reader will recall that silence is an important factor in the performance of the *siguiriya gitana,* of which Silverio was, perhaps, the leading interpreter in his day.

The last four lines form an epilogue separated from the preceding verses by double spacing to indicate a pause. In this case, the pause increases the solemn tone of the foregoing strophe. The theme is again Silverio's art which triumphs over death; the purity and definitive quality of his style still linger in the last echoes. The use of periods after the sixth and seventh verses slows the tempo of the image and brings the poem to a close with a gradual diminuendo. The impression of finality, evoked by the preterite tense in the preceding image, is continued here, even though the verb is now in the present. Paradoxically, it is precisely the use of the present tense which reinforces this feeling, because it tends to fix the action in a continuous present, in an unending reality that is extensive rather than momentary and passing. The finality of the past becomes permanent by being part of the continuing present.

There are several other poetic techniques employed in this final phase. We find a possible use of intervalence in that his song or art is referred to as a «bower,» a metaphor involving materialization of an abstract concept. There are three sense perceptions: sight, hearing, and touch (the kinesthetic relaxation implied in *duerme*.) Personification is also implied, since the verbal metaphor, «su melodía duerme,» suggests the sleep of the

---

[42] *Op. cit.,* pp. 220-221.
[43] CORREA, *La poesía mítica,* p. 18.
[44] MOLINA and MAIRENA, *op. cit.,* p. 58.

dead. There is a possible synecdoche because *melodía,* an aspect of Silverio's musical art, stands for his artistic talent as a whole rather than for just one part of it. Auditory contrast is present in the use of *silencio* as opposed to *melodía* and *ecos.* There is also an implied contrast between the symbols *glorietas* (that which will preserve or hold his art to give it permanence) and *silencio* (death or the denial of permanence.) Finally, we note an enjambement between verses three and four and five and six, as well as an anaphora (the repetition of *y*) in lines one and two.

The book's final section, «Seis caprichos,» contains six short poetic fantasies describing various aspects of Gypsy life, flamenco music and dance, and the Andalusian countryside. «Candil,» the second of these «caprichos,» deals not with the *cante jondo,* but with a scene from the lives of the Andalusian Gypsies. It begins with the image:

¡Oh, qué grave medita
la llama del candil!

which contains a verbal metaphor, «medita la llama,» and two contrasting symbols: *llama,* representing transcendency or life,[45] and *candil,* symbolizing death.[46] The metaphor may also be a *visión* in that an unreal, illogical function is attributed to an inanimate object, an attribution based on the like emotional response (a sensation of peace and calm) that both the flame and the act of meditating elicit from the poet. Furthermore, the fact that the flame is «gravely meditating» suggests a meditation about life in the midst of death, an interpretation that is verified by the poem's final lines. The first image becomes an «extended image» in that it dominates the rest of the poem and provides the metaphorical basis for the other images that follow. It involves personification since the flame is performing a human function. There are three sense perceptions: sight, hearing (the entire scene is pervaded by an intense silence), and touch (the heat of the flame), as well as an implied aura of mystery concerning the cause of the frame's intense meditation.

Como un faquir indio
mira su entraña de oro
y se eclipsa soñando
atmósferas sin viento.

The basic poetic element in this next image is the simile «Como un faquir indio,» which is reinforced by two subordinate metaphors and two symbols: «mira su entraña de oro,» a substantival metaphor, and

[45] CIRLOT, *op. cit.,* p. 299.
[46] CORREA, *La poesía mítica,* pp. 14-15.

«se eclipsa soñando,» a verbal metaphor which is also a *visión*. The two symbols are: «entraña de oro,» which represents the flame's inner being or spiritual essence, and «atmósferas sin viento» that stands for a transcendent sphere of perfect calm. The two events depicted are closely related, so that the second («se eclipsa sollando») follows as a logical outcome of the first («mira su entraña de oro»). These actions seem to represent two stages of a mystical progression resembling that of an Indian fakir who, by inner contemplation, attains a state of spiritual perfection during which he transcends («se eclipsa») the material, physical world to contemplate a realm of eternal and perfect peace which, as we shall see in the following image, may be that of death.

There is alliteration in the third verse through the repetition of the «s» sound, and an enjambement between the third and fourth lines. We also find a possible example of metonymy or antonomasia in that the transcendent sphere of perfect calm may be said to be symbolized by something associated with it or by one of its qualities: «atmósferas sin viento.» The image utilizes sight, touch (the sensation of hardness implied in gold) and hearing (intense silence). There is a partial contrast: the bright sensation of color suggested by *oro* in the first half of the image is in contrast to the complete absence of color in the second half. Personification is used, because the flame gazes, dreams, and is compared to an Indian fakir. This comparison also implies intervalence in that a man-made object is transformed into a human figure. The image conveys a feeling of mystery because of the highly abstract nature of the «atmósferas sin viento.» Finally, we note that the lack of sound and movement add immeasurably to the atmosphere of profound concentration and suspense.

The last image represents a further transformation of the lamp's flame. Its wavering is now said to be like an incandescent stork that pecks at the massive shadows and peers out trembling at the open but unseeing eyes of a dead Gypsy boy:

> Cigüeña incandescente
> pica desde su nido
> a las sombras macizas,
> y se asoma temblando
> a los ojos redondos
> del gitanillo muerto.

This stanza forms a partial contrast to the preceding, insofar as it is concerned with the concrete reality of a Gypsy wake rather than with more abstract, spiritual considerations. Furthermore, the still, motionless quality of the previous image has now been replaced with limited movement by the lamp's flame, probably caused by a wind whose absence was stressed in the foregoing verses. There are five metaphors and one possible symbol: (1) the flame equals a «cigüeña incandescente» (substantival metaphor); (2) it is said to «picar» (verbal metaphor); (3) the lamp, or at least a portion of it, is referred to as a «nido» (substantival metaphor); (4) the shadows are described as «macizas» (adjetival metaphor); and finally, (5) the flame, like a human being, «se asoma temblando» (verbal metaphor). The *sombras* are a possible death symbol.[47]

The poem's internal drama and emotional tension increase considerably in these final six lines. This intensification is due to several factors. There is, first of all, the quality of the lamp's flame. It was previously described as golden, a pleasing color, but here it has acquired a greater degree of intensity; it is now incandescent, white hot, which has an unpleasant emotional effect upon the reader akin to a sensation of pain. Secondly, the flame's intense brightness forms a chromatic contrast with the darkness of the shadows. The conflict between these visual sensations is dramatized by the fact that the «incandescent stork» is pecking at the *sombras macizas*. Thus, objects of animate and inanimate nature combine in such a way as to produce a feeling of tension, even antagonism between them. Thirdly, there is a suggestion of fear and mystery in the verb *temblando*, which implies that the flame is witnessing an awesome event. It is only in the last verse that we learn what the flame is seeing, a spectacle that is also the cause of its «grave meditation» at the beginning of the poem. The preceding images were merely a preparation for this final revelation, and all the phenomena witnessed were *signos de sugestión* leading up to the discovery of the *gitanillo muerto*. This disclosure at the very end forces us to view the poem in an entirely new perspective. We realize for the first time that we have been witnessing a scene at a Gypsy wake. And this fact creates a new sense of mystery, for not only is the reader forced to confront a new affective reality, but it raises an unanswerable question concerning the cause of the Gypsy boy's death.

The diminutive, *gitanillo,* also contributes to the affective qualities of these verses, for it expresses not only size but youth, which elicits feelings of pity or tenderness. Furthermore, there is an enjembement between lines five and six, which aids in bringing the poem to a rapid close. The image is perceived by three senses: sight, hearing (an intense silence has been present throughout) and touch (heat and pain from *incandescente,* a sensation of pain from *pica,* and heaviness implied in *sombras macizas*). Personification is

---

[47] *Ibid.,* p. 17.

utilized in converting the flame into a spectator fearfully peering at the child. Materialization is employed in transforming the flame into a stork (a change that also involves animation) and in giving mass or substance to shadows. Finally, the metaphoric conversion of a man-made object (lamp) into objects of nature (nest and stork) provides an example of plurivalence.

CONCLUSION

In conclusion, we should like to emphasize that in spite of the limitations imposed by brevity and thematic restriction, the *Poema del Cante Jondo* exhibits an extraordinary richness of imagery and poetic techniques. The highly complex nature of this poetry may be due in large measure to the fact that García Lorca was attempting to convey in visual, plastic terms the emotional and spiritual essence of a musical genre, the *cante jondo*, whose medium of expression is primarily auditory, and to avoid, at the same time, a facile, superficial imitation of its outward forms. Thus, there is a constant blending of sight and sound as the *cante* is «translated,» as it were, into a new artistic medium via the interpretative genius of the poet who transforms the songs' raw emotions into a highly personalized, sophisticated creation that combines the original, pristine, folklore spirit of the *cante* with the most modern poetic processes. At times these poems seem to be a series of random mental reflections produced by the ever changing mood of the music. But at other times, the *cante jondo* is only the pretext for examining the spirit of the region and its people who were the *cante*'s originators and present-day continuers. Hence, the poems in this collection go beyond the thematic limitations of music and dance and evoke a wider, more general Andalusian setting.

Many of these compositions utilize the landscape as their theme. This landscape, however, is not so much described as it is interpreted by the poet who infuses it with the sense of tragedy inherent in the people themselves. Lorca's Andalusian countryside is both realistic and symbolic in that the features he selects are often symbols for the dynamic struggle between self-expression and annihilation, between life and death, a struggle which permeates the very essence of the *cante jondo* as well. To this poet the land embodies a dark and mysterious, ageless force that inexorably influences the lives and destinies of its inhabitants. The human figures, particularly the Gypsies who pass through the pages of the *Poema del Cante Jondo,* are, therefore, usually little more than symbolic projections of this same tellurian force. They are elementary creatures of nature whose lives have been preordained to follow an appointed course dictated by the earth; hence, the frequency of such symbols as the *olivos, naranjos, viento,* the endless *caminos* leading to a *laberinto* or an *encrucijada,* the cemetery cross. These typical features of the landscape represent various stages of life, and they serve as guideposts to the human drama unfolding within the musical-poetic world of the *cante jondo*.

BIBLIOGRAPHY

A. E.: «Sobre Federico García Lorca.» *La Gaceta Literaria* (Madrid), 1 August 1931.

AGUIRRE, J. M.: «El sonambulismo de Federico García Lorca.» *Bulletin of Hispanic Studies*, XLIV, 4 (1967), 267-285.

ALBERTI, Rafael: «García Lorca» in *Los Hombres de la Historia*, 14. Buenos Aires: Centro Editor de América Latina, 1968.

ALCALÁ, Manuel: «García Lorca y la poesía francesa.» *Insula*, 103 (1954), 11.

ALEIXANDRE, Vicente: «Epílogo» a las *Obras completas de Federico García Lorca*. Madrid: Aguilar, 1963.

ALMUY, Camille: «Lorca, poète andalou espagnole, universel.» *Archivum de Oviedo*, VII, 1-3 (1957), 205-230.

ALONSO, Dámaso: *Poetas españoles contemporáneos*. Madrid: Gredos, 1952.

ALVAREZ DE MIRANDA, Angel: *La metáfora y el mito*. Madrid: Ediciones Taurus, 1963.

AMAYA, J.: *Gitanos y cante jondo*. Barcelona: Dux, n.d.

APARICIO, Antonio: «Federico García Lorca y su época.» *Ateneo*, XCIII, 286 (1949), 41-61.

AUCLAIR, Marcelle: *Enfances et Mort de García Lorca*. Paris: Editions du Seuil, 1968.

AZARA, Medina: «Cante jondo y cantes sinagogales.» *Revista de Occidente*, XXX, 88 (Oct.-Dec. 1930), 53-84.

BABIN, María Teresa: *García Lorca, vida y obra*. New York: Las Américas Publishing Co., 1955.

— «El hombre y el mundo social en la obra de Federico García Lorca.» *La Nueva Democracia* (New York), XXXV, 3 (1955), 18-22.

— «La metáfora y la imagen de García Lorca.» *Isla* (San Juan, P. R.), I, 3 (1939), 11-12.

— «La mujer en la obra de García Lorca.» *La Torre*, 34 (1961), 125-137.

— *El mundo poético de Federico García Lorca*. San Juan: Biblioteca de Autores Puertorriqueños, 1954.

BALBONTÍN, J. A.: *Three Spanish Poets: Rosalía de Castro, García Lorca, and Antonio Machado*. Cambridge: Cambridge University Press, 1960.

BALOCH, Aziz: *Spanish Cante Jondo and its Origin in Sindhi Music*. Hyderabad, Pakistan: The Mehran Arts Council, 1968.

BARDI, U.: «Materiaux pour une bibliographie italienne de Federico García Lorca.» *Bulletin Hispanique*, LXIII (1961), 88-97.

BAREA, Arturo: *Lorca, the Poet and his People*. London: Faber & Faber, 1944.

— «Las raíces del lenguaje poético de Lorca.» *Bulletin of Spanish Studies* (Liverpool), XXII (1945), 3-15.

BARROW, Leo, and OLSTAD, Charles: *Aspectos de la literatura española*. Lexington, Massachusetts: Xerox College Publishing, 1972.

BARTRA, A.: «Los temas de la vida y de la muerte en la poesía de Antonio Machado, García Lorca, y Miguel Hernández.» *Cuadernos Americanos*, XXI, 5 (1962), 191-212.

BELAMICH, André: *Lorca*. Paris: Gallimard, 1962.

BENET, William Rose: *The Reader's Encyclopedia*. 2nd ed. New York: Thomas Y. Crowell Co., 1965.

BOSCÁN, Lilia V.: «La muerte en la poesía de Lorca. La luna y el jinete, símbolos representativos.» *AFZ*, IV, 4 (1965), 281-295.

BOSCH, Rafael: «El choque de imágenes como principio creador de García Lorca.» *Revista Hispánica Moderna*, XXX, 1 (enero 1964), 35-44.

— «Los poemas paralelísticos de García Lorca.» *Revista Hispánica Moderna*, XXVIII, 1 (1962), 36-48.

BOUSOÑO, Carlos: *Teoría de la expresión poética*. 2 vols. Madrid: Gredos, 1970.

CAMPBELL, Roy: *Lorca: an Appreciation of His Poetry*. Cambridge: Bowes & Bowes, 1952.

Cano, José Luis: *García Lorca: biografía ilustrada.* Barcelona: Ediciones Destino, 1962.

Cano Ballesta, Juan: «Una veta reveladora en la poesía de García Lorca (Los tiempos del verbo y sus matices expresivos).» *Romanische Forschungen,* LXXVII, 1-2 (1965), 75-107.

Cernuda, Luis: «Federico García Lorca, 1898?-1936» in *Estudios sobre poesía española contemporánea.* Madrid: Ediciones Guadarrama, 1957.

Chase, Gilbert: *The Music of Spain.* 2nd rev. ed. New York: Dover Publ., 1959.

Cirlot, Juan Eduardo: *Diccionario de símbolos.* Barcelona: Editorial Labor, 1969.

Cirre, José Francisco: «El caballo y el toro en la poesía de García Lorca.» *Cuadernos Americanos,* XI, 6 (Nov.-Dec. 1952), 231-245.

— *Forma y espíritu de una lírica española.* Mexico City: Gráfica Panamericana, 1950.

Cobb, Carl W.: *Federico García Lorca.* New York: Twayne, 1967.

Comincioli, Jacques: «En torno a García Lorca. Sugerencias. Documentos. Bibliografía.» *Cuadernos Hispanoamericanos,* XLVII, 139 (1961), 37-76.

— *Federico García Lorca.* Luysanne: Editions Rencontre, 1970.

Conde, Eduardo: «Duende y hechizo de Federico García Lorca.» *Universal* (Caracas), 17 octubre 1961.

Correa, Gustavo: *La poesía mítica de Federico García Lorca.* Eugene: Univ. of Oregon Publications, 1957.

— «El simbolismo de la luna en la poesía de Federico García Lorca.» *PMLA,* LXXII, 5 (1957), 1060-1084.

— «El simbolismo del mar en la poesía española del siglo XX.» *Revista Hispánica Moderna,* XXXII, 1-2 (1966), 62-86.

— «El simbolismo del sol en la poesía de Federico García Lorca.» *Nueva Revista de Filología Hispánica,* XIV, 1-2 (1960), 110-119.

— «El simbolismo religioso en la poesía de Federico García Lorca.» *Hispania,* XXXIX, 1 (March 1956), 41-48.

Couffon, Claude: *Granada y García Lorca.* Madrid: Losada, 1967.

Cremer, Victoriano: «Los mundos oscuros de Federico García Lorca y el 'Romancero gitano.'» *La Estafeta Literaria,* 424, 15 julio 1969.

Crow, James A.: *Federico García Lorca.* Los Angeles: Univ. of California Press, 1945.

Cuartas Arboleda, Conrado: «Símbolo en la poesía de Federico García Lorca.» *Universidad de Antioquía,* 96 (1950), 541-547.

Debicki, Andrew P.: «Federico García Lorca: estilización y visión de la poesía» in *Estudios sobre poesía española contemporánea.* Madrid: Gredos (Biblioteca Románica Hispánica), 1968.

De Ory, Carlos Edmundo: *Federico García Lorca.* Paris: Editions Universitaires (Classiques du XXᵉ Siècle), 1967.

Del Río, Angel: «A los sesenta años del nacimiento de un poeta que no llegó a cumplirlos» in *Estudios sobre literatura contemporánea española.* Madrid: Gredos, 1966.

— *Federico García Lorca (1899-1936), vida y obra. Bibliografía. Antología. Obras inéditas. Música popular.* New York: The Hispanic Institute, 1941.

Del Río, A., et al.: *Antonia Mercé. La Argentinita.* New York: Instituto de las Españas en los E.E. U.U., Columbia Univ., 1930.

Devoto, Daniel: «Notas sobre el elemento tradicional en la obra de García Lorca.» *Filología* (Buenos Aires), II, 3 (1950), 292-341.

Díaz-Plaja, Guillermo: *Federico García Lorca, su obra e influencia en la poesía española.* 2nd ed. Buenos Aires: Espasa-Calpe, 1954.

Diccionario de Literatura Española. Madrid: Revista de Occidente, 1964.

Díez-Canedo, E.: Review of «Poema del cante jondo.» *El Sol* (Madrid), 28 junio 1931.

Durán, Manuel: «García Lorca, poeta entre dos mundos.» *Asomante,* 1 (1962), 70-77.

— *Lorca, A Collection of Critical Essays.* Englewood Cliffs, N. J.: Prentice-Hall (a Spectrum Book), n.d.

Eich, Cristoph: *Federico García Lorca, poeta de la intensidad.* Madrid: Gredos, 1958.

FALLA, Manuel de: «El cante jondo. Sus orígenes. Sus valores. Su influencia en el arte europeo» in *Escritos sobre música y músicos*. Madrid: Espasa-Calpe, n.d.

Falla y Granada. Vitoria, España: H. Fournier, 1963.

FERGUSON, George: *Signs and Symbols in Christian Art*. New York: Oxford University Press, 1954.

FERNÁNDEZ DEL VALLE, Agustín B.: «Sentido de la muerte en Andalucía.» *VUM*, 25 octubre 1964.

FERNÁNDEZ-GALIANO, Manuel: «Los dioses de Federico.» *Cuadernos Hispanoamericanos*, 217 (1968).

FERRIS, Evylyn M. V. D.: «Federico García Lorca: A Study of the Popular and Traditional Inspiration of his Poetry.» Master's essay, Columbia University 1941.

FLECNIAKOSKA, Jean L.: *L'Univers poétique de Federico García Lorca*. Bordeaux: Briere, 1952.

FLYS, Jaroslaw M.: *El lenguaje poético de Federico García Lorca*. Madrid: Gredos, 1955.

FORSTER, Jeremy C.: «El 'Caballista' de Lorca.» *Romance Notes* (Univ. of N.C.), IX, 1 (1967).

FUSERO, Clemente: *García Lorca*. n. p.: Dall-Oglio, 1969.

GALLEGO MORELL, Antonio: «Concurso de Cante Jondo en la Granada de 1922.» *ABC* (Madrid), 6 noviembre 1960.

— ed. *García Lorca, cartas, postales, poemas y dibujos*. Madrid: Editorial Moneda y Crédito (Colección Letras Amigas), 1968.

GARCÍA LORCA, Federico: *Obras completas*, 6th ed. Madrid: Aguilar, 1963.

— *Poema del cante jondo*. Madrid: Ediciones Ulises, 1931.

— «Viñetas flamencas.» *Verso y Prosa, Boletín de la Joven Literatura* (Murcia), Año 1, núm. 4 (abril 1927), 1.

GICOVATE, Bernardo: «Serenidad y conflicto en la poesía de Federico García Lorca.» *Asomante*, 1 (1962), 7-13.

GONZÁLEZ CLIMENT, Anselmo: *Andalucía en los toros, el cante y la danza*. Madrid: Imprenta Sánchez Leal, 1953.

— ed. *Antología de poesía flamenca*. Madrid: Escelicer, 1961.

— *Bibliografía flamenca*. Madrid: Escelicer, 1965.

— *Bulerías, un ensayo jerezano*. Jerez de la Frontera: Editorial Jerez Industrial, 1961.

— *Flamencología*. Madrid: Escelicer, 1964.

— *¡Oído al cante!* Madrid: Escelicer, 1960.

— *Segunda Bibliografía flamenca*. Málaga: Ediciones de Libros de Málaga, 1966.

GONZÁLEZ MUELA, Joaquín: «El aspecto verbal en la poesía moderna española.» *Revista de Filología Española*, XXXV (1951), 75-91.

— *El lenguaje poético de la generación Guillén-Lorca*. Madrid: Insula, 1955.

GRAY, Eden: *A Complete Guide to the Tarot*. New York: Crown Publishers, 1970.

GUARDIA, Alfredo de la: *García Lorca: Persona y creación*. Buenos Aires: Editorial Schapire, 1952.

GUEREÑA, Jacinto Luis: «El agua y Federico García Lorca.» *Cuadernos Hispanoamericanos*, LXX, 209 (1967), 392-406.

GUILLÉN, Jorge: *Federico en persona*. Buenos Aires: Emecé, 1959.

— «Prólogo» a las *Obras Completas de Federico García Lorca*. Madrid: Aguilar, 1963.

GULLÓN, Ricardo: «Motivos en la poesía de Lorca.» *Insula*, IX, 103 (julio 1954).

HECHT, Paul: *The Wind Cried*. New York: The Dial Press, 1968.

HENRY, Albert: «Les grands poèmes andalous de Federico García Lorca.» *Romanica Gandensia* (Gant, Belgium), VI (1958), 236-246.

HIERRO, José: «El primer Lorca.» *Cuadernos Hispanoamericanos*, LXXV (1968), 224-225.

«Homenaje a Federico García Lorca.» *ABC* (Madrid), 6 noviembre 1966.

HONIG, Edwin: «Dimensions of Imagery and Action in the Work of García Lorca.» *Poetry*, LXIII, 1 (October 1943), 32-44.

— *Federico García Lorca*. Norfolk, Conn.: New Directions, 1963.

IGLESIAS RAMÍREZ, M.: *Federico García Lorca, el poeta universal*. Barcelona: Dux, 1963.

LLIE, Paul: *The Surrealist Mode in Spanish Literature.* Ann Arbor: The Univ. of Michigan Press, 1968.

INFIESTA, Roberto: «Itinerario lírico,» a lecture given in the Club Femenino de Cuba. La Habana, 30 octubre 1951.

LAFFRANQUE, Marie: *Les idées esthétiques de Federico García Lorca.* Paris: Centre de Recherches Hispaniques, 1967.

— «Lorca: Etudes, souvenirs et documents.» *Bulletin Hispanique,* LXIX, pp. 195-197.

— «Pour l'Etude de Federico García Lorca. Bases Chronologiques.» *Bulletin Hispanique,* LXV, 3-4 (1963), 333-377.

LAFUENTE, Rafael: *Los gitanos, el flamenco y los flamencos.* Barcelona: Editorial Barna, 1955.

LAMURAGLIA, Nicolás: «Del sentido musical en la obra de Federico García Lorca.» *La Nación,* 31 March 1963.

LARREA PALACÍN, A. de: *La canción andaluza.* Jerez de la Frontera: Centro de Estudios Históricos Jerezanos, 1961.

LATCHAM, Ricardo A.: «Notas sobre García Lorca.» *Ateneo* (Caracas), XXXVI, 136 (1936).

LÁZARO, Fernando: «Baudelaire y García Lorca.» *Insula,* 98 (1954), 2.

LICHTMAN, Celia S.: «Federico García Lorca: A Study in Three Mythologies.» Doctoral diss. New York University, 1965.

LIRA ESPEJO, Eduardo: «Federico García Lorca en el rumor de la música.» *Ateneo* (Caracas), III, 7 (octubre 1957).

LÓPEZ CHIVARRI, Eduardo: *Música popular española.* Barcelona: Editorial Labor, 1927.

LUNA, José Carlos de: *De cante grande y cante chico.* Madrid: Escelicer, 1942.

MACHADO Y ÁLVAREZ, Antonio, ed.: *Cantes flamencos.* Buenos Aires: Espasa-Calpe Argentina, S. A., 1947.

— *Cantes flamencos, colección escogida.* Madrid: Imprenta Popular, n.d.

— *Colección de cantes flamencos recogidos y anotados por Demófilo.* Sevilla: Imprenta y Lit. de El Porvenir, 1881.

MACRÌ, Oreste: *Canti Gitani e Andalusi.* Bologna: Guanda (Collezione Fenice), 1961.

MADARIAGA, Salvador de: *De Galdós a Lorca.* Buenos Aires: Dolphin, 1960.

MAGARIÑOS, Santiago: «García Lorca y la muerte.» *Revista Nacional de Cultura,* XXIV, 148-149 (1961), 107-115.

MANFREDI, Domingo: *Geografía del cante jondo.* Madrid: Colección «El Grifón,» XXVI, 1955.

MANZANO, Rafael: *Cante jondo.* Barcelona: Editorial Barna, n.d.

MARTÍNEZ LÓPEZ, Enrique: «Aljibe y surtidor, o la Granada de Federico García Lorca.» *La Torre,* X, 40 (1962), 11-45.

MARTÍNEZ TORNER, Eduardo: «La canción tradicional española,» in *Folklore y costumbres de España.* T. II, 6-166. Barcelona, 1931.

— *Lírica hispánica (relación entre lo popular y lo culto).* Madrid: Castalia, 1966.

MOLINA FAJARDO, Eduardo: *Manuel de Falla y el «cante jondo.»* Madrid: Imprenta Urania, 1962.

MOLINA, Ricardo: *Cante flamenco.* Madrid: Ediciones Taurus, 1965.

— «Dos estudios sobre arte flamenco.» *Cuadernos Hispanoamericanos,* 217 (1968).

MOLINA, R., and MAIRENA, Antonio: *Mundo y formas del cante flamenco.* Madrid: Revista de Occidente, 1963.

MONLEÓN, José: «Cante y sociedad española.» *Cuadernos Hispanoamericanos,* 222 (1968).

MONTES, Eugenio: Review of «Poema del cante jondo.» *El Sol* (Madrid), 18 julio 1931.

MORA GUARNIDO, José: *Federico García Lorca y su mundo: Testimonio para una biografía.* Buenos Aires: Losada, 1958.

MORLA LYNCH, Carlos: *En España con Federico García Lorca.* Madrid: Aguilar, 1958.

MORRIS, C. B.: *A Generation of Spanish Poets 1920-1936.* Cambridge: Cambridge Univ. Press, 1969.

MUÑOZ CORTÉS, Manuel, and CASALDUERO, Joaquín G.: «Notas sobre el diminutivo en García Lorca.» *Archivum,* IV (1954), 277-304.

NAVARRO GONZÁLEZ, Alberto: «Gitanos, pícaros y flamencos.» *La Estafeta Literaria* (Madrid), 432 (15 noviembre 1969).

NAVARRO TOMÁS, Tomás: «La intuición rítmica en Federico García Lorca.» *Revista Hispánica Moderna*, XXXIV, 1-2 (1968), 362ff.

— *Manual de la entonación española.* New York: The Hispanic Institute, 1944.

PARROT, Louis: *Federico García Lorca (Extracts, Documents, Bibliography).* Paris: Pierre Seghers, 1947.

PEMARTÍN, Julián: *El cante flamenco, guía alfabética.* Madrid: Afrodisio Aguado, 1966.

Pequeño Larousse Ilustrado. Paris: Editorial Larousse, 1964.

PEREDA VALDÉS, Ildefonso: «García Lorca y la muerte.» *La Nueva Democracia* (New York), XIX, 9 (1938).

PÉREZ MARCHAND, Monelisa Lina: «La inquietud existencial en la poesía de Federico García Lorca.» *Asomante* (San Juan, P.R.), V, 3 (1949), 72-86.

PHILLIPS, Allen W.: «Sobre la poética de García Lorca.» *Revista Hispánica Moderna*, XXIV, 1 (1958), 36-48.

PICAZO CARBALLO, Alfredo: *Métrica española.* Madrid: Instituto de Estudios Madrileños, 1956.

POHREN, D. E.: *Lives and Legends of Flamenco: A Biographical History.* Seville: Society of Spanish Studies, 1964.

— *The Art of Flamenco.* Jerez de la Frontera: Editorial Jerez Industrial, 1962.

PONCE RIVADENEIRA, Alfredo: «Evocación de García Lorca», conferencia pronunciada en el Club Femenino de Cultura. Quito: Editorial La Unión, 1964.

PRADAL, Gabriel R.: «Las cosas de Federico García Lorca.» *Cuadernos Americanos*, 5 (sept.-oct. 1953), 271-280.

— «La paloma y el leopardo; o lo humano y lo inhumano en la obra de Federico García Lorca.» *Cuadernos Americanos*, XVI, 4 (1957), 193-207.

RAMOS-GIL, Carlos: *Claves líricas de García Lorca.* Madrid: Aguilar, 1967.

— *Ecos antiguos, estructuras nuevas y mundo primario en la lírica de Lorca.* Bahía Blanca, Argentina: Cuadernos del Sur, 1967.

REAL ACADEMIA ESPAÑOLA: *Diccionario de la Lengua española.* 18th ed. Madrid: Espasa-Calpe, 1956.

RÍOS RUIZ, Manuel: *Introducción al cante flamenco.* Madrid: Ediciones Istmo, 1972.

RIVERA, Modesto: «Federico García Lorca: Motivos naturales. Sevilla, Córdoba, Granada.» *Brújula* (San Juan, P. R.), II, 3-4 (1936), 29-34.

RIZZO, Gino L.: «Poesía de Federico García Lorca y poesía popular.» *Clavileño*, VI, 36 (nov.-dec. 1955), 44-51.

ROBERTS, Gemma: «La intuición poética del tiempo finito en 'Canciones' de Federico García Lorca.» *Revista Hispánica Moderna*, XXXIII, 3-4 (1967), 250-261.

ROCAMORA, Pedro: «Imagen lírica y teatro pasional en García Lorca.» *Arbor*, LXVIII, 264 (1967).

ROSSY, Hipólito: *Teoría del cante jondo.* Barcelona: Credsa, 1966.

RUIZ DE LA SERNA, E.: Review «Poema del Cante Jondo por Federico García Lorca.» *Heraldo de Madrid.* 20 junio 1931.

SALINAS, Pedro: «García Lorca y la cultura de la muerte» in *Ensayos de Literatura Hispánica.* Madrid: Aguilar, 1961.

— *Literatura española del siglo XX.* Mexico: Antigua Librería Rebredo, 1949.

SCARPA, Roque Esteban: *El dramatismo en la poesía de Federico García Lorca.* Santiago de Chile: Editorial Universitaria, 1961.

SCHONBERG, Jean-Louis: *A la Recherche de Lorca.* Neuchatel, Swisse: Editions de la Baconnière, 1966.

— *Federico García Lorca.* Mexico: Compañía General de Ediciones, 1959.

SCHOPF, Federico: «La esencia de la metáfora.» *Anales de la Universidad de Chile*, CXXIII, 134 (1965), 125-147.

SENDER, Ramón: «Sobre los gitanos cantores.» *DH*, 19 julio 1953.

SOLA GONZÁLEZ, A.: «La adjetivación en la poesía de Federico García Lorca.» *Cántico, poesías y poetas* (Tucumán), 1 (1940), 29-44.

SOMMAVILLA, G., and COLOMBO, A.: «Dei e demoni di F. García Lorca.» *Letture*, 15 (1960), 163-182.

SORIA, Andrés: «El gitanismo de Federico García Lorca.» *Insula*, IV, 45 (1949).

STANTON, Edward F.: «Federico García Lorca and 'Cante Jondo'.» Doctoral diss. University of California, Los Angeles, 1972.

THOMPSON, Stith: *Motif Index of Folk Literature.* Bloomington: Indiana Univ. Press, 1955.

TORRE, Guillermo de: «Así que pasen veinte años, presencia de Federico García Lorca» in *El fiel de la balanza,* pp. 169-199. Madrid: Taurus, 1961.

— *Tríptico del sacrificio: Unamuno, García Lorca, Machado.* Buenos Aires: Losada, 1960.

TORRES VIERA, J. M.: «Signo lírico de García Lorca.» *El Universal* (Caracas), 30 julio 1950.

TREND, J. B.: *Lorca and the Spanish Poetic Tradition.* Oxford: Blackwell, 1955.

— *Manuel de Falla and Spanish Music.* New York: Alfred A. Knopf, 1934.

— *The Music of Spanish History to 1600.* New York: Oxford Univ. Press, 1926.

— *Spain from the South.* New York: Oxford Univ. Press, 1928.

TURCATO, Bruno: «Struttura ed evoluzione delle prime metafore lorquiane.» *Quaderi Ibero-Americani,* 4 (1960-1962), 129-142.

UMBRAL, Francisco: *Lorca, poeta maldito.* Madrid: Biblioteca Nueva, 1968.

VALBUENA Y PRAT, Angel: «La poesía popular de Federico García Lorca» in *Historia de la literatura española,* t. II, 924-933, 970. Barcelona, 1937.

VÁZQUEZ OCAÑA, Fernando: *García Lorca: vida, cántico y muerte.* México: Biografías Gandesa, 1957.

VIAN, Cesco: *Federico García Lorca, poeta e drammaturgo.* Milan: Edizioni Universitarie, n.d.

VILAR, Sergio: «Los toros, el sexo y la muerte (apuntes a modo de introducción al tema).» *Sur,* 278 (Sept.-Oct. 1962), 36-43.

VIVANCO, Luis Felipe: «Federico García Lorca, poeta dramático de copla y estribillo» in *Introducción a la poesía española contemporánea,* pp. 385-456. Madrid: Ediciones Guadarrama, 1957.

XIRAU, Ramón: «La relación metal-muerte en los poemas de García Lorca.» *Nueva Revista de Filología Hispánica,* VII (1953), 364-371.

YAHNI, Roberto: «Algunos rasgos formales en la lírica de García Lorca: función del paréntesis.» *Bulletin Hispanique,* LXVI, 1-2 (1964), 106-124.

YOUNG, Howard T.: «Lorca and the Deep Song.» *Claremont Quarterly,* XI, 2, pp. 5-14.

— *The Victorious Expression: A Study of Four Contemporary Spanish Poets: Miguel de Unamuno, Antonio Machado, Juan Ramón Jiménez, Federico García Lorca.* Madison: Univ. of Wisconsin Press, 1964.

ZARDOYA, Concha: «Los espejos de Federico García Lorca» in *Poesía española del 98 y del 27.* Madrid: Gredos (Biblioteca Románica Hispánica), 1968.

— «La técnica metafórica de Federico García Lorca» in *Poesía española contemporánea.* Madrid: Gredos, 1962.

INDEX